Milton & Others

MILTON & OTHERS

George Williamson

And one remarks about the
Puritan mythology its thinness
T. S. Eliot

THE UNIVERSITY OF
CHICAGO PRESS

The University of Chicago Press, Chicago 37
Faber and Faber Limited, London, W.C.1, England

56387

Library of Congress Catalog Card Number: 65–26302

Foreword

My acknowledgments are due to *Modern Language Notes*, *Modern Philology*, and *Philological Quarterly*, in which the dated essays originally appeared. The others are unpublished. Most of them have some relation to Milton. Essays on *Lycidas* and Milton's mortalism are found in my *Seventeenth Century Contexts*.

G.W.

Contents

MILTON THE ANTI-ROMANTIC

MILTON'S allusions to the romances of chivalry are often treated as evidence of an earlier love, but little attention is paid to their function in his major poetic works. Miss Brinkley in her *Arthurian Legend in the Seventeenth Century* has given the fullest treatment of Milton's relation to the Arthurian material and his later opposition, but she underrates his repudiation of romance in his *Apology* of 1642, which is emphasized by his 'retraction' of the *Elegies* in 1645, and she does not consider the use to which he puts romance after renouncing the Arthurian legend. This seems to include the satiric use of its literary trappings and its normative use as a foil to his true hero and wisdom. In his chief works, for example, romantic embellishments are stripped from war, romantic love becomes a foil to true love, romantic aspirations are rebuked. However, even if these effects were allowed, the cause would still be disputed by Milton critics.

I

No doubt it would be granted that the cause was somehow related to his national epic ambition. But what are the significant facts? We know from Milton's 'Vacation Exercise' that he was early inclined to epic poetry. We know from *Elegia Sexta*, where he opposes the muses of water and wine, that he required sobriety of life for such creation. We know from the Cambridge Manuscript that he was interested in both national and Biblical subjects. And we know from his *Mansus* and *Epitaphium Damonis* that he at first intended to treat the Arthurian story. But his plans were interrupted by a new war of Reformation.

To this cause Milton then turned his pen, but he occasionally reminded his audience of his neglected ambitions. He is most specific in *The Reason of Church Government* (Bk. II), where he outlined early in 1642 the plans that he ultimately fulfilled. There he defined his ambition 'to be an interpreter and relater of the best and sagest things among mine own citizens throughout this island in the mother dialect'; mentioned his uncertainty about 'what king or knight, before the conquest, might be chosen in whom to lay the pattern of a Christian hero'; confessed his hope to present, like Tasso, the choice of either a secular or a religious subject 'in our own ancient stories'. And in making it 'doctrinal and exem-plary to a nation', he wanted to choose the most persuasive way: 'teaching over the whole book of sanctity and virtue, through all the instances of example, with such delight to those especially of soft and delicious temper, who will not so much as look upon truth herself, unless they see her elegantly dressed; that whereas the paths of honesty and good life appear now rugged and difficult, though they be indeed easy and pleasant, they will then appear to all men both easy and pleasant, though they were rugged and difficult indeed'. This is another 'reason why our sage and serious poet Spenser' was 'a better teacher than Scotus or Aquinas', since readers like young Cowley found his 'Stories of the Knights, and Giants, and Monsters, and brave Houses' irresistible.

Naturally Milton followed 'our own ancient stories' in history. He begins his *History of Britain* with this sentence: 'The beginning of Nations, those excepted of whom sacred Books have spoken, is to this day unknown.' This reminds us of the priority which Ralegh gave the Scriptures as historical records in his *History of the World*. Despite the fabulous character of early British history, Milton concludes, for the sake of possible vestiges of truth: 'I have therefore determined to bestow the telling over even of these reputed tales; be it for nothing else but in favour of our English poets and rhetoricians, who by their art will know how to use them judiciously.' This certainly does not suggest that Milton now (about 1646–7 per Edward Phillips) believed documentary truth essential to poetry.

Nevertheless, Milton had the Baconian urge to improve the writing of English history and so to 'endeavour that which hitherto hath been needed most, with plain and lightsome brevity, to relate well and orderly things worth the noting, so as may best instruct and benefit them that read'. But his addition is Miltonic:

'Which, imploring divine assistance, that it may redound to his glory, and the good of the British nation, I now begin.' Thus he began the prose epic that he was never to bring to a triumphant conclusion. And his frustration is diagnosed in the famous suppressed introduction to Book III, written about the time of his Sonnet to Fairfax (1648), which connects eventually with *Paradise Lost* by the question, 'For what can Warr, but endless warr still breed', and points back to the 'Digression' in these lines,

> Till Truth, & Right from Violence be freed,
> And Public Faith cleard from the shamefull brand
> Of Public Fraud.

Moreover, Milton, like Ralegh, saw in history the workings of Providence, and so he too ultimately turned back to the Creation for the beginning of history. But Milton began his *History of Britain* where Ralegh was to end, and ended where Ralegh began. There the lesson was clearer or 'more doctrinal and exemplary' than 'in our own ancient stories'. Milton is like Ralegh in beginning history with the fall of man, except that Milton finally made it the focus or cynosure of all history.

Apparently in 1670, however, Milton sharpened his moral in the *History of Britain* by adding this postscript: 'If these were the Causes of such misery and thraldom to those our Ancestors, with what better close can be concluded, then here in fit season to remember this Age in the midst of her security, to fear from like Vices, without amendment, the Revolutions of like Calamities.' Then in *Samson Agonistes* the moral of the *History* was pointed against those who would rather have 'bondage with ease than strenuous liberty'. Moreover, the close of the *History* and *Paradise Lost* both teach the same moral, the relation between vice and servitude.

By 1649 Milton's belief in the reformation of England had become a feeling of 'ridiculous frustration'. He understood how desperately the people needed moral instruction for civil wisdom. In *The Tenure of Kings and Magistrates* he confronts the problem of heroism which he later developed in *Samson Agonistes*. Now the 'true warfaring Christian' is seen in those who 'for the deliverance of their country endued with fortitude and heroic virtue to fear nothing but the curse written against those "that do the work of the Lord negligently", would go on to remove, not only the

13

calamities and thraldoms of a people, but the roots and causes whence they spring'. Marvell never forgot 'their bloody hands'. Yet before Samson could appear in this role he had to learn to govern himself by reason.

In the 'Digression' (1648) of his *History of Britain* Milton criticizes both ancient and modern Britons for their waste or abuse of liberty: because they succumbed to the vices they had defeated in the field; because they took to force rather than to reason; because they failed to balance liberty and discipline. 'But to do this and to know these exquisite proportions, the heroic wisdom which is required surmounted far the principles of narrow politicians.' The British were 'Valiant indeed and prosperous to win a field but to know the end and reason of winning, unjudicious and unwise, in good and bad success alike unteachable.' As a remedy mother wit was not enough: 'so must ripe understanding and many civil vertues be imported into our minds from foreign writings and examples of best ages: we shall else miscarry still and come short in the attempt of any great enterprise'.

But Hobbes believed Milton's remedy to be the cause of rebel-lion. In the *Leviathan* (Part 2, Chapter 21) he concludes: 'And by reading of these Greek and Latin Authors, men from their childhood have gotten a habit (under a false shew of Liberty) of favouring tumults, and of licentious controlling the actions of their Soveraigns; and again of controlling those controllers, with the effusion of so much blood; as I think I may truly say, there was never any thing so dearly bought, as these Western parts have bought the learning of the Greek and Latin tongues.'

Yet Milton, explaining why he defended liberty by reason rather than by arms, projects his *Second Defence of the English People* (1654) into the 'high strains' he had anticipated in *Of Reformation*. Almost in the mood of *Paradise Lost* he asserts that he has had his 'share of human misery' and then claims divine support 'to defend the dearest interests, not merely of one people, but of the whole human race, against the enemies of human liberty'.

This defence is centred on Cromwell, whose self-discipline made him the 'true warfaring Christian' of *Areopagitica*: 'for he was a soldier disciplined to perfection in the knowledge of himself'. This was the key to his success: 'He first acquired the government of himself, and over himself acquired the most signal victories;

so that on the first day he took the field against the external enemy, he was a veteran in arms, consummately practised in the toils and exigencies of war.'

Nevertheless, Milton preaches liberty to Cromwell: 'You cannot be truly free unless we are free too; for such is the nature of things, that he who entrenches on the liberty of others, is the first to lose his own and become a slave.' And then he teaches the wisdom of peace which the ancient Britons lacked. In both the *Second Defence* and Marvell's *Horatian Ode* Cromwell's claim to leadership is founded on self-mastery and sanctioned by Providence. And both suggest that this sanction must be maintained by the same virtue that brought him to power. Indeed the lesson of the 'Digression' is writ large in the *Second Defence*, because the possibility of ultimate failure was now very real to Milton. At least he can say: 'If the conclusion do not answer to the beginning, that is their concern; I have delivered my testimony, I would almost say, have erected a monument, that will not readily be destroyed, to the reality of those singular and mighty achievements.' It sounds like a fulfilment of the promise in *Of Reformation*.

Indeed it was now the only possible redemption of his promise of a national epic: 'As the epic poet, who adheres at all to the rules of that species of composition, does not profess to describe the whole life of the hero whom he celebrates, but only some particular action of his life, as the resentment of Achilles at Troy, the return of Ulysses, or the coming of Aeneas into Italy; so it will be sufficient, either for my justification or apology, that I have heroically celebrated at least one exploit of my countrymen; I pass by the rest, for who could recite the achievements of a whole people?' The propagandist added the rhetorical question; the man might have stopped with, 'I pass by the rest.'

II

Now if we turn back to the poet who followed Spenser, we find the abstemious muse ('Spare Fast') associated in *Il Penseroso* with a complex of Plato and romance:

> And if aught else great Bards beside
> In sage and solemn tunes have sung,
> Of Tourneys and of Trophies hung,

> *Of Forests, and enchantments drear,*
> *Where more is meant than meets the ear.*

Milton comes nearest to representing such a blend in *Comus*, where the muses of water and wine are opposed in the 'casta iuventus' story. But after this attempt he left the path of the romantic Spenser.

Comus and his rout are inspired by the Bacchic muse of 'elegia levis', but the abstinent muse dictates what

> *must be utter'd to unfold the sage*
> *And serious doctrine of Virginity.*

Comus and his rout illustrate how

> *The soul grows clotted by contagion,*
> *Imbodies, and imbrutes, till she quite loose*
> *The divine property of her first being,*

which the Lady illustrates. In this Platonic vein the Lady refutes the 'dazling fence' of Comus's amatory argument with its familiar topics. Another Puritan, however, could address such an argu-ment 'To his Coy Mistress'. From the enchantments of Comus the Lady is finally released by the water nymph Sabrina, who derives from British legend and completes this Spenserian complex.

In *The Reason of Church Government* we have seen that Milton's plans involved a national epic; in his *History of Britain*, however, we have seen that he found a pattern of failure rather than of a Christian hero. Arthurian romance was involved in British his-tory, but it was rejected by Milton on moral rather than historical grounds. This becomes apparent in *An Apology for Smectymnuus*, which contains his second literary confession. Here we may learn why Milton became anti-romantic: though he still admired the 'sage and serious' Spenser, he rejected the romances because of their extramarital 'defilement' of his 'casta' theme. But he did not carry the marriage of the soul to the extreme of Crashaw's 'Hymn to Saint Teresa'.

In his *Apology* (1642) Milton describes the growth of his abstemious doctrine and discipline, first mentioned in 'Elegy VI'. At first he was enamoured of 'the smooth elegiac poets' and sought to emulate them, but he deplored them when they abused 'those high perfections, which under one or other name they took to celebrate'. He emphasized his attitude by saying that he 'preferred the two famous renowners of Beatrice and Laura, who never write but honor of them to whom they devote their verse, displaying sublime and pure thoughts, without transgression'. Milton, however, outside of a few sonnets, never put woman on a pedestal except as a sign of weakness or effeminacy in man.

In *Paradise Lost* (IV, 750) when he exalts marriage because it distinguished men from animals by founding love in Reason, he pushes romantic love into 'the society of bordellos' by his contrast:

> *Here Love his golden shafts imploies, here lights*
> *His constant Lamp, and waves his purple wings,*
> *Reigns here and revels; not in the bought smile*
> *Of Harlots, loveless, joyless, unindeard,*
> *Casual fruition, nor in Court Amours,*
> *Mixt Dance, or wanton Mask, or Midnight Bal,*
> *Or Serenate, which the starv'd Lover sings*
> *To his proud fair, best quitted with disdain.*
> *These lulld by Nightingales imbraceing slept,*
> *And on thir naked limbs the flourie roof*
> *Showrd Roses, which the Morn repair'd.*

Here the married lover gets many of the embellishments of romance, and the Petrarchan is the saddest figure of all. Later the opposition to animals is extended by Raphael's rebuke (VIII, 579) to Adam's view of passion:

> *But if the sense of touch whereby mankind*
> *Is propagated seem such dear delight*
> *Beyond all other, think the same voutsaf't*
> *To Cattel and each Beast; which would not be*
> *To them made common & divulg'd, if aught*
> *Therein enjoy'd were worthy to subdue*
> *The Soule of Man, or passion in him move.*

The rebuke ends by elevating love to the Platonic level. But a son of Adam had written Donne's 'Farewell to love' because man's curse distinguished him from the animals.

After the elegiac poets, says Milton, 'I betook me among those lofty fables and romances, which recount in solemn cantos the deeds of knighthood founded by our victorious kings, and from hence had in renown over all Christendom.' This no doubt reflects his recent announcement of an ambition to write a national epic, but it also proceeds to reflect the Reformation sentiment against romances. Here he learnt his 'casta' doctrine and developed his revulsion against its violators. But note his apology: 'So that even these books, which to many others have been the fuel of wantonness and loose living, I cannot think how, unless by divine indulgence, proved to me so many incitements, as you have heard, to the love and steadfast observation of that virtue which abhors the society of bordellos.' This providential escape might not have satisfied Roger Ascham.

Then, he says, 'riper years and the ceaseless round of study and reading led me to the shady spaces of philosophy; but chiefly to the divine volumes of Plato, and his equal Xenophon: where, if I should tell ye what I learnt of chastity and love, I mean that which is truly so, whose charming cup is only virtue, which she bears in her hand to those who are worthy; (the rest are cheated with a thick intoxicating potion, which a certain sorceress, the abuser of love's name, carries about;) and how the first and chiefest office of love begins and ends in the soul, producing those happy twins of her divine generation, knowledge and virtue . . .' This is the stage of *Comus*, and we should remember that Milton (*Animadversions*, xiii) also learnt Socratic teaching from Xenophon.

Lastly, Milton crowns the 'casta' doctrine with the authority of the Bible, where it brings the highest rewards, but where 'defilement' is not allowed to include marriage. Subsequently the 'retraction' which Milton printed at the close of his 'Elegies' in 1645 rejects the 'elegia levis' and reflects the first two stages of the development described in his *Apology*, ending in its Socratic defence against Cupid and Venus. But carnality is a lesson that Adam still has to learn in *Paradise Lost*, beginning with Book VIII.

III

When we consider Milton's use of romance in his major poetic works, we should remember that ultimately for him the British past and present are alike and need the same lesson. The expectation in *Of Reformation* finally recites the moral of British history in the *Second Defence*. The moral story of both times is the same: both need to learn the meaning of the Fall of man and the providence of God, for they too were not ready for it. The pattern of a

Christian hero is the same for both times, but it is not Arthurian. The basic problem is to learn how to stand against temptation. But the basic question takes a new form: Is Adam, like the British, finally unteachable? Yet to 'assert Eternal Providence' reaffirms *Of Reformation* in a sadder key. And to 'justifie the wayes of God to men' now means not to defend God but to instruct man. The hero of Christian patience is an older and wiser form of his 'true warfaring Christian'.

When Milton first described this hero in *Areopagitica* he made liberty essential to virtue, to Providence, to the story of Adam: 'God therefore left him free', for 'he had been else a mere artificial Adam', a puppet. In *Paradise Lost* the critical moment before the Fall comes when Adam gives Eve her liberty. Hence the story of liberty began with Adam and its failure with the Fall of man. No wonder, then, that in the bitterness of experience Milton should turn back to that story for the lesson of British failure. In the 'Digression', which was not published in the *History* of 1670, but appeared in 1681 as a 'Character of the Long Parliament and Assembly of Divines', his later feeling finds moral expression. There he looked for the lesson of history: 'And no less to purpose if not more usefully to us it may withal be enquir'd, since God after 12 ages and more had drawne so neare a parallel betweene their state and ours in the late commotions', why the British had again failed; and why it was no less necessary, 'whosoever shall write thir storie, to revive those antient complaints of Gildas as deservedly on these lately as on those his times'.

The lesson was also to be found in other history: 'For stories teach us that libertie sought out of season in a corrupt and degenerate age brought Rome it self into further slaverie. For libertie hath a sharp and double edge fitt onelie to be handl'd by just and vertuous men, to bad and dissolute it becomes a mischief unwieldie in thir own hands.' Only 'just and virtuous men' can legislate liberty so 'that good men may enjoy the freedom which they merit and the bad the curb which they need'. Thus the lessons of Roman and British history are the same, but the moral basis connects the argument of *Areopagitica* with that of *Paradise Lost*: both show why force is useless in ethics, and is only to be applied to bad men who refuse reason for their law. Hence it was logical that Milton should ultimately turn to the original story of this failure, where he could teach the lesson of national failure above the level of national passions. Here his national subject and his Biblical subject became one; here he found the most persuasive way of being 'doctrinal and exemplary to a nation'.

Thus the Fall of man became the original story of the lost cause and Adam rather than Arthur its protagonist. The pattern of a Christian hero was not to be realized

> *till one greater Man*
> *Restore us, and regain the blissful Seat.*

Meanwhile man had to learn again and again the sad lesson of the Fall; its consequences remained in human misery and the 'loss of Eden'; its romantic elements, if any, belonged to the forces of evil. If the 'true warfaring Christian' had once been a 'Knight in Arms', he had defected to the other side by the time of *Paradise Lost.*

Thus in *Paradise Lost* (Bk. I) Milton not only includes the pagan gods of the *Nativity Ode* among Satan's cohorts, but magnifies the 'horrid Front' by comparison with the heroes of epic and romance (579):

> *and what resounds*
> *In Fable or* Romance *of* Uthers *Son*
> *Begirt with* British *and* Armoric *Knights;*
> *And all who since, Baptiz'd or Infidel*
> *Jousted in* Aspramont *or* Montalban,
> Damasco, *or* Marocco, *or* Trebisond,
> *Or whom* Biserta *sent from* Afric *shore*
> *When* Charlemain *with all his Peerage fell*
> *By* Fontarabbia.

If not actually pygmean, their 'mortal prowess' is now a feeble comparison for the infernal warriors. The romantic heroes are further tarnished when 'the Hall of that infernal Court' is given romantic properties in a parenthesis (763):

> (*Though like a cover'd field, where Champions bold*
> *Wont ride in arm'd, and at the Soldans chair*
> *Defi'd the best of* Panim *chivalry*
> *To mortal combat or career with Lance.*)

But Milton never exorcized the romance of names or their Marlovian magic.

Yet he did thoroughly exorcize war as the romantic glorification of force in Book VI. We may remember that Milton in his
History found the British fit for war but not for peace. The war in
Heaven is concerned with Milton's basic thesis of reason versus
force; it illustrates the futility of the appeal to force, which is most
glamorous in the romantic trial by combat. Even the angels in
Hell, where heroic combat is simulated but not ridiculed, pervert
this thesis in debate. In heaven Abdiel has fought 'the better fight'
of reason, and now (40) prepares for 'the easier conquest' of force,

> *and to subdue*
> *By force, who reason for thir Law refuse.*

Thus force is a last resort, but it fails in this instance. Although
Abdiel is to return more glorious than he departed, only the
power of Christ is able to subdue Satan. And so the war of the
angels comes to an inglorious conclusion (695): 'Warr wearied
hath perform'd what Warr can do.' Only divine power can drive
the rebels out of Heaven, but expulsion by force is not a final
solution. The war, as many have said, degenerates into a primitive
battle of Titans; it declines from a dignified or heroic representation of war to a satiric one, because it is illustrative of Milton's
thesis about war and hence evaluative. Thus war is caricatured by
the action and mocked by the presumptuous dialogue, raucous
cannon, sarcastic puns, and undisciplined uproar without end.
Thus it becomes a lesson not only for Adam, who exhibits some
romantic aspirations, but also for the British, whom Milton
thought too ready to resort to force.

When in Book IX Milton says, 'I now must change / Those
Notes to Tragic', he comes to the heroic theme he announced at
the beginning of the poem: 'Sad task, yet argument / Not less but
more Heroic' than the subjects of classical epic. Then he justifies
himself:

> *Not sedulous by Nature to indite*
> *Warrs, hitherto the onely Argument*
> *Heroic deem'd, chief maistrie to dissect*
> *With long and tedious havoc fabl'd Knights*
> *In Battels feign'd;*

but Milton had already turned the usual heroics into the unheroic
war in Heaven. Then he names his own theme:

> *the better fortitude*
> *Of Patience and Heroic Martyrdom.*

Adam is the hero in this sense, like Samson—of valiant submis, sion to God, in doing or enduring what is required. To say that Adam is too unheroic to be the hero may be true in the usual sense, but not in Milton's. Adam is later warned (XI, 685):

> *For in those dayes Might onely shall be admir'd,*
> *And Valour and Heroic Vertu call'd.*

Finally in Book IX Milton becomes scornful in renouncing heroic trappings:

> *or to describe Races and Games,*
> *Or tilting Furniture, emblazon'd Shields,*
> *Impreses quaint, Caparisons and Steeds;*
> *Bases and tinsel Trappings, gorgious Knights*
> *At Joust and Torneament; then marshal'd Feast*
> *Serv'd up in Hall with Sewers, and Seneshals;*
> *The skill of Artifice or Office mean,*
> *Not that which justly gives Heroic name*
> *To Person or to Poem.*

The embellishments of romantic epic here sink lowest in the scale.

Adam's 'Patience and Heroic Martyrdom' are developed by consequences of the Fall and his responses to them; they produce lessons of moral growth rather than heroic action. The lament of Adam after the Fall (X, 720) grounds the theme of 'Heroic Martyrdom'. It leads to his awareness of the nature of their martyr, dom or their punishment; he replies to Eve (950),

> *alas,*
> *Beare thine own first, ill able to sustaine*
> *His full wrauth whose thou feelst as yet lest part,*
> *And my displeasure bearst so ill. If Prayers*
> *Could alter high Decrees, I to that place*
> *Would speed before thee, and be louder heard,*
> *That on my head all might be visited.*

The hero of patience counsels Eve against

> *impatience and despite,*
> *Reluctance against God and his just yoke*
> *Laid on our Necks.*

When the loss of Eden draws a cry of anguish from Eve, the Angel says (XI, 287):

> *Lament not Eve, but patiently resigne*
> *What justly thou hast lost.*

And Michael teaches Adam the same lesson (360):

> *thereby to learn*
> *True patience, and to temper joy with fear*
> *And pious sorrow, equally enur'd*
> *By moderation either state to beare,*
> *Prosperous or adverse.*

When Adam later (779) expresses Milton's feeling of 'ridiculous frustration',

> *But I was farr deceav'd; for now I see*
> *Peace to corrupt no less then Warr to waste.*
> *How comes it thus?*

Michael repeats the story of disillusionment expressed in the 'Digression' of Milton's *History of Britain*. Whether Milton came to share Adam's feeling of martyrdom we do not know, but Adam strikes the tragic note just before this last question:

> *better had I*
> *Liv'd ignorant of future, so had borne*
> *My part of evil onely, each dayes lot*
> *Anough to bear.*

In that counterpart to *Paradise Lost*—and we would be more perceptive if we considered the extent to which *Paradise Regained* is a counterpart—we find romance again on the side of the devil. First, temptation is pointed by contrast:

> *Alas how simple, to these Cates compar'd,*
> *Was that crude Apple that diverted* Eve!

Then the demonic banquet (II, 354) is made alluring by allusions to myth embellished by Malory:

> *Under the Trees now trip'd, now solemn stood*
> *Nymphs of* Diana's *train, and* Naiades
> *With fruits and flowers from* Amalthea's *horn,*
> *And Ladies of th'* Hesperides, *that seem'd*

23

> *Fairer then feign'd of old, or fabl'd since*
> *Of Fairy Damsels met in Forest wide*
> *By Knights of* Logres, *or of* Lyones,
> Lancelot *or* Pelleas, *or* Pellenore.

Here romance, which was identified long ago, helps to colour the Satanic temptation.

In the temptation of empire, likewise known to Eve, romance also finds its place (III, 337):

> *Such forces met not, nor so wide a camp,*
> *When* Agrican *with all his Northern powers*
> *Besieg'd* Albracca, *as Romances tell;*
> *The City of* Gallaphrone, *from thence to win*
> *The fairest of her Sex* Angelica
> *His daughter, sought by many Prowest Knights,*
> *Both* Paynim, *and the Peers of* Charlemane.
> *Such and so numerous was thir Chivalrie.*

Of course Christ rejects this 'Luggage of war' as evidence 'Of human weakness rather then of strength', and quite irrelevant to power in his kingdom.

In *Samson Agonistes* the Harapha incident is treated to the full irony of romantic contrast as the giant affects knighthood. Samson is scornful (1116):

> *Therefore without feign'd shifts let be assign'd*
> *Some narrow place enclos'd, where sight may give thee,*
> *Or rather flight, no great advantage on me;*
> *Then put on all thy gorgeous arms, thy Helmet*
> *And Brigandine of brass, thy broad Habergeon,*
> *Vant-brass and Greves, and Gauntlet, add thy Spear*
> *A Weavers beam, and seven-times-folded shield,*
> *I only with an Oak'n staff will meet thee,*
> *And raise such out-cries on thy clatter'd Iron . . .*

Samson's contempt for knights of romance is answered by Harapha's effort to disparage Samson's strength:

> *Thou durst not thus disparage glorious arms*
> *Which greatest Heroes have in battel worn,*
> *Thir ornament and safety, had not spells*
> *And black enchantments, some Magicians Art*

> *Arm'd thee or charm'd thee strong, which thou from Heaven*
> *Feigndst at thy birth was giv'n thee in thy hair . . .*

Thus 'celestial vigour' is reduced to black magic.

But Samson is reserved for 'the better fortitude / Of Patience and Heroic Martyrdom', not the mockery of 'fabl'd Knights / In Battels feign'd'. Though subjected to humiliation, Samson fulfils the requirements better than Adam. In the equivocal terms of the Chorus (1277) action may be his lot:

> *He all thir Ammunition*
> *And feats of War defeats*
> *With plain Heroic magnitude of mind*
> *And celestial vigour arm'd. . . .*
> > *But patience is more oft the exercise*
> *Of Saints, the trial of thir fortitude,*
> *Making them each his own Deliverer,*
> *And Victor over all*
> *That tyrannie or fortune can inflict.*

Having redeemed himself in the trial of patience, he is granted 'heroic martyrdom' rather than a romantic trial by combat. Now the 'invincible might' hailed by the Chorus imposes upon him blind the bloody heroism required by *The Tenure of Kings and Magistrates* and justified against bad men. Yet in *Samson Agonistes* Milton offers the English people his final lesson in servitude and true 'Heroic magnitude of mind'. This he sets off by the ironic figure of chivalry exhibited in the rival Giant. For Milton the romantic lady ends in Dalila and the romantic hero in Harapha.

2

THE CONTEXT OF *COMUS*

MILTON once contemplated a play on the destruction of Sodom to be entitled *Cupids Funeral Pile*. In his statement of its 'economy' or disposition the action begins thus: 'By then supper is ended, the Gallantry of the town passe by in Procession with musick and song to the temple of Venus Urania or Peor'; they invite two noble strangers (Angels) to their solemnities, because all fair personages are sacred to their goddess. The argument is summarized thus: 'The first Chorus beginning may relate the course of the citty, each evening every one with mistresse, or Ganymed, gitterning along the streets, or solacing on the banks of Jordan, or down the stream. At the preists inviting the Angels to the Solemnity, the Angels, pittying thir beauty, may dispute of love & how it differs from lust, seeking to win them.' In *Elegia Septima* Milton presents an English form of this social scene. But instead of this play we have *Comus*, another form of Cupid's funeral pile.

I

This surmise is based on evidence of Milton's poetic development such as the palinode which in 1645 recants his elegiac wantonness (*nequitia*). In *Elegia Sexta* this opposition was defined but not established. It is explained by the subsequent confession in *An Apology for Smectymnuus* (1642), made in response to the charge of a licentious life, frequenting playhouses and brothels. There he confesses his attraction to the love poets, the smooth elegiac poets 'whom both for the pleasing sound of their numerous writing, which in imitation I found most easy, and most agreeable to nature's part in me, and for their matter, which what it is, there be few who know not, I was so allured to read, that no recreation came to me better welcome. For that it was then those years with me which are excused, though they be least severe, I may be saved the labor to remember ye.' No doubt he now felt that some of his own elegies made him vulnerable. But then he was persuaded that 'not to be sensible when good and fair in one person meet, argues both a gross and shallow judgment, and withal an ungentle and swainish breast'. Consequently, if he 'found those authors anywhere speaking unworthy things of themselves, or unchaste of those names which before they had extolled . . . from that time forward their art he still applauded, but the men he deplored'. This is why he 'preferred the two famous renowners of Beatrice and Laura', who never dishonoured their subjects. And this experience led him to the belief 'that he who would not be frustrate of his hope to write well hereafter in laudable things, ought himself to be a true poem; that is, a com, position and pattern of the best and honorablest things'.

Likewise he excuses his taste for the romances. There he 'learnt what a noble virtue chastity sure must be, to the defence of which so many worthies, by such a dear adventure of themselves, had sworn'. And if any betrayed his ideal, Milton regarded it the same as profanation in the poet. 'So that even these books, which to many others have been the fuel of wantonness and loose living', proved to him so many incitements 'to the love and steadfast observation of that virtue which abhors the society of bordelloes'. Again we have both the expression of a taste and the ethical judgment of that taste.

So far Milton has been on the defensive. The rest of his progress is unobjectionable. Next his reading led him to philosophy; 'but chiefly to the divine volumes of Plato, and his equal Xenophon: where, if I should tell ye what I learnt of chastity and love, I mean that which is truly so, whose charming cup is only virtue, which she bears in her hand to those who are worthy; (the rest are cheated with a thick intoxicating potion, which a certain sorceress, the abuser of love's name, carries about;) and how the first and chiefest office of love begins and ends in the soul, producing those happy twins of her divine generation, knowledge and virtue . . .' Thus he extends the lesson of the romances, and in terms that suggest *Comus*. But something more seems intended: 'with such abstracted sublimities as these, it might be worth your listening readers, as I may one day hope to have ye in a still time, when there shall be no chiding'. Whether these abstracted sublimities were to sound like the Angels of *Cupids Funeral Pile* remains a question, but their subject is also found in *Comus*.

Thus before Milton had learnt much of Christian doctrine, a certain natural reserve and moral discipline were 'enough to keep him in disdain of far less incontinences than this of the bordello'. Then from St Paul he learnt that unchastity in man is a sin 'against the image and glory of God, which is in himself'. And he did not slumber over the passage in Revelation xiv 'expressing such high rewards of ever accompanying the Lamb with those celestial songs to others inapprehensible, but not to those who were not defiled with women . . .' This reward, we may recall, was given to Damon in *Epitaphium Damonis*, but here it is risked by Milton's qualification of Scripture: 'which doubtless means fornication; for marriage must not be called a defilement'. When he said, 'Nor did I slumber over that place', he was preparing the reader for his reduction of chastity from virginity to continence. Thus chastity and love were harmonized by a union of philosophy and religion that issued in a doctrine of continence or temper-ance.

But the scene of Milton's ethical development is found in his Latin elegies, where he imitated the smooth elegiac poets because they were 'most agreeable to nature's part' in him, not only for 'their numerous writing' but, as even his shy opacity reveals, for 'their matter'. Thus it is the context of Milton's own work with which we must be concerned, not those writers to whom he is indebted.

In his first youthful elegy Milton gives an attractive picture of his devotion to the Muses, his enjoyment of Spring, and especially his sensitiveness to beauty: 'Here often one may see groups of maidens go by, stars breathing soft flames. Ah, how many times have I been entranced by the miracle of some wondrous beauty such as might make even aged Jove a youth again. Ah, how many times have I seen eyes that surpassed gems and all the stars that either pole keeps in revolution, necks that outshone the arms of Pelops twice alive and the Way that flows moist with pure nectar; how many times exquisite beauty of brow and waving tresses, golden snares that deceiving Love spreads, and alluring cheeks in comparison with which the crimson of the hyacinth and even the blush of thy flower, Adonis, lack lustre.'

28

Many years later, in *Paradise Regained* (II), Milton set this theme
to another key when Belial proposed it as a temptation to Christ:

> *Many are in each Region passing fair*
> *As the noon Skie; more like to Goddesses*
> *Then Mortal Creatures, graceful and discreet,*
> *Expert in amorous Arts, enchanting tongues*
> *Perswasive, Virgin majesty with mild*
> *And sweet allay'd, yet terrible to approach,*
> *Skill'd to retire, and in retiring draw*
> *Hearts after them tangl'd in Amorous Nets.*

By then love had become 'terrible as an army with banners'.
But even now it is a theme of temptation employing the Circe
myth that finds its chief place in *Comus*: 'But I, while the indul-
gent mood of the blind boy permits, am preparing to leave these
happy precincts with all convenient speed, and to keep far away
from the ill-famed halls of treacherous Circe, using the help of the
divine plant moly.' For this youth mythology was a language, not
mimicry; his Muse could not simply 'look in thy heart and write'.

Elegy VII, although given a terminal position, resumes his
susceptibility to love in the vernal scene of *Elegy I*. Milton, like
Donne in *Love's Exchange*, has provoked Cupid by putting him
to unusual trouble: 'Sometimes, in the city where our citizens
promenade, sometimes where the fields near the town give pleasure, groups of maidens with goddess-like faces move radiantly to
and fro along the walks; and with this accession of brightness the
day shines with double splendor . . . These pleasing sights I did
not shun through any austerity; and I followed instinctively the
suggestion of my youthful impulses; and taking no thought of the
future I sent my glances to meet theirs; I could not control my
eyes.' This is the excuse offered in his *Apology for Smectymnuus*.
But Cupid has yet to play his trump: 'As it chanced, I noted one
maiden who outshone all the rest; that radiance was the beginning
of my trouble. So Venus herself might wish to appear to mortals;
so the queen of the gods should be the cynosure of all eyes.'

This time he was caught in the snare of beauty: 'Straightway,
unwonted ardors filled my heart. I was consumed within with
love and was all flame. Meantime, to my misery she who now
alone pleased me, vanished, never again to meet my eyes . . .
What am I to do, unhappy man that I am, o'ercome with sorrow?

I may neither put away the love that has begun nor follow it up. Oh, that I may have the privilege of seeing once again that beloved face, and of telling her my sad tale. Perhaps she is not made of unimpressionable adamant, perhaps she would not be deaf to my prayers! Believe me, no one has ever burned with love so unhappily; I shall be put down as the first and only example.' In submitting to this sweet wretchedness, he prays for mercy and one concession from Cupid: 'Do thou only graciously grant that if hereafter any maiden is to be mine, a single arrow shall pierce both the hearts whose destiny is love.' For Milton the 'burning' of these elegies had two consequences: one was the palinode which epitomizes the *Apology*; the other was the Pauline bias of *The Doctrine and Discipline of Divorce*.

In *Elegy V* his imagination becomes truly erotic in its response to Spring. It is said that later in life 'his vein never happily flowed but from the autumnal equinox to the vernal'. Now he finds his inspiration vernal, but the vein of youth makes it Cybelene; sensual figures dominate as he sings the amatory rites of Spring. The opening of his contest with Philomel is later translated to the beginning of his sonnet on the Nightingale. Now Nature becomes a virtual feast of the senses and a riot of fertility: 'Thus the wanton earth sighs forth her love, and all her children tumultuously follow the example of their mother.' Now Cupid 'essays to conquer even unconquerable Diana, even chaste Vesta, as she sits by her hallowed hearth'.

As for Milton's elegiac maidens: 'In crowds the maidens with gold-cinctured breasts go forth to gain the joys of the lovely spring. Each has her own prayer; still the prayer of all is one and the same, that Cytherea may give her the man that she desires.' Even the Oread of *L'Allegro*, 'sweet Liberty', becomes a little wanton: 'Faunus, love-possessed, would fain ravish some Oread, while the trembling nymph takes to her heels for safety; now she hides, and though she does so, desires, since she is poorly concealed, to be seen; and flees, and though she flees, is anxious to be caught.' Indeed, Milton had only to return to this elegy for both the fertility theme and the eloquence that animate Comus.

Elegy VI, on the other hand, reveals Milton's sensitivity to moral discipline. Here the possibility of the elegiac palinode emerges and the moral development of the *Apology* is anticipated. In fact the muse of elegy is contrasted with the muse of epic, and

their regimens related to wine and to water respectively. Light
elegy may invoke Bacchus, the erotic Muse, fertile Ceres, or Venus
and Cupid, for song has been inspired by wine and feasting. But
the epic poet requires a stricter regimen: 'that poet should live
sparingly as did the Samian teacher and should find in herbs his
simple food. Let the crystal water stand beside him in a beechen
cup, and let him drink only sober draughts from a pure spring.
Let him have, in addition, a youth chaste and free from evil,
uncompromising standards, and stainless hands.' These requirements project the stage of moral development that crowns the
progress described in his *Apology for Smectymnuus.*

They are also reflected in the covenant made in *The Reason
of Church Government* (II): 'Neither do I think it shame to covenant with any knowing reader, that for some few years yet I may
go on trust with him toward the payment of what I am now indebted, as being a work not to be raised from the heat of youth, or
the vapors of wine; like that which flows at waste from the pen of
some vulgar amorist, or the trencher fury of a rhyming parasite;
nor to be obtained by the invocation of dame memory and her
siren daughters, but by devout prayer to that eternal Spirit, who
can enrich with all utterance and knowledge, and sends out his
seraphim, with the hallowed fire of his altar, to touch and purify
the lips of whom he pleases.' This pledge brings decision to
Elegy VI and confirmation to the moral progress outlined in the
Apology.

II

The opposed Muses of *Elegy VI* are later divided between the
moods of Mirth and Melancholy, which are personified in
variants of Marlowe's invitation to a mode of life, 'Come live
with me and be my love.' The muse of *L'Allegro* is a nymph
'fair and free', the daughter of Venus and Bacchus, or of Zephyrus
and Aurora; by either lineage related to Cupid or Eros. Spenser
had suggested that mirth could become wanton (*F.Q.*, II, vi):
'Guyon is of immodest Merth led into loose desire.' Milton made
this transition through the lineage of Comus, son of Circe and
Bacchus, who lives with licence, not 'sweet Liberty'. The opposite muse of *Il Penseroso* is 'sage and holy', lives with 'Spare Fast',
and is thus addressed: 'Com pensive Nun, devout and pure.' Her

lineage is equally appropriate, the daughter of Saturn and Vesta, who resisted the lust of *Elegy V*. She descends to *Comus* as the Lady, and the Platonism of *Il Penseroso* relates it not only to *Comus* but also to the *Apology* and the elegiac palinode.

Sir Henry Wotton's letter about *Comus* may serve to define the nature of Milton's poetic achievement before *Comus*. It is pointed by Wotton's emphasis: 'Wherin I should much commend the Tragical part, if the Lyrical did not ravish me with a certain Dorique delicacy in your Songs and Odes, wherunto I must plainly confess to have seen yet nothing parallel in our Language: *Ipsa mollities*.' *Arcades* would have given him much less reason to 'commend the Tragical part' as compared with the Lyrical. No doubt Dr Johnson would have regretted this passage of rhymed dramatic verse:

> *Stay gentle Swains, for though in this disguise,*
> *I see bright honour sparkle through your eyes,*
> *Of famous* Arcady *ye are, and sprung*
> *Of that renowned flood, so often sung,*
> *Divine* Alpheus, *who by secret sluse,*
> *Stole under Seas to meet his* Arethuse.

The last couplet is redeemed in *Lycidas*. But here the Lyrical part sounded with his best music, and no less in proper names:

> *Nymphs and Shepherds dance no more*
> *By sandy* Ladons Lillied *banks.*
> *On old* Lycæus *or* Cyllene *hoar,*
> *Trip no more in twilight ranks,*
> *Though* Erymanth *your loss deplore,*
> *A better soyl shall give ye thanks.*

Milton, however, still had much to learn in the Tragical part, but *Comus* revealed the nature of his ultimate achievement.

Milton's explicit definition of dramatic form is found, of course, in his Preface to *Samson Agonistes*. But it is possible to infer his conception of that form from his plans in the Cambridge Manuscript and their reflection in *The Reason of Church Government* (II). In the latter he already finds the Greek dramatic form in the Bible: 'The Scripture also affords us a divine pastoral drama in the Song of Solomon, consisting of two persons, and a double chorus, as Origen rightly judges.' And the Cambridge plans already reflect the definition of plot in the *Samson* preface as the 'oeconomy, or disposition of the fable as may stand best with verisimilitude and decorum'; at least the argument of *Abram from Morea* is introduced as follows: 'The oiconomie may be thus . . .'

Milton's 'disposition' of the dramatic *Paradise Lost* and *Adam Unparadiz'd* depends upon two speakers and a chorus, the basic form of *Samson Agonistes*. But the plan of *Adam Unparadiz'd* also mentions the masque: 'The Angel is sent to banish them out of paradise; but before, causes to passe before his eyes in shapes a mask of all the evills of this life & world.' Even in the epic form of *Paradise Lost* Milton kept this masque. Moreover, in its dramatic form these 'shapes' appeared as 'mutes' in Act V: 'Adam and Eve, driven out of Paradice praesented by an angel with Labour greife hatred Envie warre famine Pestilence sicknesse discontent Ignorance Feare Death.' This morality play, which is close to Spenserian allegory, shows more personifications as actors, but neither God nor Christ; later its epic form gives personified roles to sin and death. For Milton it seems the masque is like allegory, a moral presentation of life, not a mimetic representation; its plot is a disposition of the fable as may stand best with the ideal, with decorum, not verisimilitude; it is motivated by its argument.

Spenser had set an example of the epic use of such a masque in the third book of his *Faerie Queene*. It is more suggestive, however, for *Comus*, since this book deals with the legend of 'Chastitie' and ends with 'The maske of Cupid' or the release of a Lady from enchantment. This lady, Amoret, was born in the Garden of Adonis and reared by Psyche at the behest of Venus. In order to adapt this masque to his theme and occasion, Milton had only to change the personifications, Comus for Cupid, Sabrina for Britomart, and incorporate the Circe myth informed by his Platonism. The relation of his *Maske* to the Spenserian tradition had even been suggested in *Il Penseroso*:

> *Of Forests, and inchantments drear,*
> *Where more is meant then meets the ear.*

III

Much of Milton's earlier work bore fruit in *Comus*. *Elegy VI*, for example, had concluded by exemplifying the poet as *vates*: 'So

Homer, the spare eater and the water-drinker, carries Ulysses through vast stretches of ocean, through the monster-making hall of Circe, through the seas made treacherous by the songs of the Sirens, and through your mansions, O infernal King, where he is said to have held the hosts of shades by means of black blood.' Thus the myth of Circe offered a basic myth or trial for the moral hero of Milton. But in his *Maske* it is extended by elements borrowed from Spenser. In *Elegy V* he had already exploited the fertility theme and made the satyrs and Sylvanus participate in its rites. Only the Platonism of his *Apology* was lacking among the basic ingredients of *Comus*, and it had appeared in *Il Penseroso*.

In *Comus* we may detect a licentious form of *L'Allegro* opposed by the sober muse of *Il Penseroso*. This opposition first became possible in *Elegy VI*. We should recall that *L'Allegro* descends from Venus and Bacchus, who belong to 'light elegy', but that Comus is degraded by having Circe rather than Venus for his mother. The Platonic opposition to the Circe myth in *Comus* finds its appropriate descent in the Vesta and Saturn lineage of *Il Penseroso*. In his own moral drama, however, Milton professes in *Elegy VII* finally to have succumbed to Venus and Cupid, and in the palinode later to have triumphed over them by means of Platonism. Perhaps his *Maske* may be regarded as a dramatization of his defence against the temptations to which he replies in the *Apology for Smectymnuus*. At any rate the elements of this *Maske* are clearly apparent in his earlier work.

How this argument was to be deployed in the masque form was limited by external requirements of the occasion, especially with respect to the actors and the compliment of patrons. The basic action obviously concerns Comus and the Lady; the others are used to develop its significance. On the other hand, Milton puts external features of the masque to dramatic use: song and dance are extended to characterization, for characters are discriminated by their sounds and rhythms, even to the point of marking entrances. The anti-masque is also put to moral purpose in Comus's rout so as to illustrate the consequence of succumbing to Circe's son. Thus Comus and his rout present the same contrast between seductive and repulsive vice that Satan and Sin represent in *Paradise Lost*.

Comus is a morality in masque form introduced by a prologue and concluded by an epilogue. First the attendant Spirit reminds men, or rather the worthy, of the theme of the *Maske*:

> *Unmindfull of the crown that Vertue gives*
> *After this mortal change, to her true Servants*
> *Amongst the enthron'd gods on Sainted seats.*

This theme rests on Revelation (iv and xiv) and repeats the reward with which his confession in the *Apology* concluded. The protective genius of the good provides the necessary exposition for the action, which centres in the Circe myth. Comus as Circe's son has a 'charmed Cup' that is subsequently countered, here as in the *Apology*, by the 'charming cup' of Plato's *Symposium*, which distinguished between the physical and spiritual ends of love. Now the jollity of *L'Allegro* becomes less innocent; instead of such lines as

> *Haste thee nymph, and bring with thee*
> *Jest and youthful Jollity,*
> *Quips and Cranks, and wanton Wiles,*
> *Nods, and Becks, and Wreathed Smiles,*

we find less 'unreproved pleasures':

> *Mean while welcom Joy, and Feast,*
> *Midnight shout, and revelry,*
> *Tipsie dance, and Jollity.*
> *Braid your Locks with rosie Twine*
> *Dropping odours, dropping Wine.*

Restraining factors are personified and put to bed. '*Venus* now wakes, and wak'ns Love.' For "Tis onely day-light that makes Sin' and the wanton rites of *Elegy V* belong to 'Dark vaild Co-tytto'. Comus breaks off the dance because his art enables him to detect 'som chast footing neer'. The Lady enters, guided by her ear to 'the sound / Of Riot', expecting to find rustics as 'In wan-ton dance they praise the bounteous *Pan*, / And thank the gods amiss.' Here the fertility theme of *Elegy V* emerges before the 'chaste footing' of the Lady introduces a morality figure. In terms of the *Apology* she is a Laura and unafraid of the Riot:

> *These thoughts may startle well, but not astound*   (210)
> *The vertuous mind, that ever walks attended*
> *By a strong siding champion Conscience.—*

O welcom pure-ey'd Faith, white-handed Hope,
Thou hovering Angel girt with golden wings,
And thou unblemish't form of Chastity . . .

Obviously she is conceived in the morality tradition or Spenserian
vein, and the shortest answer to those who bewail the decline of
charity into chastity is that the Lady is about to face a trial of
chastity, not charity, and that Comus certainly knew the difference. In the dramatic plan of *Paradise Lost* Milton retained both
Conscience and Faith, Hope, and Charity. And of course it is
not dramatic verisimilitude, but the masque convention that permits a lady in danger to make her presence known by singing a
song. Although the song concerns her lost brothers, romantic love
finds a place in it:

> *Where the love-lorn Nightingale* (234)
> *Nightly to thee her sad Song mourneth well.*

Aside from compliment, Comus feels that this song surpasses the
singing of Circe and the Sirens, and even moves him to express
an honourable intention: 'she shall be my Queen'. But the Lady
is far more suspicious of flattery than Mother Eve, and much more
aware of her trial (329): 'Eie me blest Providence, and square my
triall / To my proportion'd strength.'

The anxiety of the two brothers for their lost sister is developed
rather more ethically than dramatically, or at least on two levels,
the natural and the philosophical. The confidence of the Elder
Brother is ethical; he does not think his sister 'so unprincipl'd in
vertues book' as to fall a victim to Comus's night. Echoes of *Il
Penseroso* are heard in his speech on virtue, and they continue in
the reply of the second brother, leading to a theme that is to echo
in the Epilogue:

> *But beauty like the fair Hesperian Tree* (393)
> *Laden with blooming gold, had need the guard*
> *Of dragon watch with uninchanted eye,*
> *To save her blossoms, and defend her fruit*
> *From the rash hand of bold Incontinence.*

But the Elder Brother insists that their sister is not defenceless
against incontinence, that she has a hidden strength other than
divine grace, the chastity of Diana. Ultimately this strength rests

(439) upon 'the old Schools of Greece', as it did in Milton's *Apology* and elegiac palinode.

Obviously the Elder Brother, despite some natural anxiety, does not regard rape as a trial of virtue, even though chastity is made as magical as other elements of the *Maske*. Clearly the culmination of Milton's confession in the *Apology* touches this crucial passage:

> So dear to Heav'n is Saintly chastity, (453)
> That when a soul is found sincerely so,
> A thousand liveried Angels lacky her,
> Driving far off each thing of sin and guilt,
> And in cleer dream, and solemn vision
> Tell her of things that no gross ear can hear . . .

The Elder Brother continues to suggest the *Apology*, but chiefly in terms of Plato's *Phaedo* on the relation of body and soul:

> Till oft convers with heav'nly habitants (459)
> Begin to cast a beam on th'outward shape,
> The unpolluted temple of the mind,
> And turns it by degrees to the souls essence,
> Till all be made immortal: but when lust
> By unchaste looks, loose gestures, and foul talk,
> But most by leud and lavish act of sin,
> Lets in defilement to the inward parts,
> The soul grows clotted by contagion,
> Imbodies, and imbrutes, till she quite loose
> The divine property of her first being.

Thus it is lust rather than woman that defiles. Moreover, moral qualities have had their effect on 'the outward shape' of characters in the *Maske* so that unpolluted shapes belong to the Lady and her brothers, but shapes of lust to Comus and his rout. Thus Milton presents the basic doctrine of the morality in his *Maske*. Now the second brother forgets his fear enough to praise philosophy and its temperance, 'Where no crude surfet raigns'.

When the attendant Spirit gives substance to the second brother's fears, he describes the great sorcerer Comus and how he bewitches his victims:

> And here to every thirsty wanderer, (524)
> By sly enticement gives his banefull cup,

37

> *With many murmurs mixt, whose pleasing poison*
> *The visage quite transforms of him that drinks,*
> *And the inglorious likenes of a beast*
> *Fixes instead, unmoulding reasons mintage*
> *Character'd in the face . . .*

This magic translates Milton's Platonism into masque terms most obviously in Comus's rout, but it also represents his evil, or descent in the scale of being. Hardly less magical is the role of music in this masque, especially when the Spirit hears 'strains that might create a soul / Under the ribs of Death'. The danger that now threatens the Lady gives the Elder Brother an opportunity to reaffirm his faith:

> *Vertue may be assail'd, but never hurt,*   (589)
> *Surpriz'd by unjust force, but not enthrall'd,*
> *Yea even that which mischief meant most harm,*
> *Shall in the happy trial prove most glory.*
> *But evil on it self shall back recoyl,*
> *And mix no more with goodness, when at last*
> *Gather'd like scum, and setl'd to it self*
> *It shall be in eternal restless change*
> *Self-fed, and self-consum'd, if this fail,*
> *The pillar'd firmament is rott'nness,*
> *And earths base built on stubble.*

Virtue can never be forced, by whatever means; it can only be lost by consenting to evil. The magnificence of this passage rests upon the necessity of moral choice to a rational world. This is why Comus employs what the younger brother must regard as his weakest weapon, persuasion. But in planning to rescue the Lady, the Spirit offers her brothers a protection against enchant-ment like that which Milton used against Circe in *Elegy I*.

The temptation scene, which appears again in *Paradise Regained*, is set out in masque elements that justify the final song of triumph 'O're sensual Folly, and Intemperance'. The Lady, now 'set in an inchanted Chair', responds to Comus's threat with the very ground of virtue for Milton (603): 'Thou canst not touch the freedom of my minde / With all thy charms.' Comus resorts to sensuous appeals and the refreshment of nature as persuasions to the Lady, but she rebukes him for his deception and rejects his baits, because none

> *But such as are good men can give good things,* (703)
> *And that which is not good, is not delicious*
> *To a well-govern'd and wise appetite.*

If Milton's elegies show that he was familiar with what Comus calls 'youthfull thoughts', they also show the growth of such ideas of continence.

Comus counters with the speech that has won the admiration even of Leavis. It is an argument from Nature's fertility, which Milton had celebrated in *Elegy V*, where even Diana and Vesta had to resist its devotees. This argument is related to providence by Comus and directed against the severe regimen of *Elegy VI*:

>   *if all the world* (720)
> *Should in a pet of temperance feed on Pulse,*
> *Drink the clear stream, and nothing wear but Freize,*
> *Th'all-giver would be unthank't, would be unprais'd . . .*

Neither God nor nature is niggardly, and we should not 'live like Natures bastards'. His picture of nature 'strangl'd with her waste fertility' is not to be equalled even in *King Lear*, but it had already been sketched in *Elegy V*. Milton also knew the corollary against coyness, that 'Beauty is natures brag', and love's lure.

But the Lady is ready for Comus's attempt to charm reason, which is the real danger for Milton: nature's providence is not an invitation to riotous excess. As for his contemptuous words against chastity:

> *Thou hast nor Eare, nor Soul to apprehend* (784)
> *The sublime notion, and high mystery*
> *That must be utter'd to unfold the sage*
> *And serious doctrine of Virginity.*

Aside from answering magic with magic in masque fashion, this alludes to the 'high mysteries' which crowned Milton's confession in the *Apology*. Although Comus is impressed by her counter-magic, he retorts: 'This is meer moral babble.'

When the brothers bungle the release of the Lady, the attendant Spirit offers to borrow another means of rescue from old Melibœus or Spenser:

> *And, as the old Swain said, she can unlock* (852)
> *The clasping charm, and thaw the numming spell,*
> *If she be right invok't in warbled Song . . .*

Thus Sabrina is given a role like that of Britomart and adapted to
the requirements of Milton's *Maske*. She had been 'made Goddess
of the River' as Lycidas became 'the Genius of the shore', both
to succour others, Sabrina being partial to virgins in distress. She
is invoked in the manner required and releases the Lady with
appropriate magic. Physical release from Comus's magic is
achieved not by reversing his magic, which cannot enthral her
mind, but by the application of Sabrina's lustral element.

If *Comus* ends within the convention of the pastoral masque, the
Epilogue of the Spirit extends its theme into Elysium. The night
of Comus gives way to eternal day or summer, where beauty is
unguarded:

> *All amidst the Gardens fair*   (981)
> *Of* Hesperus, *and his daughters three*
> *That sing about the golden tree.*

Gone is the dragon watch, and Iris, a virgin goddess, 'drenches
with *Elysian* dew' the bed and flower of two victims of love, whose
flowers were foils to beauty in *Elegy I*. Again (cf. 784) apprehension depends upon an ear for high mystery—the physical and
spiritual ends of love. As Adonis recovers, Venus mourns; not
as Comus said, 'Venus now wakes, and wak'ns Love.' The
higher love appears above:

> *But far above in spangled sheen*   (1003)
> *Celestial* Cupid *her fam'd son advanc't,*
> *Holds his dear* Psyche *sweet intranc't*
> *After her wandring labours long,*
> *Till free consent the gods among*
> *Make her his eternal Bride . . .*

This marriage is to produce 'Youth and Joy' after 'wandring
labours long'. Such are the rewards of the lower and higher love
of Plato's *Symposium*. Only the love of virtue can teach you 'how
to clime / Higher then the Spheary chime' to the ultimate happiness.

IV

The conflict between the muse of elegy and the muse of epic,
which Milton stated in *Elegy VI*, appears briefly in *Lycidas* as the
famous question about strictly meditating the thankless Muse:

The Context of Comus

Were it not better don as others use,
To sport with Amaryllis *in the shade,*
Or with the tangles of Neaera's *hair?*

But desire for fame ('That last infirmity of Noble mind') spurred him 'To scorn delights, and live laborious dayes.' Here the temptations of 'light elegy' are opposed to the requirements of a stricter Muse. Both his *Apology* and his elegiac palinode tell us that Platonism taught Milton how to escape from these temptations of youth, and yet when he defined poetry in *Of Education* he used such terms as 'more simple, sensuous, and passionate'. But neither his Platonism nor his poetics ever divorced the spiritual and the physical.

Milton again dramatized the story of a character dedicated to virtue in *Samson Agonistes*. Samson, vowed to abstinence but seduced by his Circe, presents the final form of this myth in Milton. Both the Lady and the Nazarite undergo trials of temperance or continence in the broad sense. Criticism has been harder on the Lady than on Samson, but Milton obviously did not think it less praiseworthy for the Lady to stand when Samson fell than for Christ to stand when Adam fell. Yet the world has continued to find the sinners more interesting or more sympathetic. But a famous sinner could damn Cowley by saying, 'Not being of God, he could not stand.'

3

THE EDUCATION OF ADAM

WHEN Milton decided to make the Fall of Man 'doctrinal and exemplary to a nation' by 'teaching over the whole book of sanctity and virtue', we may be sure that he wanted to make his teaching effective. But too often his teaching in *Paradise Lost* has seemed tedious to the reader, especially after the brilliance of the opening action. Indeed, for several books the story suspends that action to the point of seriously abating the epic suspense. Was this a consequence of following the principle of beginning *in medias res*? Or was it the result of Milton's epic strategy?

The suspense could not turn on the uncertainty of the outcome, but rather must turn upon the interpretation of the Fall. Why Adam would fall, not how, alone gave scope to the poet. For Milton was limited as the Greek dramatists were limited, free only to interpret a known story. In making it 'doctrinal and exemplary' he could develop tension in the story only in terms of its characters, their motives, and their moral behaviour. The impressiveness of Satan is Milton's tribute not only to the power of evil but also to the glory of moral warfare. The education of Adam must prepare him for his ordeal as well as the reader for its significance. Thus his education seems both intrinsic and extrinsic to the plot; doctrine and example unite in the epic strategy. If the education of Adam teaches over 'the whole book of sanctity and virtue', it also includes 'all the instances of example' necessary for his instruction. In Milton's strategy the didactic element is intended both to motivate and to amplify the tragic consequences of the fall of man. At the same time it must leave man with more hope than Satan was able to muster after the fall of the angels. This is achieved by the ambiguity of the so-called 'fortunate fall', which Satan inverts in Hell (II, 14–17).

I

In the Argument prefixed to Book I of *Paradise Lost* we read: 'Which action past over, the Poem hasts into the midst of things, presenting Satan with his Angels now fallen into Hell.' The action past over is Satan's revolt from God and expulsion from Heaven, or 'the prime cause' of man's fall from obedience. The ensuing action depends upon Satan's report of a prophecy in Heaven about 'a new World and new kind of Creature to be created'. This report introduces the story of man as sequel to the fall of the angels. And this conjunction of the two stories necessi/ tates the 'relations' of Books V to VIII, which suspend the seduc/ tion of man and prepare for his loss of Paradise. Moreover, for the education of Adam these relations narrate both the 'action past over' and the creation of 'a new World and new kind of Creature'. At the same time they explore the potentialities of human nature which the Fall will exhibit.

Then in Book IX the action which joins the two stories is resumed and carried to its tragic consequence. The education of Adam, however, as well as the ultimate significance of his story, requires the further relations—or vision and relation—of the last two Books. His education serves first as the dramatic prepara/ tion for the catastrophe and then as the moral extension of its consequences. Thus the education of Adam becomes both a structural element in the epic plot and a didactic element in the meaning of *Paradise Lost*. If his education is carried on by relations, his catastrophe belongs to the main action; but without the rela/ tions his catastrophe would be lacking in what Dryden called concernment. Since the relations are narrated between the begin/ ning and end of the main action, they naturally raise questions about their dramatic function. To answer that their function is doctrinal is to beg the poetic question. Moreover, Milton's insis/ tence on the freedom of moral choice subordinates his doctrine to character and the agency of plot.

Of course the creation of 'a new World and new kind of Creature' introduced Sir Thomas Browne's other book of divinity, Nature. It added what Bacon called 'the book of God's works' to 'the book of God's word', and it taught the same lesson. When a man, says Bacon's *Advancement of Learning*, 'seeth the dependence of causes, and the works of Providence; then, according to the allegory of the poets, he will easily believe that the highest link of nature's chain must needs be tied to the foot of Jupiter's chair'. Sir Thomas Browne found the first Cause of Common Errors in the common infirmity of Human Nature, and so directed an inquiry into the reasons for the Fall of Man. Milton was also concerned with the relations between the two kinds of learning.

In *Paradise Lost* Milton followed the aim and principle of education which he set forth in *Of Education*. First the aim: 'The end then of learning is to repair the ruins of our first parents by regaining to know God aright, and out of that knowledge to love him, to imitate him, to be like him, as we may the nearest by possessing our souls of true virtue, which being united to the heavenly grace of faith makes up the highest perfection.' But, as Donne explained in his *Second Anniversarie*, the mind of man limits his method of learning: 'But because our understanding cannot in this body found itself but on sensible things, nor arrive so clearly to the knowledge of God and things invisible as by orderly conning over the visible and inferior creature, the same method is necessarily to be followed in all discreet teaching.'

For Milton, however, this principle finally rested upon his so-called materialism as set forth in *Paradise Lost* (V, 469 ff.). Patrick Hume, Milton's first annotator, explained this materialism as the consequence of Scripture and the Scale of Nature or chain of being. Hume calls this 'a real visible Ladder' which 'leads us by *Steps in Contemplation of Created Things up to God*, the Invisible Creator of all Things'. This is why Raphael's concrete approach to Adam's instruction is something more than a pedagogic fiction. For Milton it was not an allegory of the poets that tied the highest link of nature's chain to the foot of Jupiter's chair, but neither did nature yield the highest wisdom; as *The Reason of Church Government* (II) said, 'the contemplation of natural causes and dimensions . . . must needs be a lower wisdom, as the object is low'. Although Bacon could also deceive Uriel, the study of God's works became for him a way to acquire power; for Milton it could also lead to the sin of pride.

Before Satan alights on the World in Book III, Milton presents the theological scheme that is basic to the meaning of his poem. Although animated in presentation, it is expository in nature and hence not dramatic in purpose or feeling. As dignified exposition rather than debate, it lacks the intensity of the Council in Hell, but it gives intensity to the consequences of that Council. God as the *deus ex machina* plays a role of expositor rather than manipulator. Man's fate will turn on the idea (ll. 100 ff.) that rational liberty makes obedience a manifestation of love; God cannot compel service.

By the close of Book IV Satan's plan of temptation has been formed and his action, 'tempting her in a dream', has been interrupted by the guardian angels. This plan centres on the 'fatal Tree', the only sign of their obedience left (ll. 522 ff.):

> *Hence I will excite thir minds*
> *With more desire to know, and to reject*
> *Envious commands, invented with designe*
> *To keep them low whom knowledge might exalt*
> *Equal with Gods; aspiring to be such,*
> *They taste and die.*

Already the first epic relation of matter not covered by the action proper (ll. 440 ff.) has revealed Eve's vanity, which opens her to the temptation of pride. Now she reveals a desire to know by her question about the moon and stars (ll. 657–8):

> *But wherfore all night long shine these, for whom*
> *This glorious sight, when sleep hath shut all eyes?*

Her question implies the need for admiration and is turned to flattery by Satan in her dream. But Adam replies that light is necessary for life and that God is not dependent on man for praise. When Satan's action is interrupted, the outlines of the temptation are clear; but his action has to be suspended both for the education of Adam and for the preparation of the audience. While the didactic purpose is being served, dramatic tension is developed by our growing insight into Adam and Eve.

If the tree of knowledge gives Satan the grounds of temptation, Eve first directs speculation towards the heavens. Both the reply of Adam and the dream inspired by Satan suggest the involvement of pride in Eve's question. Thus when Raphael is sent to prepare Adam for his trial, the reader is prepared to follow and interpret Adam's response to the lessons of the 'action past over' and to the 'new World and new kind of Creature'. The path of temptation has been defined enough to arouse the reader's apprehension.

II

Book V opens with Adam and Eve's first experience of evil and the beginning of trouble in the form of Eve's dream. This antici-pates the tragic temptation in its essentials, but it also reflects and alters her past experience. First she thought her seducer's voice that of Adam, and its question related to her question of the night, that the moon and stars shone 'in vain, / If none regard'. And then its flattery harmonized with her own first experience of vanity (ll. 44–47):

> *Heav'n wakes with all his eyes,*
> *Whom to behold but thee, Natures desire,*
> *In whose sight all things joy, with ravishment*
> *Attracted by thy beauty still to gaze.*

Adam had exhibited this capacity while Eve was still dreaming. Now he explains her dream as a manifestation of evil created out of past experience by faculties usually subordinate to reason (ll. 114–16):

> *Som such resemblances methinks I find*
> *Of our last Eevnings talk, in this thy dream,*
> *But with addition strange.*

Now both are troubled and their trouble finds expression in a prayer for help (ll. 205 ff.). And so God sends Raphael to fulfil the providence expressed in Book III, chiefly by recounting the 'action past over'. As 'the sociable Spirit' he is most sympathetic to Adam's deepest need, and so enables Milton to explore the human condition.

For Milton the prodigality of nature provides not only a mani-festation of God's providence but also a constant trial of temper-ance. This topic motivates the encounter between Comus and the Lady; it becomes the field of trial to which Adam is related in *Areopagitica*; it supports much of the education of Adam in human nature. It is manifest in the Garden of Eden and in the prepara-tions to entertain Raphael. The angelic supper provides the occa-sion for Raphael to satisfy Adam's desire to know by explaining the scale of Nature by which matter works up to spirit (as in *Comus*). Its importance is emphasized by Adam (ll. 508 ff.):

The Education of Adam

> *Well hast thou taught the way that might direct*
> *Our knowledge, and the scale of Nature set*
> *From center to circumference, whereon*
> *In contemplation of created things*
> *By steps we may ascend to God.*

This is the principle of education set forth in Milton's tract of that name; it may also lead to undue aspiration. But Raphael had imposed a condition on man's future that worries Adam: 'What meant that caution joind, *if ye be found / Obedient?*' Raphael explains that our service of God must be voluntary, the effect of love, not of necessity, if it is to be acceptable. As in *Areopagitica* freedom of will is a necessary condition of virtue as of love. Adam's desire to hear more of what 'Hath past in Heav'n' gives Raphael the opportunity to exemplify the meaning of obedience, which Milton has translated into love.

But first Raphael lays down the assumption of his teaching (ll. 571 ff.):

> *what surmounts the reach*
> *Of human sense, I shall delineate so,*
> *By lik'ning spiritual to corporal forms,*
> *As may express them best.*

It is the assumption found in *Of Education*, but Raphael extends it to express a possibility which he had already suggested in his comparison of man and angel:

> *though what if Earth*
> *Be but the shaddow of Heav'n, and things therein*
> *Each to other like, more then on earth is thought?*

Now the action past over becomes a great lesson in obedience to God, and a graphic answer to Adam's question (ll. 514 ff.):

> *can wee want obedience then*
> *To him, or possibly his love desert*
> *Who formd us from the dust, and plac'd us here*
> *Full to the utmost measure of what bliss*
> *Human desires can seek or apprehend?*

The human situation is related to the trial of virtue in *Areopagitica*: 'This justifies the high providence of God, who, though he command us temperance, justice, continence, yet pours out before us, even to a profuseness, all desirable things, and gives us minds that can wander beyond all limit and satiety.' And Belial reminds us how easily our minds succumb to romantic aspiration:

> *for who would loose*
> *Though full of pain, this intellectual being,*
> *Those thoughts that wander through Eternity?*

How such a desertion could happen is exemplified by the revolt in Heaven, with Satan as the great model of disobedience and Abdiel as the great model of obedience, one whom pride alienates from God and one who cannot 'his love desert'. The emphasis on love in *Paradise Lost* belongs to the emphasis on the social nature of man and the bonds that produce society or relate man to the good. By love he may ascend the scale of being as well as descend it by lust. Thus 'the sociable Spirit' Raphael becomes the best interpreter of the human condition. As the proud Spirit, Satan represents the perversion of virtue and his followers the more negative sins; together they animate the sins that produce alienation from God.

Book VI reveals the significance of Abdiel's stand: Abdiel is an example of the moral courage that enables one to stand against evil. He embodies Milton's favourite moral doctrines; his example corrects the argument in Hell that force is stronger than reason. Here 'the easier conquest' is that of force, the necessity of the fallen Angels, 'who reason for thir Law refuse'. Yet force does not and cannot resolve the war with evil; for Milton believed that force can curb or punish evil, but only reason can conquer it. Comus, we may recall, could neither force nor persuade virtue. Adam is taught that God and Nature (reason) both bid us follow virtue: to serve vice is to be enslaved (ll. 174 ff.). Evil is born of disobedience and produces violence and war (ll. 262 ff.). When the war in Heaven degenerates into a primitive battle of Titans, uncontrolled force threatens Heaven with ruin, and shows that 'Warr wearied hath perform'd what Warr can do'. When Christ drives out the forces of evil, for Heaven 'Brooks not the works of violence and Warr', Christ manifests the punishment of God rather than the triumph of force. And so Adam learns 'By terrible Example the reward / Of disobedience'; learns about the first cause of his story (ll. 900 ff.):

> Satan, *hee who envies now thy state,*
> *Who now is plotting how he may seduce*
> *Thee also from obedience, that with him*
> *Bereavd of happiness thou maist partake*
> *His punishment, Eternal miserie.*

We know that at best this tragic consequence may be shortened but not escaped. And since this mitigation is theological rather than dramatic, our concern has to centre in the troubles of the human characters.

Book VII deals with the Creation which is God's answer to Satan's revolt, and which makes possible the conclusion of the Conclave in Hell. But its revelation is motivated by Adam's human nature:

> *Led on, yet sinless, with desire to know*
> *What neerer might concern him,*

he returns to his early curiosity about the world (ll. 84 ff.):

> *Deign to descend now lower, and relate*
> *What may no less perhaps availe us known,*
> *How first began this Heav'n which we behold*
> *Distant so high, with moving Fires adornd.*

Possibly that 'perhaps' intimates doubt on Milton's part, but for the reader it continues the revelation of human nature upon which our concern must be founded. Here Milton's imagination returns to his Native Element (ll. 23 ff.):

> *Standing on Earth, not rapt above the Pole,*
> *More safe I sing with mortal voice, unchang'd*
> *To hoarce or mute, though fall'n on evil dayes,*
> *On evil dayes though fall'n, and evil tongues;*
> *In darkness, and with dangers compast round,*
> *And solitude.*

And every detail of his own fallen state brings new sympathy to his voice and new understanding to his theme.

Adam disclaims any intention to seek forbidden knowledge, but offers the same excuse that Satan addressed to Uriel (ll. 95–97):

> *not to explore the secrets aske*
> *Of his Eternal Empire, but the more*
> *To magnifie his works, the more we know.*

Bacon in answering the Divines in his *Advancement of Learning* not only distinguished between philosophy and revelation but used St Paul to distinguish between pride and charity as ends of knowledge. Although he thought the study of nature ought to produce wonder with respect to God, it should not be limited: 'To conclude therefore, let no man upon a weak conceit of sobriety or an ill-applied moderation think or maintain, that a man can search too far, or be too well studied in the book of God's word, or in the book of God's works; divinity or philosophy.' Milton, however, would impose some restraint in line with St Paul's charge that 'Knowledge puffeth up' (ll. 126 ff.):

> But Knowledge is as food, and needs no less
> Her Temperance over Appetite, to know
> In measure what the mind may well contain,
> Oppresses else with Surfet, and soon turns
> Wisdom to Folly, as Nourishment to Winde.

Thus Milton's 'conceit of sobriety' connects the spiritual and the physical.

Creation culminates in the new creature man, 'self-knowing', made in the image of God, brought into (ll. 538 ff.)

> This Garden, planted with the Trees of God,
> Delectable both to behold and taste;
> And freely all thir pleasant fruit for food
> Gave thee, all sorts are here that all th'Earth yeelds,
> Varietie without end; but of the Tree
> Which tasted works knowledge of Good and Evil,
> Thou mai'st not; in the day thou eat'st, thou di'st;
> Death is the penaltie impos'd, beware,
> And govern well thy appetite, least sin
> Surprise thee, and her black attendant Death.

Milton has already established the metaphorical range of 'appetite' and now he translates the test of obedience into a test of temperance. The penalty imposed is the main one, death, without mention of the contingent ones of "all our woe, / With loss of *Eden*'. This omission leaves open an extension of the tragic consequences which may become significant. Book VII ends with a limited invitation to Adam's curiosity: 'if else thou seek'st / Aught, not surpassing human measure, say'.

Book VIII centres on man, and human nature is put into sharp focus. Here we are initiated more specifically into grounds for the fall of man. On Adam's thirst for knowledge the Argument is suggestive: 'Adam inquires concerning celestial Motions, is doubt- fully answer'd, and exhorted to search rather things more worthy of knowledg.' His question merely extends the question raised by Eve and altered in her dream, but this repetition also enhances its significance. Adam's concern about celestial motions no doubt exceeds sobriety, but it is related to the prodigality argument of Comus, for he finds excess in the macrocosm and wonders (ll. 26 ff.)

> *How Nature wise and frugal could commit*
> *Such disproportions, with superfluous hand*
> *So many nobler Bodies to create,*
> *Greater so manifold to this one use,*
> *For aught appears . . .*

This disproportion of means to end seems to Adam wasteful, but his implied moral challenges the wisdom of nature rather than temperance. The prodigality of nature serves more than one pur- pose in *Paradise Lost*.

Milton's treatment of Eve at this juncture is worth notice. When she perceives Adam 'Entring on studious thoughts ab- struse', and departs to her gardening, Milton saves her from condescension (ll. 48 ff.):

> *Yet went she not, as not with such discourse*
> *Delighted, or not capable her eare*
> *Of what was high.*

If this makes Eve worthy of being Adam's helpmeet, her preference for Adam rounds out Milton's view of marriage:

> *hee, she knew would intermix*
> *Grateful digressions, and solve high dispute*
> *With conjugal Caresses, from his Lip*
> *Not Words alone pleas'd her.*

The consequence of Eve to Adam turned the words, 'and solve high dispute / With conjugal Caresses', into irony at the Fall. But Eve anticipated Marvell's 'Coy Mistress' (IV, 310):

> *Yeilded with coy submission, modest pride,*
> *And sweet reluctant amorous delay.*

Raphael's reply to Adam's question is intended to discourage Adam's curiosity. Positively Raphael uses the occasion to point a lesson in values; negatively he uses the conflicts between the Ptolemaic and Copernican systems to point the futility of such knowledge. He concludes by warning Adam not to aspire too high (l. 173): 'be lowlie wise: / Think onely what concernes thee and thy being'. In acquiescing Adam seems to join Eve: 'nor with perplexing thoughts / To interrupt the sweet of Life'. Yet as he surrenders what Belial would not lose, 'Those thoughts that wander through Eternity', he admits (l. 188), 'But apte the Mind or Fancie is to roave', and hence it must be taught that the prime wisdom is 'That which before us lies in daily life'. But Adam was not ready to understand Donne's conclusion to his satiric *Progress of the Soul* when he says, 'wonder with me, why'

> *most of those arts, whence our lives are blest,*
> *By cursed* Cain's *race invented be,*
> *And blest* Seth *vexed us with Astronomy.*

Although Adam is willing to change the subject and speak of useful knowledge, he does not surrender his curiosity (ll. 200–2):

> *whence haply mention may arise*
> *Of something not unseasonable to ask*
> *By sufferance, and thy wonted favour deign'd.*

And so, prompted by an even deeper need, he tells his story in order to detain Raphael. Beginning as a subterfuge it culminates in the revelation of his craving for rational society. In exploring the problem of solitude Milton lays the basis for Adam's fall. After his creation Adam also dreams of the tempting fruit, but wakes in time to be warned by God about the pledge of obedience. In pronouncing the penalty of death God adds what the Angel omitted (ll. 331–3):

> *From that day mortal, and this happie State*
> *Shalt loose, expell'd from hence into a World*
> *Of woe and sorrow.*

Then in 'the Garden of bliss' Adam discovers a deficiency in his relation to the animals (l. 354): 'but in these / I found not what me thought I wanted still'. And so after thanking God for his bounty, he presumes to object:

> *In solitude*
> *What happiness, who can enjoy alone,*
> *Or all enjoying, what contentment find?*

For he cannot find rational society among the animals (ll. 389–92):

> *Of fellowship I speak*
> *Such as I seek, fit to participate*
> *All rational delight, wherein the brute*
> *Cannot be human consort.*

Of course all this is a trial in self-knowledge, for God 'Knew it not good for Man to be alone', and so creates his 'other self'. In his sleep Adam sees a ravishing vision, and as he wakens Milton projects her importance to Adam (ll. 478–80):

> *She disappeerd, and left me dark, I wak'd*
> *To find her, or for ever to deplore*
> *Her loss, and other pleasures all abjure.*

Although Eve brings his 'Storie to the sum of earthly bliss', she presents a new problem in self-knowledge (ll. 530 ff.):

> *here passion first I felt,*
> *Commotion strange, in all enjoyments else*
> *Superior and unmov'd, here onely weake*
> *Against the charm of Beauties powerful glance.*

But this father of Samson has his own explanation: nature again used more than she needed:

> *Or Nature faild in mee, and left some part*
> *Not proof enough such Object to sustain,*
> *Or from my side subducting, took perhaps*
> *More then enough; at least on her bestow'd*
> *Too much of Ornament, in outward shew*
> *Elaborate, of inward less exact.*

Now Adam finds disproportion in the microcosm: reason is not equal to passion, so that higher faculties seem inferior to lower, and beauty makes wisdom look like folly.

Raphael gives the same answer as before to Adam's charge against nature: 'Accuse not Nature.' Wisdom is not to be doubted but obeyed; otherwise he will lose the sense of proportion, and make false judgments, take the seeming good for the real good. As with celestial motions, Raphael argues that 'Bright inferrs not Excellence', but that Eve was 'Made so adorn for thy delight the more, / So awful, that with honour thou maist love.' He tells Adam that physical desire is shared by the animals, and is not worthy to subdue (ll. 585 ff.)

> *The Soule of Man, or passion in him move.*
> *What higher in her societie thou findst*
> *Attractive, human, rational, love still;*
> *In loving thou dost well, in passion not,*
> *Wherein true Love consists not.*

Thus Adam's weakness is rebuked as Raphael proceeds to give love a Platonic bias:

> *love refines*
> *The thoughts, and heart enlarges, hath his seat*
> *In Reason, and is judicious, is the scale*
> *By which to heav'nly Love thou maist ascend,*
> *Not sunk in carnal pleasure, for which cause*
> *Among the Beasts no Mate for thee was found.*

This scale, in effect, connects human and divine love.

By this rebuke Adam is 'half abash't' and hastens to disclaim any delight (ll. 597–9)

> *In procreation common to all kindes*
> *(Though higher of the genial Bed by far,*
> *And with mysterious reverence I deem).*

If Adam seems reluctant to leave the *lectus genialis*, he none the less describes the feminine ways and signs of union that attract but do not subject. Indeed the unabashed half of Adam insists that Raphael ascend the scale to heavenly love and report on its relation to the sense of touch. Whereupon Raphael blushed 'Celestial rosie red, Loves proper hue', and answered (ll. 620–1):

> *Let it suffice thee that thou know'st*
> *Us happie, and without Love no happiness.*

If Adam learned no more about angelic love than that it did not leave the physical entirely behind, he did get a strong reaffirmation of love, which Raphael incorporated into his parting advice:

The Education of Adam

> Be strong, live happie, and love, but first of all
> Him whom to love is to obey, and keep
> His great command; take heed least Passion sway
> Thy Judgement to do aught, which else free Will
> Would not admit; thine and of all thy Sons
> The weal or woe in thee is plac't; beware.

This sums up Adam's predicament. His fundamental weakness is born out of the greatest human need, relief from solitude. If there is no happiness without love, Adam's position between God and woman will become a tragic dilemma and as full of ambiguity as the so-called fortunate fall.

III

In Book IX the tragic action is resumed. All the preparations have been made, and Milton must now change the notes to tragic. For him the argument is 'Not less but more Heroic then the wrauth / Of stern Achilles.' He declares that he was

> Not sedulous by Nature to indite
> Warrs, hitherto the onely Argument
> Heroic deem'd, chief maistrie to dissect
> With long and tedious havoc fabl'd Knights
> In Battels feign'd; the better fortitude
> Of Patience and Heroic Martyrdom
> Unsung.

This is the fortitude of his early thought which he came to know better through blindness.

Satan's eulogy of the Earth (ll. 99 ff.) magnifies our sense of Adam's bliss while it expands Satan's motives for revenge upon Adam. The luxuriance of the Garden in turn becomes Eve's excuse to Adam for the separation of their labours. Adam replies that God has not imposed labour upon them strictly (ll. 242–3). Although 'solitude sometimes is best societie', he fears the attempt of Satan upon her; for he is uncertain (ll. 261 ff.)

> Whether his first design be to withdraw
> Our fealtie from God, or to disturb
> Conjugal Love, then which perhaps no bliss
> Enjoy'd by us excites his envie more.

Adam thinks in terms of his dilemma. Notice how Milton weaves his themes of prodigality, labour, solitude, society, love, into his preparation for the Fall.

This is how the Argument phrases the beginning of Eve's defection: 'Eve loath to be thought not circumspect or firm enough, urges her going apart, the rather desirous to make tryal of her strength.' In Book IV Satan had sought to arouse discontent and inordinate desires in Eve; now she seems to exhibit over-confidence rather than strength, and to argue 'Vertue unassaid' into tempting evil through pride. Adam answers Eve in the vein of *Comus* that man is (ll. 348 ff.)

> *Secure from outward force; within himself*
> *The danger lies, yet lies within his power:*
> *Against his will he can receave no harme.*
> *But God left free the Will, for what obeyes*
> *Reason is free, and Reason he made right*
> *But bid her well beware, and still erect,*
> *Least by some faire appeering good surpris'd*
> *She dictate false, and missinforme the Will*
> *To do what God expressly hath forbid.*

Adam is now perfect in his lesson: Will is free when it obeys reason, not the passions; but reason can be deceived, and so he warns against deception. But if Eve's will cannot be persuaded, Adam can only say, 'Go; for thy stay, not free, absents thee more.' The potentialities of their separation—their tragedy on the human level—are all in that line.

Satan's seduction of Eve (ll. 532 ff.) appeals to her original experience of self-awareness and translates her effect upon Adam into general flattery. But when Eve repeats the command of God, Satan questions their pride of place, the penalty of God, and even His omnipotence. When Eve is seduced by rational deception, desire, and appetite, she reduces the prohibition to that of knowledge and its potentialities. Finally she puts aside the temptation to keep this boon to herself out of love for Adam (ll. 832-3):

> *So dear I love him, that with him all deaths*
> *I could endure, without him live no life.*

The Argument describes Adam's reception of her fall in these words: 'Adam at first amaz'd, but perceiving her lost, resolves through vehemence of love to perish with her; and extenuating the trespass, eats also of the Fruit.' But in the poem when she tells Adam she has eaten of the fruit and its effects are not what they have been told, Adam (ll. 890 ff.)

> *Astonied stood and Blank, while horror chill*
> *Ran through his veins, and all his joynts relax'd;*
> *From his slack hand the Garland wreath'd for* Eve
> *Down drop'd, and all the faded Roses shed.*

Thus the effect of her fall passes through Adam and his flowers, and continues into his cry of pain:

> *How art thou lost, how on a sudden lost,*
> *Defac't, deflourd, and now to Death devote?*

And then the first want that he knew in Paradise undoes him (ll. 906 ff.):

> *And mee with thee hath ruind, for with thee*
> *Certain my resolution is to Die;*
> *How can I live without thee, how forgoe*
> *Thy sweet Converse and Love so dearly joyn'd,*
> *To live again in these wilde Woods forlorn?*

In that last line her loss already transforms Paradise.

Then Adam extenuates the trespass by arguments like those of Eve and Satan (ll. 921 ff.). Neither one as yet suspects Satan in the Serpent. Eve takes Adam's resolution as a trial of love or separation (ll. 975–6):

> *This happie trial of thy Love, which else*
> *So eminently never had bin known.*

This is the Happy Fall on the human level. Adam fell (ll. 998–9)

> *Against his better knowledge, not deceav'd,*
> *But fondly overcome with Femal charm.*

For he chose 'to incurr / Divine displeasure for her sake, or Death'. And the fall first betrays itself in their love: 'in Lust they burne'. In terms of *The Doctrine and Discipline of Divorce* (IV) their rational burning sinks into sensual burning and they experience shame. Reason and Will fall into subjection to sensual appetite, and high passions begin to separate them and alienate their love.

Both the ethos and the magnitude of the original tragedy of love remove it from romantic descendants like *All for Love, or the World Well Lost.* Milton's eloquent gloss on St Paul's 'burning' is fundamental to the human drama of *Paradise Lost*: 'What is it then but that desire which God put into Adam in Paradise, before he knew the sin of incontinence; that desire which God saw it was not good that man should be left alone to burn in; the desire and longing to put off an unkindly solitariness by uniting another body, but not without a fit soul to his, in the cheerful society of wedlock? Which if it were so needful before the fall, when man was much more perfect in himself, how much more is it needful now against all the sorrows and casualties of this life, to have an intimate and speaking help, a ready and reviving associate in marriage? Whereof who misses, by chancing on a mute and spiritless mate, remains more alone than before, and in a burning less to be contained than that which is fleshly, and more to be considered; as being more deeply rooted even in the faultless innocence of nature.' Thus solitude or loneliness becomes the basic affliction of human life.

In Book X, before man's Redeemer prepares to mitigate his doom, we are reminded that man's fall was also a test of faith. Now since obedience is love, the appearance of Adam and Eve is revealing (ll. 111 ff.):

> *Love was not in thir looks, either to God*
> *Or to each other, but apparent guilt,*
> *And shame, and perturbation, and despaire,*
> *Anger, and obstinacie, and hate, and guile.*

Adam blames Eve and is rebuked by Christ; Eve admits her guilt. Man's redemption is concealed in the enigmatic judgment of Satan. Man is to live with pain and sorrow, and eat by the sweat of labour; his death is postponed. Sin and death prepare to extend their reign over the new world. Satan returns to Hell triumphant, only to experience a degradation of form corresponding to his degradation of soul (like Comus's rout) and to become a victim of his own deception.

In his lament (ll. 720 ff.) Adam complains against Providence, yearns for death as an escape, fears that death may be 'endless miserie', is torn by the dilemma of the fallen angels. Finally he admits his guilt, and both desires and fears the punishment (ll. 837–9):

> *Thus what thou desir'st,*
> *And what thou fearst, alike destroyes all hope*
> *Of refuge . . .*

His bitter tirade against Eve ends with some general reflections on
the misfortunes of love for later men, including Milton. While
Adam seeks to shift the blame, Eve strikes the note of true repentance and craves forgiveness; she is ready to bear the punishment
for both. Eve's penitence softens Adam, and he professes (ll.
952 ff.):

> *If Prayers*
> *Could alter high Decrees, I to that place*
> *Would speed before thee, and be louder heard,*
> *That on my head all might be visited,*
> *Thy frailtie and infirmer Sex forgiv'n . . .*

Adam, however, had exhibited himself as somewhat less firm
before his outburst against Eve. His wisdom is more evident when
he urges that they strive

> *In offices of Love, how we may light'n*
> *Each others burden in our share of woe;*
> *Since this days Death denounc't, if ought I see,*
> *Will prove no sudden, but a slow-pac't evill,*
> *A long days dying to augment our paine,*
> *And to our Seed (O hapless Seed!) deriv'd.*

Adam's lament is enough to show us how the postponement of
death may add to their tragic suffering. This extension of woe
prompts Eve to suggest that they remain childless or seek death,
Belial's 'sad cure'. But Adam finds a safer resolution when he
realizes that Satan was in the Serpent and that God's sentence
depends upon Eve's 'Seed'. He concludes (ll. 1043 ff.) that Eve's
course

> *cuts us off from hope, and savours onely*
> *Rancor and pride, impatience and despite,*
> *Reluctance against God and his just yoke*
> *Laid on our Necks.*

This is not 'the better fortitude / Of Patience and Heroic Martyrdom'.

Instead of 'immediate dissolution' their doom now has brought
them pain in childbirth and the curse of labour, neither the worst

of misfortunes. In contrast to Book IX this one ends with the cessation of mutual blame and the beginning of sincere repentance as they

> *Repairing where he judg'd them prostrate fell*
> *Before him reverent, and both confess'd*
> *Humbly thir faults, and pardon beg'd . . .*

Although the Fall threatened to alienate Adam and Eve from each other as well as from God, their moral drama—at least as a mode of 'prevenient Grace'—prepared them for divine reconcilia‑tion. But the final blow has not yet fallen.

IV

In Book XI God adds the final consequence of man's fall, the loss of Eden. Nature's Law, which Adam has twice criticized, forbids him (ll. 48–52) 'longer in that Paradise to dwell', for 'Those pure immortal Elements . . . Eject him tainted now.' As God explains, man now finds himself in a new dilemma:

> *I at first with two fair gifts*
> *Created him endowed, with Happiness*
> *And Immortalitie: that fondly lost,*
> *This other serv'd but to eternize woe;*
> *Till I provided Death; so Death becomes*
> *His final remedie . . .*

Now Adam has to learn the meaning of 'all our woe', for which sin is the cause and death the relief. Michael, the warrior of Heaven, is sent to exile Adam and Eve; and if they are patient, to dismiss them, 'though sorrowing, yet in peace'. Eve expresses the state of mind upon which their banishment is to fall (ll. 179–80):

> *What can be toilsom in these pleasant Walkes?*
> *Here let us live, though in fall'n state, content.*

Thus exile is to continue the undiminished tragic note: on the human side by Eve, on the theological side by Adam.

If the Vision shows Adam that his exile is not from God, it also shows him that his exile is to a world of sin and death. Indeed the Vision is like a great Morality teaching patience. The opera‑tion of original sin introduces the 'shapes of death', the wages of sin. After the spectacle of Cain and Abel, Adam cries (l. 462), 'But have I now seen Death?' Then Adam learns that temperance leads to painless death. The next spectacle shows what Donne calls 'those arts, whence our lives are blest', culminating in 'A Beavie of fair Women'. This scene pleases Adam (ll. 594 ff.):

> *Those were of hate and death, or pain much worse,*
> *Here Nature seems fulfilld in all her ends.*

If these lines emphasize the morality nature of the episodes, Adam's response suggests the original Adam: 'Female charm' still 'attach'd the heart / Of *Adam*' and earned him another rebuke. For Adam has seen 'the Tents / Of wickedness', of Cain's race, who for Donne also were inventors 'Of Arts that polish Life'. After the next scene Adam, in tears, learns that he has seen War, and Michael stresses the theme of heroic patience by saying (ll. 685–6):

> *For in those dayes Might onely shall be admir'd,*
> *And Valour and Heroic Vertu call'd.*

Then a scene of luxury and riot multiplies vice until the Deluge, and Adam exclaims (ll. 759–62):

> *better had I*
> *Liv'd ignorant of future, so had borne*
> *My part of evil onely, each dayes lot*
> *Anough to bear.*

Thus Adam learns the burden of 'all our woe' as he learns the meaning of death.[1] But the last scene also taught him a lesson about his hope for peace (ll. 779–80):

> *But I was farr deceav'd; for now I see*
> *Peace to corrupt no less then Warr to waste.*

If this corruption suggests Belial, Noah as 'the onely Son of light / In a dark Age' suggests Abdiel and becomes the means to grace (ll. 886 ff.):

> *Such grace shall one just Man find in his sight,*
> *That he relents, not to blot out mankind . . .*

---

[1] Thus Milton used part of the dramatic design for *Adam Unparadiz'd* found in his Trinity Manuscript: 'The angel is sent to banish them out of Paradise; but before causes to pass before his eyes, in shapes, a mask of all the evils of this life and world.' These evils were 'Mutes' in his earlier dramatic version: 'Labour, Grief, Hatred, Envy, War, Famine, Pestilence, Sickness, Discontent, Ignorance, Fear, Death.'

Thus 'one just Man' brings 'peace from God' and revives Adam by the assurance 'that Man shall live'. But the assurance of 'one greater Man' is still unrevealed.

To this revelation Book XII proceeds. To Adam it is another world in more than one sense:

> *Thus thou hast seen one World begin and end;*
> *And Man as from a second stock proceed.*
> *Much thou hast yet to see, but I perceave*
> *Thy mortal sight to faile; objects divine*
> *Must needs impaire and wearie human sense.*

Such matter is beyond Adam's ken and so it is narrated. First Michael represents the origin of tyranny in Nimrod, and extends the doctrine of rational liberty to show how tyranny from without may enslave one who is enthralled by tyranny within. After the extension of tyranny from ethics to politics, Michael epitomizes (ll. 105 ff.):

> *Thus will this latter, as the former World,*
> *Still tend from bad to worse . . .*

until God withdraws his presence to 'one peculiar Nation', and makes faithful Abraham the promise of a messiah (ll. 147 ff.):

> *This ponder, that all Nations of the Earth*
> *Shall in his Seed be blessed; by that Seed*
> *Is meant thy great deliverer, who shall bruise*
> *The Serpents head; whereof to thee anon*
> *Plainlier shall be reveald.*

This revelation proceeds by various types of Christ, as sin did by the shapes of death, until Adam understands 'Why our great expectation should be call'd / The seed of Woman', but not how the prophecy is to be fulfilled. Finally Adam learns that Christ will save man from death (ll. 394 ff.)

> *Not by destroying* Satan, *but his works*
> *In thee and in thy Seed: nor can this be,*
> *But by fulfilling that which thou didst want,*
> *Obedience to the Law of God, impos'd*
> *On penaltie of death, and suffering death,*
> *The penaltie to thy transgression due,*
> *And due to theirs which out of thine will grow:*
> *So onely can high Justice rest appaid.*

This is the supreme example of 'Patience and Heroic Marytrdom'
instead of the duel of force which Adam expected. But it is also
the supreme example of love:

> *The Law of God exact he shall fulfill*
> *Both by obedience and by love, though love*
> *Alone fulfill the Law.*

This is the New Testament abridgement of the Law for which
Donne is thankful in *Holy Sonnet XVI*, and this is the sacrifice
which elicits Adam's wonder at the paradox of his fall—or at
God (ll. 470–1)

> *That all this good of evil shall produce,*
> *And evil turn to good.*

When Adam asks about the fate of the faithful after Christ
ascends to Heaven, Michael returns to the course of original sin,
which does not exempt the church but ends with the last judgment (ll. 537 ff.):

> *so shall the World goe on,*
> *To good malignant, to bad men benigne,*
> *Under her own waight groaning, till the day*
> *Appeer of respiration to the just,*
> *And vengeance to the wicked, at return*
> *Of him so lately promiss'd to thy aid . . .*

History had finally taught Milton not to expect in this world
'that good men may enjoy the freedom which they merit and the
bad the curb which they need'.

In Adam's summary of what he has learned from Michael we
should notice the repetition of the heroic theme which Milton
stated before the Fall (ll. 569 ff.):

> *that suffering for Truths sake*
> *Is fortitude to highest victorie,*
> *And to the faithful Death the Gate of Life;*
> *Taught this by his example whom I now*
> *Acknowledge my Redeemer ever blest.*

Thus to the faithful death becomes the gate of life. Michael
replies that Adam has now acquired wisdom rather than the
knowledge he sought, but adds a further injunction (ll. 581 ff.):

> *onely add*
> *Deeds to thy knowledge answerable, add Faith,*
> *Add Vertue, Patience, Temperance, add Love,*
> *By name to come call'd Charitie, the soul*
> *Of all the rest: then wilt thou not be loath*
> *To leave this Paradise, but shalt possess*
> *A Paradise within thee, happier farr.*

Wisdom is not enough, one must add works, and works answer-able to the virtues that summarize this wisdom; then the mind will have created a new Paradise instead of the one lost. Meanwhile Eve has been 'composed to meek submission' in a dream, unlike the effect of her earlier dream.

Michael's instruction plays a role similar to that of Raphael's, except that it ends with the wisdom necessary for the world and a happy ending. The purpose of the last two books is to unfold the consequences of the Fall—again as moral preparation, but this time for the loss of Eden and happiness, though with the ultimate hope of a happy ending. Both books bring home the meaning of Adam's doom or judgment, which he has not understood, and both prepare him for new trials. They develop the tragedy of his loss of Eden or happiness, not least by giving perspective to that loss. Adam's new awareness adds to his martyrdom as much as to his ultimate hope. Finally, these revelations themselves become a trial of patience for his dismissal from Eden.

Adam and Eve depart in mingled hope and sadness:

> *They looking back, all th' Eastern side beheld*
> *Of Paradise, so late thir happie seat,*
> *Wav'd over by that flaming Brand, the Gate*
> *With dreadful Faces throng'd and fierie Armes.*

The aspect of justice is obvious in this scene, but it does not inhibit grief:

> *Som natural tears they drop'd, but wip'd them soon;*
> *The World was all before them, where to choose*
> *Thir place of rest, and Providence thir guide:*
> *They hand in hand with wandring steps and slow,*
> *Through Eden took thir solitarie way.*

This prospect, 'The World was all before them', could bring no quickening to Adam's heart, and though Providence was their guide, their steps were wandering and slow. The last two lines epitomize their tragedy: 'their solitary way' touches a basic human need, emphasizes their loss of society, which Adam feared might include God, and describes their exile to an alien world alone but mutually supported. Thus Adam enters upon the life of Everyman in a world of woe, where he must prove himself. We must not forget that the action of the poem ends with paradise lost, and that the 'relations' of the poem are subordinate to that action and its characters.

4

PLOT IN *PARADISE REGAINED*

In *Paradise Lost* (XII) Adam learns that Christ will save man from death 'Not by destroying *Satan*, but his works / In thee and in thy Seed'. This can only be achieved 'by fulfilling that which thou didst want, / Obedience to the Law of God', and by 'suffering death, / The penaltie to thy transgression due'. Only thus 'can high Justice rest appaid'. The Miltonic view of Christ is explained by the next lines:

> *The Law of God exact he shall fulfill*
> *Both by obedience and by love, though love*
> *Alone fulfill the Law . . .*

That is, after Christ abridged the Law. *Paradise Regained* is indeed Milton's epic of obedience and *Paradise Lost* his epic of love. Both epics deal with a limited action foreshadowing its sequel, and in both the Passion is postponed. Where obedience failed, love was more urgent; where obedience prevailed, plot became univocal; and this explains the emphasis in each epic. Yet the impulse to conflate the two poems often leads critics of *Paradise Regained* into equivocal views of the nature and characters of its action, which need to be discriminated by its own 'verisimilitude and decorum'.

Book I

Milton's treatment of the Temptation is based on Luke supplemented by Matthew. He states a limited theme: to recover Paradise, not to save man from the penalty of his disobedience:

> *Recover'd Paradise to all mankind,*
> *By one mans firm obedience fully tri'd*

Through all temptation, and the Tempter foil'd
In all his wiles, defeated and repuls't,
And Eden *rais'd in the wast Wilderness.*

In the world of man's exile Christ is to raise the moral Eden
which *Paradise Lost* called 'happier farr'; he is to prepare the way
from Law to love. Milton invokes the Holy Spirit that led Christ
into the desert 'and broughtst him thence / By proof the undoubted
Son of God'. This line shows that Satan is not alone in requiring
proof from Christ. And again Milton insists that he is 'to tell of
deeds / Above Heroic'. But these deeds are not therefore miracles.
God has permitted this new trial of man by Satan, and hence
we know that it will not involve divinity, which would nullify
its end. In his divine aspect Christ defeated Satan in *Paradise
Lost*.

After Christ has been proclaimed by John the Baptist, Satan
reports to his followers his renewed anxiety about his 'dread',
because events have led to divine recognition of Christ:

> *And what will he not do to advance his Son?* (88)
> *His first-begot we know, and sore have felt,*
> *When his fierce thunder drove us to the deep;*
> *Who this is we must learn . . .*

Satan must learn whether this is the Seed of Eve who is to inflict
'that fatal wound' upon his head. But his kind of proof will differ
from that which concerns man. Satan argues the urgency of the
occasion and the need of fraud, and is again chosen to undertake
the mission.

God tells Gabriel that Satan will now prove Christ worthy of
his destiny and a greater man than Adam. Then he limits the
action:

> *But first I mean* (155)
> *To exercise him in the Wilderness,*
> *There he shall first lay down the rudiments*
> *Of his great warfare, e're I send him forth*
> *To conquer Sin and Death the two grand foes,*
> *By Humiliation and strong Sufferance.*

Sin and death are finally to be conquered on the Cross, by the
Passion of Christ, the hero of patience. Now he is limited to the

'rudiments' of his warfare with Satan. God's present purpose is to show him exercised in his human role:

> *From what consummate vertue I have chose*   (165)
> *This perfect Man, by merit call'd my Son,*
> *To earn Salvation for the Sons of men.*

It is not to show the full achievement of that salvation. The action is not defined as the Atonement: 'But to vanquish by wisdom hellish wiles'. Obviously the action is limited to the moral warfare by which Christ will earn salvation for man by fulfilment rather than redemption. This limitation also restricts him to his human capacity; divine prerogative would defeat Milton's purpose.

Meanwhile the Son of God considers how best he might begin his work. As he is led into the desert by the Holy Ghost, we learn of his devotion to the Law of God and the public good, of his aspiration to subdue 'Brute violence and proud Tyrannick pow'r,/ Till truth were freed, and equity restor'd':

> *Yet held it more humane, more heavenly first*   (221)
> *By winning words to conquer willing hearts,*
> *And make perswasion do the work of fear;*
> *At least to try, and teach the erring Soul*
> *Not wilfully mis-doing, but unware*
> *Misled: the stubborn only to subdue.*

Here the Miltonic emphasis on persuasion prepares us for the nature and drift of his coming trial. After hearing from his mother the prophecy of his Kingdom, he turned again to

> *The Law and Prophets, searching what was writ*   (260)
> *Concerning the Messiah, to our Scribes*
> *Known partly, and soon found of whom they spake*
> *I am; this chiefly, that my way must lie*
> *Through many a hard assay even to the death,*
> *E're I the promis'd Kingdom can attain,*
> *Or work Redemption for mankind, whose sins*
> *Full weight must be transferr'd upon my head.*

But that transfer is not embraced by the present action; here the fulfilment of the Law is to be by obedience. This relation of prior events culminates in his baptism and divine recognition, and concludes with this recapitulation:

68

And now by some strong motion I am led   (290)
Into this wilderness, to what intent
I learn not yet, perhaps I need not know;
For what concerns my knowledge God reveals.

The purpose of his trial Christ does not know; but, unlike Adam, he trusts God for what concerns his knowledge, which is limited as we have seen.

Before he hungered, Christ passed forty days in the desert; 'Nor tasted humane food, nor hunger felt'. The basic propriety of food to his trial is thus established, and we can expect it to become a recurrent symbol. As so often in Milton, Satan begins by questioning Providence: 'what ill chance hath brought thee to this place?' And Satan poisons his question by saying that he has lately heard him called Son of God. Christ replies by expressing faith in his Guide, whose intent is still unknown to him. Satan objects that it will take a miracle to save him, and adds:

But if thou be the Son of God, Command   (342)
That out of these hard stones be made thee bread.

Christ's reply, however, immediately lifts the bread to a symbolic level: 'Think'st thou such force in Bread?' Man does not live by bread alone, but also by the word of God; and Christ develops this lesson from the context in which it was first taught (Deuteronomy viii). Deuteronomy is the great Mosaic context of obedience, and thus Christ's first temptation is oriented towards obedience to the Law. The force of the question, 'Why dost thou then suggest to me distrust?' depends upon the fact that Moses and Elijah survived similar trials, and so the Son of God need not fear. If Satan knows Christ's identity in part, he does not know his power, and this ignorance makes Christ's question, 'Think'st thou such force in Bread?' dissemble the force Satan is trying to discover. Various allusions show that mutual knowledge comes gradually and dramatically to the two adversaries.

Satan, now recognized but still of unknown guile, admits to being 'that Spirit unfortunate', and proceeds to become a sophistic example of obedience to God. Although God has said otherwise, Satan declares that God 'Gave up into my hands Uzzean Job / To prove him, and illustrate his high worth'. When he adds, 'For what he bids I do', we know that he is not aware of its irony. And when Satan professes both admiration for Christ and friendship for man, we realize that his temptation is not grounded on any certainty about the divine nature of Christ.

Christ's stern reprimand elaborates God's remark about Satan's 'over-weening' and translates his boasts into deceits, culminating in this pretence:

> *Wilt thou impute to obedience what thy fear*   (422)
> *Extorts, or pleasure to do ill excites?*

And here Milton's basic metaphor reappears: 'For lying is thy sustenance, thy food.' Then 'His gray dissimulation' makes a submissive reply turning on Medea's famous excuse (Ovid, *Met.* vii, 20):

> *I see the Right, and I approve it too,*
> *Condemn the Wrong—and yet the Wrong pursue.*

Finally, Christ sharply rejects Satan's mocking obeisance:

> *I bid not or forbid; do as thou find'st*
> *Permission from above; thou canst not more.*

And we know that God will continue access to Christ so that Satan may exercise him in the Wilderness.

Book II

Meanwhile the 'new-baptiz'd' and plain fishermen lament the disappearance of their Messiah, and his mother is moved by the troubles foretold by Simeon. However, they all resign themselves to Providence. Satan, with a 'slye preface' towards his return, had left Christ to his meditations and returned to the evil Spirits for help.

In council Belial proposes the lure of woman, which underlines the contrast with Adam that Satan has already made, but Belial uses the shrewd example of 'wisest Solomon'. In replying to Belial, Satan delivers a diatribe against feminine beauty that affords an odd contrast with the Choric recognition of its power in *Samson Agonistes*. Indeed, Satan makes Belial and his crew ('false titl'd Sons of God') responsible for most of the mythological seductions, and (worst of all) 'then lay'st thy scapes on names ador'd'.

Satan seems to admire Christ more than Solomon or beauty: 'for Beauty stands / In the admiration of weak minds'. Certainly the devastating love of the Restoration heroic play was not a proper heroic theme for Satan, but 'a trivial toy'.

> *Therefore with manlier objects we must try*   (225)
> *His constancy, with such as have more shew*
> *Of worth, of honour, glory, and popular praise;*
> *Rocks whereon greatest men have oftest wreck'd;*
> *Or that which only seems to satisfie*
> *Lawful desires of Nature, not beyond.*

Satan will begin with the last temptation: that which really goes beyond the 'lawful desires of Nature'. For he knows that Christ now 'hungers where no food / Is to be found'. If Satan has rebuked Belial, he has also outlined further temptations.

Meanwhile Christ has begun to hunger: 'But now I feel I hunger, which declares, / Nature hath need of what she asks.' Thus he is ready for Satan's last kind of temptation. But he is not afraid of famine:

> *Nor mind it, fed with better thoughts that feed*   (258)
> *Mee hungring more to do my Fathers will.*

Again he prefers obedience, or to live by the Word of God.

Against Satan's return he 'dream'd, as appetite is wont to dream', of food but not of the Biblical parallels that attend his dream. Then Satan appears, no longer the rustic, 'but seemlier clad', sophisticated beyond nature. Using Biblical parallels, Satan renews his attack on Christ's faith in Providence. Now he wonders even more at the plight of the Son of God:

> *Of thee these forty days none hath regard,*   (315)
> *Forty and more deserted here indeed.*

Matthew reports that Christ felt such neglect upon the Cross, but here he replies: 'They all had need, I as thou seest have none.' Satan's telling retort is then why are you hungry?

When asked if he would not eat if food were set before him, Christ responds that it depends on the giver. The subtle Fiend then tries to make Nature appear to be the giver, although he has said that Christ hungers where no food is to be found:

> behold   (331)
> *Nature asham'd, or better to express,*
> *Troubl'd that thou should'st hunger, hath purvey'd*
> *From all the Elements her choicest store*
> *To treat thee as beseems, and as her Lord*
> *With honour, only deign to sit and eat.*

Moreover, Nature cares for his want and honours him, says Satan, beginning the temptation to empire. Of course this sumptuous banquet is not given by Nature, and Milton places its character by contrast:

> *Alas how simple, to these Cates compar'd,*   (348)
> *Was that crude Apple that diverted Eve!*

Then Satan tries to induce Christ to eat by embellishing this contrast to the temptation of man.

When Milton says, 'thus Jesus temperately reply'd', he labels the nature of the temptation; he emphasizes the excess, beyond 'lawful desires of Nature', represented by the banquet. Christ answers, in effect, that he is not dependent on Satan's gifts, and that he does not like the giver: 'And with my hunger what hast thou to do?' Moreover, he does not like this gift of 'pompous' luxury or its deception:

> *Thy pompous Delicacies I contemn,*   (390)
> *And count thy specious gifts no gifts but guiles.*

The bread of life becomes obsessive. But Satan, though 'male‑content', has demonstrated his power to give, and accepts his rebuff: 'I see / What I can do or offer is suspect.' Thus Jesus distrusts Satan, not God.

Satan then proceeds to build on his failure by way of praise: 'By hunger, that each other Creature tames, / Thou art not to be harm'd, therefore not mov'd.' And he is superior to other appetites: 'Thy temperance invincible besides, / For no allurement yields to appetite.' But he is not superior to higher ends:

> *And all thy heart is set on high designs,*   (410)
> *High actions: but wherewith to be atchiev'd?*

'Great acts require great means of enterprise', and these means he lacks. Satan describes him as among the lowest sons of man:

> *Thou art unknown, unfriended, low of birth,* (413)
> *A Carpenter thy Father known, thy self*
> *Bred up in poverty and streights at home;*
> *Lost in a Desert here and hunger-bit:*
> *Which way or from what hope dost thou aspire*
> *To greatness?*

Of course Satan mistakes Christ's greatness as he mistook his hunger, and so he tempts him with wealth. But Christ patiently replies that without virtue, valour, and wisdom, wealth is impotent

> *To gain dominion or to keep it gain'd.* (434)
> *Witness those antient Empires of the Earth,*
> *In highth of all thir flowing wealth dissolv'd.*

If Christ knows that he is destined to a kingdom, he also knows that there are two kinds of power or dominion. First the temporal:

> *Yet he who reigns within himself, and rules* (466)
> *Passions, Desires, and Fears, is more a King.*

This rule is basic to dominion of the body, which is 'oft by force'. Spiritual dominion is higher:

> *But to guide Nations in the way of truth* (473)
> *By saving Doctrine, and from errour lead*
> *To know, and knowing worship God aright,*
> *Is yet more Kingly . . .*

This is dominion of the soul, the object of Christ's aspiration. But his rejection of wealth does not close the subject of empire.

Book III

Satan again climbs the ladder of praise to another temptation, that of glory: 'These God-like Vertues wherefore dost thou hide?' The irony of this question escapes Satan, but he knows that he must try a higher incentive, the motive 'of most erected Spirits'. Nothing quenches the thirst for glory, and he cites great military examples.

But Christ is not to be moved by the new temptation:

> *Thou neither dost perswade me to seek wealth* (44)
> *For Empires sake, nor Empire to affect*
> *For glories sake by all thy argument.*

Thus Milton indicates the transition in temptations, for wealth in
the preceding book included all opulence or excess beyond the
needs of nature, and empire continues to describe Christ's kingdom for Satan. Christ's contempt for popular favour is a humanistic view added to the definition of true glory found earlier in
Lycidas. He responds to Satan's military heroes by describing war
as anything but glorious: 'They err who count it glorious to
subdue / By Conquest far and wide.' It is contrary to the ethical
view:

> But if there be in glory aught of good,   (88)
> It may by means far different be attain'd
> Without ambition, war, or violence;
> By deeds of peace, by wisdom eminent,
> By patience, temperance . . .

As Job suffered for God, or Socrates for truth. He concludes:

> Shall I seek glory then, as vain men seek   (105)
> Oft not deserv'd? I seek not mine, but his
> Who sent me, and thereby witness whence I am.

This states the kind of witness Christ desires to give of his descent,
but Satan cleverly turns it to his advantage: 'Think not so slight
of glory; therein least, / Resembling thy great Father.' To Satan's
charge that God 'for his glory all things made', Christ replies:
'Though chiefly not for glory as prime end, / But to shew forth
his goodness', for which he rightly expects glory as thanks. 'But
why should man seek glory? . . . Who for so many benefits
receiv'd / Turn'd recreant to God':

> Yet so much bounty is in God, such grace   (142)
> That who advance his glory, not thir own,
> Them he himself to glory will advance.

Thus Christ escapes from his dilemma and turns Satan into his
own rebuttal, who 'Insatiable of glory had lost all'.

Dropping this motivation, Satan turns back to empire: 'But
to a Kingdom thou art born.' David's throne is now under Roman
rule: 'and think'st thou to regain / Thy right by sitting still or
thus retiring?' He suggests a higher motivation: 'If Kingdom
move thee not, let move thee Zeal, and Duty . . . to free / Thy
Country from her Heathen servitude.' Christ responds that one
must await the due time of Providence:

What if he hath decreed that I shall first   (188)
Be try'd in humble state, and things adverse,
By tribulations, injuries, insults,
Contempts, and scorns, and snares, and violence,
Suffering, abstaining, quietly expecting
Without distrust or doubt, that he may know
What I can suffer, how obey?

Thus he unwittingly particularizes the trial originally set forth by
God. He concludes in the vein of Milton's new heroism:

> *who best*
> *Can suffer, best can do; best reign, who first*
> *Well hath obey'd; just tryal e're I merit*
> *My exaltation without change or end.*

In this trial he must merit his exaltation.

    Christ sees that Satan does not understand the nature of his
kingdom:

> *Know'st thou not that my rising is thy fall,*   (201)
> *And my promotion will be thy destruction?*

This is signified by the concluding action of the poem. Satan,
however, is not so ready to accept prophecy. He retorts: 'Let that
come when it comes'; grace is not for him. And 'If there be
worse, the expectation more / Of worse torments me then the
feeling can.' His dubiety is puzzled: 'If I then to the worst that
can be hast, / Why move thy feet so slow to what is best?' Then
Satan comes close to the anxiety that Christ has expressed: 'Perhaps thou linger'st in deep thoughts detain'd / Of the enterprize so
hazardous and high.' And no wonder: his experience and knowledge of the world are so limited. Of course Satan has some
disdain for 'a fugitive and cloistered virtue, unexercised and un-
breathed', but not for the same reason that God is concerned to
exercise Christ in 'the rudiments / Of his great warfare'. Hence
there is some irony in Satan's boast:

> *But I will bring thee where thou soon shalt quit*   (244)
> *Those rudiments, and see before thine eyes*
> *The Monarchies of the Earth, thir pomp and state . . .*

Satan and God could agree on the end, 'that thou may'st know /
How best their opposition to withstand', but the opposition
would belong to different kinds of warfare.

After the military vision Satan further explains 'To what end I have brought thee hither and shewn / All this fair sight'. It is to advise him how to secure his kingdom and to promise help in the deliverance of his people. Christ answers again that his time is not yet come, and when it does he will not be found wanting or in need of

> *Thy politic maxims, or that cumbersome* (400)
> *Luggage of war there shewn me, argument*
> *Of human weakness rather then of strength.*

His rejection of martial luggage gains force from the military amplification in Satan's vision of the monarchies of the earth. And Christ finds Satan's zeal for Israel both late and sophistic. 'As for those captive Tribes, themselves were they / Who wrought their own captivity'; let them serve their enemies so long as they serve idols. Again we encounter Milton's belief that moral slavery leads to political slavery, and also the conclusion of *Samson Agonistes*: 'To his due time and providence I leave them.' This is likewise the faith by which Christ acts in his own trial.

Book IV

Now Satan raises the temptation to greater kingdoms; first that of Rome. Even this enticement is given an altruistic end: to free a victor people from servile yoke:

> *And with my help thou may'st; to me the power* (103)
> *Is given, and by that right I give it thee.*
> *Aim therefore at no less then all the world,*
> *Aim at the highest, without the highest attain'd*
> *Will be for thee no sitting, or not long*
> *On Davids Throne, be propheci'd what will.*

Thus he supports ambition by prudence, and offers the power he has been unable to discover in Christ.

Milton is so careful to indicate the kinds of temptation to which Christ is subjected that one has no right to bind him to outside sources. Hence Christ's reply:

> *Nor doth this grandeur and majestic show* (110)
> *Of luxury, though call'd magnificence,*

More then of arms before, allure mine eye,
Much less my mind; though thou should'st add to tell
Thir sumptuous gluttonies, and gorgeous feasts
. . . to me should'st tell who thirst
And hunger still . . .

Thus, although you call it magnificence, man still does not live
by bread alone. After an ironic allusion to his mission, 'what if I
withal / Expel a Devil who first made him such?' he says he was
not sent to free that people 'deservedly made vassal', and then outlines their steps of moral decline from ambition to cruelty to luxury
to effeminacy. This familiar Miltonic doctrine ends with the question, who 'could of inward slaves make outward free?' Positively
Christ replies that when his kingdom comes,

Means there shall be to this, but what the means,   (152)
Is not for thee to know, nor me to tell.

What Christ knows he knows from the Word of God, the Old
Testament; but he must learn about the Temptation from experience, not from revelation. This fact limits and defines his dramatic
character in the poem, but verifies his moral example.

Now Milton indicates a change in the Tempter by calling his
response 'impudent'. Satan finds Christ too 'difficult and nice',
even obstinate; exasperation betrays him into revealing his purpose. His condition for his gifts, 'if thou wilt fall down, / And
worship me as thy superior Lord', could be called the usual
worship of the world.

But Christ becomes vehement: 'I never lik'd thy talk, thy offers
less, / Now both abhor.' Satan's abominable terms have exposed
his real motive; Christ knows his blasphemy from the Mosaic
commandments. It means to break faith with God, and so he
emphatically rejects him:

Get thee behind me; plain thou now appear'st   (193)
That Evil one, Satan for ever damn'd.

This is the first discovery of the poem, and Satan, now 'with
fear abasht', proceeds to excuse his 'test' by pleading his fear of
Christ's identity:

Who then thou art, whose coming is foretold   (204)
To me so fatal, me it most concerns.

Although he has missed his aim, he protests that he will not advise him further.

At last Satan sees that Christ is not inclined to a 'worldly Crown', but rather to contemplation:

> *Be famous then* (221)
> *By wisdom; as thy Empire must extend,*
> *So let extend thy mind o're all the world,*
> *In knowledge, all things in it comprehend,*
> *All knowledge is not couch't in* Moses *Law,*
> *The* Pentateuch *or what the Prophets wrote . . .*

There is also Gentile learning, and without it 'Ruling them by perswasion as thou mean'st' will be impossible. This is the province that Bacon took and the 'hydroptique immoderate desire' that Donne regretted. Then Satan directs Christ's vision from 'this specular Mount' towards Athens. He gives an eloquent survey of Greek learning and concludes with a home shot:

> *These rules will render thee a King compleat* (283)
> *Within thy self, much more with Empire joyn'd.*

This is the subtlest, because most congenial, lure yet offered by Satan, but the cloven hoof still lurks in the stress on empire.

Milton knows that Christ must tread warily, and so 'our Saviour sagely thus repli'd':

> *Think not but that I know these things, or think* (286)
> *I know them not; not therefore am I short*
> *Of knowing what I aught: he who receives*
> *Light from above, from the fountain of light,*
> *No other doctrine needs, though granted true.*

The opening alternatives give the humanist little comfort, but the conclusion defends the faith against deism from Bacon to Dryden. The next two lines make the humanist wince:

> *But these are false, or little else but dreams,* (291)
> *Conjectures, fancies, built on nothing firm.*

Dryden, in his *Religio Laici*, chastised the Deists for presuming to know the ends of human life without revelation, and he itemized the efforts of the philosophers as Milton does here. This is why Christ praises Socrates, and not for scepticism:

> *The first and wisest of them all profess'd*　　(293)
> *To know this only, that he nothing knew.*

The presumption to knowledge exhibited by Adam is again rebuked, and the limits of his knowledge defined. It should be added that

> *Much of the Soul they talk, but all awrie,*　　(313)
> *And in themselves seek vertue, and to themselves*
> *All glory arrogate, to God give none,*
> *Rather accuse him under usual names,*
> *Fortune and Fate, as one regardless quite*
> *Of mortal things.*

This is the faith of the fallen Angels, and so we should not be surprised that Christ concludes:

> *Who therefore seeks in these*　　(318)
> *True wisdom, finds her not, or by delusion*
> *Far worse, her false resemblance only meets . . .*

And this is why the Devil can also quote the classics. If one turns to the Greeks for pleasure, where can one find that solace better than in Hebrew arts? Indeed were they not (as commonly held) the originals? Greek poetry does not reach the highest inspiration, which Milton now requires,

> *Unless where moral vertue is express't*　　(351)
> *By light of Nature not in all quite lost.*

Hebrew literature is also superior in political wisdom, especially the Prophets: 'These only with our Law best form a King.' Thus Christ rounds to Satan's argument.

Christ also contrasts Greek and Hebrew style in a way that is suggestive for this poem. The Greek has 'swelling Epithetes thick laid / As varnish on a Harlots cheek'; the Hebrew has a 'majestic unaffected stile'. Plainness is opposed to ornament. In short, *Paradise Regained* is written in the Hebrew tradition, like the Book of Job, and *Paradise Lost* in the Greek or Roman tradition. When Milton thought of adorning his native tongue, he condemned 'verbal curiosities' in *The Reason of Church Government*. There also he mentioned the Book of Job as 'a brief model' of the epic and set Hebrew poetry against the Greek even 'in the very critical art of composition'. Already, in *Of Reformation*, he had opposed 'the sober, plain, and unaffected style' of Scripture to Patristic rhetoric. This view would explain the severer style of a poem modelled after the Hebraic mode of epic.

By this time Satan—the seducer, not the rebel—is nonplussed, and his quandary exhausts the worldly temptations:

> *Since neither wealth, nor honour, arms nor arts,*   (368)
> *Kingdom nor Empire pleases thee, nor aught*
> *By me propos'd in life contemplative,*
> *Or active, tended on by glory, or fame,*
> *What dost thou in this World? the Wilderness*
> *For thee is fittest place . . .*

Hence he reads the stars in the Gentile way and spells out a tragic fate for Christ, waxing ironic about the reality and eternity of his Kingdom. Then he brings Christ back to the Wilderness, and tries to frighten him with dreams, storms, and spectres. The next day Satan adds them to the portents of the stars, but Christ is indifferent to these terrors 'As false portents, not sent from God, but thee'; and refuses to be frightened into accepting Satan as his God.

Milton has indicated rising passion in Satan and, 'now swoln with rage', the Fiend launches into a tirade against Christ: 'For Son of God to me is yet in doubt.' His whole effort has been to find out in what sense Christ is the Son of God. He has learned at best that Christ is to be his fatal enemy:

> *Good reason then, if I before-hand seek*   (526)
> *To understand my Adversary, who*
> *And what he is; his wisdom, power, intent,*
> *By parl, or composition, truce, or league*
> *To win him, or win from him what I can.*

This is Satan's basic motivation, and he has proved that Christ is 'firm / To the utmost of meer man both wise and good, / Not more'. This may be enough to reinstate Adam, but it is not enough for Satan:

> *Therefore to know what more thou art then man,*   (538)
> *Worth naming Son of God by voice from Heav'n,*
> *Another method I must now begin.*

A hint of this method is conveyed by Satan's naming the 'voice from Heaven'.

Then he seizes Christ and takes him bodily over the 'holy City' and 'There on the highest Pinacle he set / The Son of God'. Indeed Satan acts out his scorn, for this predicament mocks Christ's destiny and his divine sanction. Satan's words amplify his scorn (like Rochester's words—'not being of God, he could not stand'):

> There stand, if thou wilt stand; to stand upright   (551)
> Will ask thee skill; I to thy Fathers house
> Have brought thee, and highest plac't, highest is best,
> Now shew thy Progeny; if not to stand,
> Cast thy self down; safely if Son of God.

Out of the Gospel Milton creates a dilemma, either horn of which may prove Christ's lineage, or more likely his death in Satan's view. For Satan, who has put Christ in jeopardy, either to stand or to fall safely exceeds the power of mere man. If the dilemma is in the Gospel at all, it has to be latent in the remark that the Angels 'shall bear thee up'. But in Milton, as in the Gospel, this remark follows the challenge to 'cast thyself down' and belongs to the promise that is written. Satan's dilemma is answered out of the Word of God:

> To whom thus Jesus: also it is written,   (560)
> Tempt not the Lord thy God, he said and stood.

Here he gives the reason for not casting himself down and also counters Satan's sardonic citation of Psalm xci. It is important to observe that Satan has forced this test of God's providence, and that Christ has chosen to try his skill rather than to presume upon God in the obvious way of the Gospel.

The unexpected reversal of fortune, 'But Satan smitten with amazement fell', accompanies Satan's discovery of Christ's true 'progeny'. Like Antaeus and yet unlike, he is defeated in the air, his own element. This turn of events is emphasized:

> So after many a foil the Tempter proud,   (569)
> Renewing fresh assaults, amidst his pride
> Fell whence he stood to see his Victor fall.

And this reversal portends their destinies:

> So struck with dread and anguish fell the Fiend . . .
> Who durst so proudly tempt the Son of God.   (580)

Satan forced the issue by his presumption. His irony about the providence of God is confounded by the Angelic rescue:

> *Who on their plumy Vans receiv'd him soft*　　(583)
> *From his uneasie station, and upbore*
> *As on a floating couch through the blithe Air,*
> *Then in a flowry valley set him down*
> *On a green bank, and set before him spred*
> *A table of Celestial Food, Divine,*
> *Ambrosial, Fruits fetcht from the tree of life.*

This is food by which man can live, given by Providence, and fetched from the other tree in the Garden of man's fall. It contains the 'force' that bread does not, but not the force that Satan looked for.

The significance of Christ's action is then reiterated:

> *now thou hast aveng'd*　　(606)
> *Supplanted* Adam, *and by vanquishing*
> *Temptation, hast regain'd lost Paradise,*
> *And frustrated the conquest fraudulent.*

Already Satan feels the effect of his defeat:

> *for proof, e're this thou feel'st*　　(621)
> *Thy wound, yet not thy last and deadliest wound*
> *By this repulse receiv'd . . .*

These words also extend the consequences of the present action. The Angelic salute to Christ concludes with these lines:

> *Hail Son of the most High, heir of both worlds,*　　(633)
> *Queller of Satan, on thy glorious work*
> *Now enter, and begin to save mankind.*

Thus it is clear that the poem centres on Christ as teacher of mankind, a role parallel to that of Job. Those who bewail the conclusion of the poem not only mistake Milton's emphasis but miss his final contrast between Christ's humility and Satan's pride. Humility and humanity are epitomized in his final action: 'hee unobserv'd / Home to his Mothers house private return'd'. No doubt Satan felt that Christ was compounding all of his shortcomings, for, unlike Satan, he affected neither godhead nor supernatural power.

*　　　　*　　　　*

Plot *in* Paradise Regained

Like *Samson Agonistes*, this poem builds to divine sanction of its protagonist. The beginning and end define the change of fortune; the middle is a series of tests by which merit earns divine favour. The unifying theme is obedience to the Law of God. The dramatic action is a contest between two adversaries whose fortunes depend upon their powers and turn upon their discoveries. In this contest, if not in theology, Christ is not both in the drama and above it. The temptation of 'bread' tests Christ's power; that of 'kingdoms' tempts him with power, which he apparently lacks; that of the 'pinnacle', which tries God's providence in the Bible, is meant to destroy Christ or force God's hand. In the development of the poem the symbolism of 'bread' is related to Christ's fasting, and that of 'kingdoms' to his destiny.

The last test is Satan's overt power play, but power is his motive throughout. His condition for giving the kingdoms reveals him as a rival to God. Before they became rewards for serving Satan, however, these temptations stood on their own as lures, without cost or condition. After this disclosure Christ endures Satan as the will of God. Until the pinnacle episode Satan doubts Christ to be more than man, and his scornful alternatives do not anticipate any contrary evidence. The temptations order the plot as well as its ethical meaning, but they are not the same for both. In tempting Christ, Satan is actually probing human nature; and in resisting Satan, Christ is instructing human nature; but these are not the primary motives of either action. Instrumental to the plot and its meaning are the discoveries. The first discovery comes when Christ learns his Tempter's true malice and rejects him rather than his gifts. The second and climactic discovery comes when Satan learns his opponent's true lineage and falls. Until then Satan had not connected him with his opponent in Heaven. The first discovery leads to open animosity between them and finally to the use of force by Satan.

Most telling, however, are the reversals. After Christ has rejected Satan as well as his temptations, he has proved himself and is ready for further recognition by God. His rising and Satan's falling produce a reversal and denouement of basic significance. This reversal brings the fall of Satan and triumph of Christ at the moment of supreme arrogance, as in *Samson Agonistes*, and is thus a fitting end to their contest. Satan thinks the situation beyond Christ's power and providence because he is unconvinced of

Christ's descent. Having failed in fraud with this second Adam, Satan has resorted to force. The act that convinces Satan also manifests divine approval of Christ and concludes his defeat of Satan. Of course the supreme reversal is that of the fall of man, and it is crossed by minor reversals in the argument. Characteristic of its pattern is the irony with which Satan brings Christ to his 'Fathers house' countered by the humility with which Christ returns to his 'Mothers house'. Here it is another way of expressing obedience to the Divine Will.

5

TENSION IN *SAMSON AGONISTES*

WHEN Milton pledged obedience to the Divine Will in his sonnet, 'How soon hath Time the suttle theef of youth', he could not foresee that he would lose patience and murmur, 'When I consider how my light is spent.' Still less could he expect the fate that moved him to dramatize this murmur and yet conclude again like the sonnets. Nor could he have anticipated the hubbub over the defective classicism of his play, especially after his casual assertion of its unity: 'It suffices if the whole Drama be found not produced beyond the fifth Act.' The trouble, we are told, is that it was not produced up to the fifth act.

But Milton was most concerned with the catharsis of tragedy, to which he gave a moral function as Dryden did, and which he interpreted in terms of Paracelsian medicine, as Puttenham did the elegiac function (*Arte of English Poesie*, I, xxiv). In 1589 Putten-ham had said the elegiac poet should 'play also the Phisitian, and not onely by applying a medicine to the ordinary sicknes of man-kind, but by making the very greef it selfe (in part) cure of the disease'. Tragic sorrows 'the noble Poets sought by their arte to remove or appease, not by any medicament of a contrary temper, as the Galenistes use to cure *contraria contrariis*, but as the Paracel-sians, who cure *similia similibus*, making one dolour to expell another, and, in this case, one short sorrowing the remedie of a long and grievous sorrow'.

Likewise Milton explains the Aristotelian power of tragedy, which he calls lustration: 'Nor is Nature wanting in her own effects to make good his assertion: for so in Physic things of melancholic hue and quality are used against melancholy, sour against sour, salt to remove salt humours.' This is the essence of tragedy for Milton and the reason why we must regard the dramatic form of his murmur against Providence from this point of view.

Now the questioning theme of *Lycidas*, 'Alas! What boots it with
uncessant care', is translated by bitter experience into Samson's
'What boots it at one gate to make defence?' Indeed this tension
becomes dramatic and makes 'one dolour to expell another' in
Samson Agonistes.

I

The classic problem of *Samson Agonistes* was neatly summarized
by Dr Johnson when he said 'the intermediate parts have neither
cause nor consequence, neither hasten nor retard the catastrophe'.
It is true that the arrangement of the incidents lacks any necessary
concatenation, because the necessary conditions of the plot are
external, not within the power of the protagonist. And as Bacon
said, things not within our command have to be dealt with 'by
way of application only'. For Milton this limitation justifies his
most intense questioning of eternal Providence, the Christian form
of Fate.[1] The strict limits of this external necessity are thus described by Milton: 'Samson made Captive, Blind, and now in the
Prison at Gaza, there to labour as in a common work-house, on a
Festival day, in the general cessation from labour, comes forth into
the open Air, to a place nigh, somewhat retired, there to sit a
while and bemoan his condition.' Thus Samson's basic situation
is one of bondage, given some respite by a Festival day which contains other potentialities; together they produce consequences
which shape the plot.

Hence the action must come to Samson and can only issue
from him when he finds a way of applying his limitations to his
own ends. But as the object of action he may resist sinking into a
bondage more shameful than the one he endures. Milton provides
us with this definition of plot: 'which is nothing indeed but such
economy, or disposition of the fable as may stand best with
verisimilitude and decorum'. Hence such probability should
govern the arrangement of the visits, and indeed they move from
the most sympathetic to the least sympathetic person who might

[1] Milton's chapter on 'Providence' in *The Christian Doctrine* says that 'the providence
of God extends to all things, and that it has enacted certain immutable laws, by
which every part of the creation is administered'. His ordinary providence is 'the
immutable order of causes' which we call nature; his extraordinary providence is
'some effect out of the usual order of nature', which we call a miracle.

visit him on this day. This hypothesis is proved by Milton's effort to explain the exception: why the visit of Samson's friends precedes that of his father. Of course the formal excuse given in the Argument is that the friends become the Chorus, but the excuse that Milton offers in the play is that of age, Manoa's feet 'cast back with age / Came lagging after'. As the Chorus, certain friends and equals 'seek to comfort him what they can'.

Then he is visited 'by his old Father Manoa, who endeavours the like, and withal tells him his purpose to procure his liberty by ransom; lastly, that this Feast was proclaim'd by the Philistines as a day of Thanksgiving for their deliverance from the hands of Samson, which yet more troubles him'. Manoa's attempt to comfort Samson succeeds in depressing him profoundly by revealing the reason for this Festival day. His bondage means their deliverance. But his father proposes to buy his liberty: 'Manoa then departs to prosecute his endeavour with the Philistian Lords for Samson's redemption.'

Yet Samson's deliverance, like his blindness, has both physical and spiritual aspects. Thus physical redemption becomes one line of action, but it proves contrary to spiritual redemption. These become the conflicting lines of action which produce the fundamental irony of the plot and finally represent the struggle between God and Dagon. Samson's true course is to bear his lot with patience, not to buy his release; thus spiritual and physical deliverance are fundamentally opposite, except as the latter becomes an 'accident' of the former.

Throughout the play Milton develops parallels into antitheses between the spiritual and the physical—in blindness, bondage, and deliverance. The conflict in Samson becomes explicit in the lines of action that constitute his drama. Of course Samson is ultimately the cause of his bondage, but the action of this play relates him to its consequences. Gradually roused from despair by opposition to the Philistines, he finally precipitates the action against him so that it culminates in physical death but spiritual deliverance, or his martyrdom for a cause. Though he falters in the trial of patience, he proves constant in his faith when the enemy scorn his right to champion his God. The Samson story reaches its supreme paradox, as well as Milton's, in 'the better fortitude / Of Patience and Heroic Martyrdom'.

After the departure of Manoa, the Argument tells us that

Samson 'in the meanwhile is visited by other persons; and lastly by a public Officer to require his coming to the Feast before the Lords and People, to play or show his strength in their presence'. Thus the Festival reveals its menace to Samson. This is the climax of his bondage and beginning of his deliverance—the point at which the enemy action crosses Manoa's attempt 'to procure his liberty by ransom'. Both actions seem to lead to the humiliation of his dedicated strength. But the Argument provides no clue to the purpose or significance of the other visits, unless it is suggested by the command to play the agonistic role.

II

As background it is useful to recall Milton's defence of his own blindness in his *Second Defence of the English People* (1654). He wished that he could deny his blindness, but he 'must submit to the affliction. It is not so wretched to be blind as it is not to be capable of enduring blindness.' Yet it is a common misfortune, and has 'been known to happen to the most distinguished and virtuous persons in history'. He mentions 'those wise and ancient bards whose misfortunes the gods are said to have compensated by superior endowments, and whom men so much revered that they chose rather to impute their want of sight to the injustice of heaven than to their own want of innocence or virtue'.

Although his enemies boast that his affliction is a punishment, he is not conscious 'of having committed any enormity which might deservedly have marked me out as a fit object for such a calamitous visitation'. And to these enemies he replies: 'Let then the calumniators of the divine goodness cease to revile, or to make me the object of their superstitious imaginations. Let them consider that my situation, such as it is, is neither an object of my shame or my regret, that my resolutions are too firm to be shaken, that I am not depressed by any sense of the divine displeasure; that, on the other hand, in the most momentous periods, I have had full experience of the divine favor and protection; and that, in the solace and the strength which have been infused into me from above, I have been enabled to do the will of God; that I may oftener think on what he has bestowed than on what he has withheld; that, in short, I am unwilling to exchange my consciousness of rectitude with that of any other person; and that I feel the recollection a treasured store of tranquillity and delight.'

On most of these points of likeness Samson becomes the anti⁄thesis of Milton, and to complete the opposition Milton gives him the blindness of his adversary: 'But, if the choice were necessary, I would, sir, prefer my blindness to yours; yours is a cloud spread over the mind, which darkens both the light of reason and of conscience; mine keeps from my view only the colored surface of things, while it leaves me at liberty to contemplate the beauty and stability of virtue and of truth.'

Milton feels that he enjoys divine favour, 'not indeed so much from the privation of my sight, as from the overshadowing of those heavenly wings which seem to have occasioned this ob⁄scurity; and which, when occasioned, he is wont to illuminate with an interior light, more precious and more pure'. Samson has to recover this vision in an obscurity more like Comus's 'wing'd air dark't with plumes'. Other consequences of divine favour may be extended by analogy to Milton's play: 'To this I ascribe the more tender assiduities of my friends, their soothing attentions, their kind visits, their reverential observances; among whom there are some with whom I may interchange the Pyladean and Thesean dialogue of inseparable friends. . . . This extraordinary kindness which I experience, cannot be any fortuitous combination; and friends such as mine do not suppose that all the virtues of a man are contained in his eyes. Nor do the persons of principal distinc⁄tion in the commonwealth suffer me to be bereaved of comfort, when they see me bereaved of sight, amid the exertions which I made, the zeal which I showed, and the dangers which I run for the liberty which I love.'

These are the brave words of a public spokesman, but in private he must later have felt less confident; indeed he expressed the darker mood which opens Book VII of *Paradise Lost* with a Biblical echo of the fall of Babylon:

> *though fall'n on evil dayes,*
> *On evil dayes though fall'n, and evil tongues;*
> *In darkness, and with dangers compast round,*
> *And solitude . . .*

In this mood the ideas of his defence could easily take equivocal form as the dramatic argument of the Samson story. In the play, indeed, his defence of Providence is no longer simply a defence of himself but also evidence of distress and a challenge to faith.

III

The dramatic problem, in terms of Milton's Argument, depends upon the physical limitations of the plot. Samson now blind, fettered, a slave, shares a holiday with the Philistines: 'unwillingly this rest / Their Superstition yields me'. He withdraws to bemoan his fate, his bondage and disgrace and misery. Knowledge of the real occasion for the Holiday of the Philistines will intensify his misery and humiliation. In fact, their superstition willingly yields him this rest, and the Holiday motivates their later attention.

In his present state Samson can be a hero of suffering, hardly a hero of action as formerly, since he is circumscribed by necessity. Hence the question he provokes is, What will happen to him and how will he bear what happens? If he lacks freedom of action, he has freedom of will, and by his choices he may influence what will happen to him. His basic choice becomes one of accepting or rejecting release from his fate, even by suicide.

As the play opens, Samson, unlike Milton, finds no comfort in memory, no ease 'to the mind / From restless thoughts'. Rather he wonders why he should have been gifted and then debased. But he checks his murmuring against Providence: 'Yet stay, let me not rashly call in doubt / Divine Prediction.' After admitting 'Whom have I to complain of but myself?' he soon falls to questioning Providence again, going so far as to hint that God has mocked him by hanging the gift in his hair. And again he checks himself: 'But peace, I must not quarrel with the will / Of highest dispensation'; and yet he concludes:

> Suffices that to me strength is my bane, (63)
> And proves the source of all my miseries;
> So many, and so huge, that each apart
> Would ask a life to wail, but chief of all,
> O loss of sight, of thee I most complain!

His complaint ends on the theme of how vulnerable blindness has made him to the miseries of captivity.

Then the Chorus develops the tragic change in the great champion, becoming uncertain:

> *Which shall I first bewail,*   (151)
> *Thy Bondage or lost Sight,*
> *Prison within Prison*
> *Inseparably dark?*
> *Thou art become (O worst imprisonment!)*
> *The Dungeon of thyself . . .*

But the Chorus modifies the medieval notion of the tragic fall to fit Samson:

> *For him I reckon not in high estate*   (170)
> *Whom long descent of birth*
> *Or the sphere of fortune raises;*
> *But thee whose strength, while virtue was her mate*
> *Might have subdued the Earth.*

Samson himself revises Milton's boast in his *Defence*: 'Your coming, Friends, revives me, for I learn / Now of my own experience, not by talk', how counterfeit some professed friends can be. And like the author of *Paradise Lost*, he feels 'How many evils have enclosed me round.' But he ends again by questioning 'yet why?' and by blaming Providence for his error:

> *Immeasurable strength they might behold*   (206)
> *In me, of wisdom nothing more than mean;*
> *This with the other should, at least, have pair'd,*
> *These two proportion'd ill drove me transverse.*

Samson is like Adam in finding disproportions in the nature of things, but the Chorus now checks him: 'Tax not divine disposal, wisest Men / Have err'd, and by bad Women been deceived.'

Yet, says the Chorus, men do wonder why he should have wed Philistian women. In his first marriage he explains, 'That what I motion'd was of God, I knew / From intimate impulse'; but of his marriage with Dalila he says, 'I thought it lawful from my former act, / And the same end.' This end was the deliverance of his people. Since these marriages broke Mosaic law, they had to be sanctioned by God, and this sanction is doubtful in the second marriage; so he accepts the blame. The Choral response adds to the potentiality of this exposition:

> *In seeking just occasion to provoke*   (237)
> *The* Philistine, *thy Country's Enemy,*
> *Thou never wast remiss, I bear thee witness:*
> *Yet* Israel *still serves with all his Sons.*

But this is not his fault, says Samson, for Israel's governors rejected him:

> *But what more oft in Nations grown corrupt,*   (268)
> *And by their vices brought to servitude,*
> *Than to love Bondage more than Liberty,*
> *Bondage with ease than strenuous Liberty.*

Although this epitomizes the alternatives of Samson as well as Israel, he warns them: 'Me easily indeed mine may neglect, / But God's proposed deliverance not so.'

The final response of the Chorus debates the justice of Providence. Only fools doubt God's existence. 'Yet more there be who doubt his ways not just. . . . But never find self-satisfying solution.' In attempting to convict God of contradiction, they are trying to confine the infinite. If God could not dispense with his own laws, he would not

> *Have prompted this Heroic* Nazarite,   (318)
> *Against his vow of strictest purity,*
> *To seek in marriage that fallacious Bride,*
> *Unclean, unchaste.*

Then Samson is exonerated in his marriage with the woman of Timna, and Reason is taught to submit to Providence.

Manoa also comes to comfort Samson, but in fact adds to his distress by making him the occasion for questioning Providence: Why do God's gifts 'draw a Scorpion's tail behind?' And Manoa concludes:

> *Alas methinks whom God hath chosen once*   (368)
> *To worthiest deeds, if he through frailty err,*
> *He should not so o'erwhelm, and as a thrall*
> *Subject him to so foul indignities,*
> *Be it but for honour's sake of former deeds.*

But Samson checks him:

> *Appoint not heav'nly disposition, Father,*   (373)
> *Nothing of all these evils hath befall'n me*
> *But justly; I myself have brought them on.*

Nevertheless, he describes himself as twice betrayed, although he ends by condemning his 'foul effeminacy':

> *The base degree to which I now am fall'n,*   (414)
> *These rags, this grinding, is not yet so base*
> *As was my former servitude . . .*

Manoa replies that 'Bitterly hast thou paid, and still art paying / That rigid score. A worse thing yet remains.' Then he discloses the reason for the Holiday, that it celebrates the Philistian triumph over Samson and his God. Samson is crushed by the weight of his shame, especially for provoking doubt of Providence; but he finds hope in that 'Dagon hath presumed, / Me overthrown, to enter lists with God.' It may be remarked that Manoa's omens contribute more to suspense than to events. Samson then rejects Manoa's proposal of ransom: 'let me here, / As I deserve, pay on my punishment'. And Manoa's advice is clearly wrong in its motivation: 'Repent the sin, but if the punishment / Thou canst avoid, self-preservation bids.' This is supported by an attempt to convict Samson of a sin of pride. Samson replies, 'His pardon I implore; but as for life, / To what end should I seek it?' He counters Manoa's argument by relating how he had behaved 'like a petty God' and 'Then swoll'n with pride into the snare I fell.'

Now the Chorus and Samson unite to praise his observance of the temperance required of the Nazarite. Samson, however, proceeds to question its value when faced by the temptation of *Lycidas*, 'To sport with Amaryllis in the shade, / Or with the tangles of Neaera's hair.' For he repeats the 'What boots it' theme:

> *But what avail'd this temperance, not complete*   (558)
> *Against another object more enticing?*
> *What boots it at one gate to make defence,*
> *And at another to let in the foe*
> *Effeminately vanquish'd?*

Now Samson feels, like Milton in the sonnet, that he can no longer serve God, but asks not 'to sit idle on the household hearth. . . . Here rather let me drudge and earn my bread.' In his despair Samson looks only to death and bewails his torment of mind:

Sleep hath forsook and giv'n me o'er (629)
To death's benumbing Opium as my only cure.
Thence faintings, swoonings of despair,
And sense of Heav'n's desertion.

As Samson falters in patience his one petition is for 'speedy death'.

Here the Chorus provides the climactic questioning of Provi-dence on the fate of dedicated spirits, and the parallels to Milton or his cause are irresistible. It begins with the inefficacy of works 'Extolling Patience as the truest fortitude'; perhaps things like Edward Sherburne's poem on 'Seneca's Answer to Lucilius his Quaere, Why Good Men suffer misfortunes seeing there is a Divine Providence?' or even Milton's own sonnet on his blind-ness. These are useless without 'Some source of consolation from above', such as Milton felt in his *Second Defence*, not the worldly source of his sonnet 'To Mr Cyriack Skinner upon his Blindness'. The vehemence of the indictment of Providence beginning 'God of our Fathers' is unparalleled in Milton and concludes its eloquence with a petition to counter Samson's prayer for speedy death: 'Behold him in this state calamitous, and turn / His labours, for thou canst, to peaceful end.'

The transition to Dalila, however, appears to mock Samson with the temptation of Amaryllis, presented as a gay, confident, and enticing object. But she is the only visitor whose reason for coming remains equivocal, perhaps because she is the bridge be-tween sympathy and antipathy in the visitors. Samson's blindness excuses her vivid description by the Chorus, but not its satire of female finery. Dalila approaches in a guise related to the Philistian 'Sea-Idol' and to Samson's feeling of shame (198):

Who like a foolish Pilot have shipwreck'd
My Vessel trusted to me from above,
Gloriously rigg'd; and for a word, a tear,
Fool, have divulged the secret gift of God
To a deceitful Woman . . .

Yet his repulse of her is followed by the Chorus's sentimental description of her distress. Some aspects of the Chorus's original comparison were put to comic use in Congreve's *Way of the World* (II, iv): 'Here she comes i' faith full sail, with her fan spread and streamers out, and a shoal of fools for tenders.'

At first Dalila professes fear, contrition, conjugal affection, doubt, and desire to comfort him. But Samson regards them as feminine wiles to play on masculine virtue or weakness:

> *That wisest and best men full oft beguiled*   (759)
> *With goodness principled not to reject*
> *The penitent, but ever to forgive . . .*

Then she admits her weakness, counters it by his, and pleads jealousy as a cause. Samson turns these excuses into bitter reproaches. Because he rejects the plea of weakness, Dalila urges the civil and religious pressures exerted upon her to surrender her private interests to the public good. But Samson then accuses her of civil impiety or religious hypocrisy and of sacrificing his love to gods who are 'the contradiction / Of their own deity'. Now it is Dalila, not Samson, who is 'motioned' by something other than love.

Finally, Dalila offers to rescue him from slavery in recompense for her mistake. And Samson, less harshly but yet firmly, rejects the 'enchanted cup', now more clearly Circean than when it was offered by Manoa: 'This Gaol I count the house of Liberty / To thine, whose doors my feet shall never enter.' This offer complicates the temptation to his amatory weakness. Her request to touch his hand, whatever its motivation, is also the way to wake 'fierce remembrance' in a blind man. But he sends her away with his forgiveness. His added taunt, however, draws from her a spirited retort of how she will be memorable among her own people.

Now Samson seems more charitable to his Circe than the Chorus: 'So let her go; God sent her to debase me, / And aggravate my folly.' He accepts her visit as part of his punishment, his humiliation. But the Chorus tries to magnify the power of beauty and then to support it by a tirade on woman and her effect on the 'wisest men and best', Samson's own phrase. This dotage evokes from the Chorus the kind of metaphor with which they first described Dalila: 'What Pilot so expert but needs must wreck / Embark'd with such a Steers-mate at the Helm?' Yet Dalila's visit is given an ambivalence that is absent from this moral against effeminacy and from Samson's earlier account of the impudence and contempt with which she had betrayed him. It is clear, however, that Dalila has not regained her power over

Samson, but instead has renewed his antagonism to the Philistines.

Where Dalila was introduced with ambiguity, 'But who is this,
what thing of Sea or Land?' Harapha is introduced in stormy
metaphor, 'But had we best retire, I see a storm?' In fact the
Chorus promises open antagonism:

> *Look now for no enchanting voice, nor fear* (1065)
> *The bait of honey'd words; a rougher tongue*
> *Draws hitherward . . .*

And Harapha immediately confirms their promise. He comes out
of incredulity about Samson's feats, and regrets that he

> *was never present on the place* (1085)
> *Of those encounters, where we might have tried*
> *Each other's force in camp or listed field.*

Samson answers that the proof is to try his strength. Surprised by
the challenge, Harapha retorts, 'I thought / Gyves and the Mill
had tamed thee.' But he disdains to fight a blind man; besides,
Samson is dirty. Then Samson proposes a contemptuous way to
even the odds. Harapha replies that he would not dare to 'disparage glorious arms' unless he owed his strength to some black
art, 'which thou from Heaven / Feign'dst at thy birth was giv'n
thee in thy hair'. Thus he questions Samson's celestial claim.

Of course Samson replies that he owes his strength to God:
'My trust is in the living God who gave me / At my Nativity
this strength.' Then he extends his challenge to Dagon to prove
himself by dissolving these alleged 'Magic spells'. Thus the contest is moved to God and Dagon by means that recall *Comus*.
Where Samson had said (462) 'Dagon hath presumed . . . to
enter lists with God', Harapha now responds:

> *Presume not on thy God, whate'er he be,* (1156)
> *Thee he regards not, owns not, hath cut off*
> *Quite from his people, and deliver'd up*
> *Into thy Enemies' hand, permitted them*
> *To put out both thine eyes, and fetter'd send thee*
> *Into the common Prison, there to grind*
> *Among the Slaves and Asses thy comrades,*
> *As good for nothing else . . .*

Harapha taunts him with his treatment by Providence, which has made him unworthy to enter the lists with a 'noble Warrior'. Samson now faces the most trying statement of a crucial issue in his own mind. Though goaded as never before, he admits his degradation and its justice, 'yet despairs not of his final pardon', and hence dares put his faith to 'the trial of mortal fight'.

Harapha retorts that Samson's God will not accept 'A Murderer, a Revolter, and a Robber' as his champion. The turns of this argument obviously centre in Samson's relation to Providence. Samson demands proof of Harapha's charges and then defends himself against them, concluding with some ambiguity: 'These shifts refuted, answer thy appellant / Though by his blindness maim'd for high attempts.' But Harapha continues to treat him as beneath the dignity of honourable combat. Samson's charges of cowardice receive answers like 'This insolence other kind of answer fits', or 'thou shalt lament / These braveries in Irons loaden on thee'.

The real force of this visit is not to be found in Harapha's cowardice but in Samson's humiliation as a champion, which puts his faith in Providence to its supreme test. The Chorus could repeat its earlier concession (237):

> *In seeking just occasion to provoke*
> *The* Philistine, *thy Country's Enemy,*
> *Thou never wast remiss, I bear thee witness.*

But, although this occasion is disguised by rules of single combat, Samson cannot escape the limitations of his punishment in his effort to enter the lists for his God. The Chorus fears that Harapha will stir the Philistines up 'Some way or other yet further to afflict thee'. Samson replies that death is 'The worst that he can give, to me the best'. Now Samson's hope of achieving his mission is rather like Hamlet's:

> *Yet so it may fall out, because their end*   (1265)
> *Is hate, not help to me, it may with mine*
> *Draw their own ruin who attempt the deed.*

The motivation here points to an act of Providence rather than of Samson, except as he may have provoked the enemy.

Then the Chorus speculates on what 'may fall out'. Will it be

the conquest of warrior or of saint? of power or of patience?
Patience is the less showy conquest:

> *But Patience is more oft the exercise*   (1287)
> *Of Saints, the trial of their fortitude,*
> *Making them each his own Deliverer,*
> *And Victor over all*
> *That tyranny or fortune can inflict.*

It is a mode of self-delivery and their conclusion is this:

> *Either of these is in thy lot,*   (1292)
> *Samson, with might endued*
> *Above the Sons of men; but sight bereaved*
> *May chance to number thee with those*
> *Whom Patience finally must crown.*

The latter alternative fits his limited sphere of action, is not beyond
the constraints imposed by his earlier lapse.

The transition to the next visit summarizes the action thus far:

> *This Idol's day hath been to thee no day of rest,*   (1297)
> *Labouring thy mind*
> *More than the working day thy hands,*
> *And yet perhaps more trouble is behind.*

With this premonition the Chorus announces the Public Officer,
whose very name suggests that Samson's labour is about to be
moved to the public stage.

Indeed Harapha is soon to get his proof of Samson's strength,
for the Philistine Lords 'now some public proof thereof require'
for 'this Idol's day'. Once more Samson stands in need of a
dispensation from Mosaic law, and again he faces personal humiliation: 'To make them sport with blind activity', not 'high
attempts', but to make a game of his calamities. When the Officer
cautions, 'Regard thyself', as Manoa had urged, Samson replies:

> *Can they think me so broken, so debased*   (1335)
> *With corporal servitude, that my mind ever*
> *Will condescend to such absurd commands?*

Debasement is the greatest trial of Samson's fortitude in patience.
The lesson with which his mind laboured was Milton's: it is
not so wretched to be afflicted as it is not to be capable of enduring

affliction. After his refusal, the Chorus counsels him to 'Expect another message more imperious', and Samson's course seems equally determined:

> Shall I abuse this *Consecrated gift*   (1354)
> *Of strength, again returning with my hair*
> *After my great transgression, so requite*
> *Favour renew'd, and add a greater sin*
> *By prostituting holy things to Idols?*

Here he reveals the basis of his returning confidence, but the Chorus objects that he already serves the Philistines with this strength. Samson answers that he is a prisoner of their civil power, not religious; and that he cannot go with the Officer unless 'outward force constrains' or God grants a dispensation. The Chorus is finally baffled, and Samson takes over the office of consoler because he again feels 'motioned' by God:

> *If there be aught of presage in the mind,*   (1387)
> *This day will be remarkable in my life*
> *By some great act, or of my days the last.*

The alternatives of this presage retain the ambiguity that has be-longed to the future for some time. We may recall that Samson was once certain of a motion from God, and once uncertain; now his feeling grows in conviction.

When the Officer returns and threatens Samson with force (the other release of conscience) Samson agrees to go with some equivocation: 'Masters' commands come with a power resistless / To such as owe them absolute subjection.' The Officer ventures the opinion that this compliance may even set him free. The ambiguities now begin to multiply potential ironies. Promising no dishonour to 'Our God, our Law, my Nation, or myself', Samson goes with the blessing of the Chorus. Simultaneously Manoa returns to report his hope 'With good success to work his liberty'. Then he is interrupted by a noise or shout that tore the sky. Continuing, he declares: 'For his redemption all my Patri-mony, / If need be, I am ready to forgo.' The Chorus sympathizes with Manoa, but Samson has already rejected this ransom, and the 'hideous noise' of his final act makes it futile.

IV

Samson's redemption did not lie in Manoa's way; nor did it depend upon the miracle to which the Chorus also looks, the restoration of his eyesight. Rather it depended upon the guidance of Providence, to which even the Messenger now feels obliged. The Messenger's account of the horrid spectacle 'still lessens / The sorrow' until it comes to Samson's death. Manoa's immediate response emphasizes its relation to the plot:

> *The worst indeed, O all my hopes defeated*   (1571)
> *To free him hence! but death who sets all free*
> *Hath paid his ransom now and full discharge.*

Then Manoa's distress turns to a vital question: 'How died he? death to life is crown or shame.' The Messenger's answer, 'By his own hands', turns his death to shame, and provokes Manoa's anguished 'what cause?' The Messenger points to fate: 'Inevitable cause / At once both to destroy and be destroyed.' But Manoa does not understand: 'O lastly over-strong against thyself!'

Finally the Messenger describes the scene, and how Samson figured:

> *At sight of him the people with a shout*   (1620)
> *Rifted the Air, clamouring their god with praise,*
> *Who had made their dreadful enemy their thrall.*

Samson, 'patient but undaunted', performed incredible feats, and at the intermission volunteered a greater feat:

> *Now of my own accord such other trial*   (1643)
> *I mean to show you of my strength, yet greater;*
> *As with amaze shall strike all who behold.*

And when he pulled the roof down upon them, 'Samson with these immix'd, inevitably / Pull'd down the same destruction on himself.' For this is the other side of his earlier resort: 'Some narrow place enclosed, where sight may give thee, / Or rather flight, no great advantage on me.'

The Choral summary defines the nature of Samson's death by explaining the role of Providence or natural necessity in his fate:

> *O dearly-bought revenge, yet glorious!*   (1660)
> *Living or dying thou hast fulfill'd*
> *The work for which thou wast foretold*
> *To Israel, and now ly'st victorious*
> *Among thy slain self-kill'd,*
> *Not willingly, but tangled in the fold*
> *Of dire necessity, whose law in death conjoin'd*
> *Thee with thy slaughter'd foes in number more*
> *Than all thy life had slain before.*

Samson paid dearly for fulfilling his work, for his crown of glory: his death appears to be an act of shame, and is indeed a consequence of the penalty for his original lapse. Thus his death is tragic in one sense and a moral victory in another. The Semichoruses give antiphonic development to the contest between Samson and the Philistines: how the Philistines 'with blindness internal struck' willed their own destruction and how Samson 'with inward eyes illuminated' executed that destruction. Thus 'His fiery virtue roused / From under ashes into sudden flame', and renewed itself like the Phoenix.

By this time Manoa understands that Samson's death is a crown rather than a shame, and proceeds to itemize its glories, concluding with Samson's greatest fear:

> *And which is best and happiest yet, all this*   (1718)
> *With God not parted from him, as was fear'd,*
> *But favouring and assisting to the end.*
> *Nothing is here for tears, nothing to wail*
> *Or knock the breast, no weakness, no contempt,*
> *Dispraise, or blame, nothing but well and fair,*
> *And what may quiet us in a death so noble.*

All of Manoa's fears of shame have been removed, and he goes to find the body and prepare the funeral. But it must be remarked that freedom for Israel is still contingent: 'let but them / Find courage to lay hold on this occasion'.

Thus Samson is delivered from bondage, but release is achieved by his own action and limited by his condition. Hence he must be freed from blame, and so is given divine sanction, which makes him both the instrument of God and a martyr by necessity. Thus he fulfils his mission as well as justice. By what happens to him he is enabled at last to make things happen to others; thereby he passes from the passive to the active role. By his moral action he puts himself in a position again to act as the champion of God. This opportunity is discovered within the limits of his punish‑ ment, at the moment of his greatest humiliation and of the enemy's greatest insolence towards his God.

The final Chorus answers the central question about Provi‑ dence:

> *All is best, though we oft doubt,*   (1745)
> *What th' unsearchable dispose*
> *Of highest wisdom brings about,*
> *And ever best found in the close.*

This will be found in the close if the whole Drama be found produced to the end. For the benevolent face of Providence is not always manifest:

> *Oft he seems to hide his face,*
> *But unexpectedly returns*
> *And to his faithful Champion hath in place*
> *Bore witness gloriously . . .*

Thus Providence returns to his faithful servant, but another face is turned to those who resist its necessity:

> *whence* Gaza *mourns*
> *And all that band them to resist*
> *His uncontrollable intent.*

These are the ways of the Christian fate or Providence. To the obedient this outcome brings catharsis:

> *His servants he with new acquist*
> *Of true experience from this great event*
> *With peace and consolation hath dismiss'd,*
> *And calm of mind, all passion spent.*

Doubt and fear of Providence are cured by the doubt and fear and grief that end in accepting its necessity. In the order of Providence also 'things of melancholic hue and quality are used against melancholy, sour against sour, salt to remove salt humours'.

6

DRYDEN'S VIEW OF MILTON

Three Poets, in three distant Ages born,
Greece, Italy, *and* England *did adorn.*
The first in Loftiness of Thought surpass'd,
The next in Majesty, in both the last:
The Force of Nature could no farther go;
To make a third she join'd the former two.

Lines on Milton, 1688

In 1667 both Milton and Dryden published an heroic poem. But Dryden calls his *Annus Mirabilis* 'historical, not epic', because, as he tells us in the preface, its action lacks unity and magnitude. He adds: 'For this reason (I mean not of length, but broken action, tied too severely to the laws of history), I am apt to agree with those who rank Lucan rather among historians in verse than epic poets.'

At this time, however, Dryden is more concerned with expres- sion. For verse he has chosen the *Gondibert* quatrain: 'or stanzas of four in alternate rhyme, because I have ever judged them more noble, and of greater dignity, both for the sound and number, than any other verse in use amongst us'. Then he seems to have been under the influence of Sir William Davenant. But he admits, more out of conviction than complaisance, that 'The learned lan- guages have certainly a great advantage of us, in not being tied to the slavery of any rhyme.' However, Dryden regards rhyme as both necessary in English and easiest in couplets: 'But in this necessity of our rhymes, I have always found the couplet verse most easy (though not so proper for this occasion).'

In elocution Dryden allows the heroic poet more liberty than the dramatic: 'he relates almost all things as from himself, and thereby gains more liberty than the other to express his thoughts

103

with all the graces of elocution, to write more figuratively, and to confess as well the labour as the force of his imagination'. Such images are proper to the end of Heroic poetry: 'for they beget admiration, which is its proper object; as the images of Burlesque, which is contrary to this, by the same reason beget laughter: for the one shows nature beautified . . . the other shows her de-formed.' The exaggeration or disparity common to both will unite them for Dryden in the mock-heroic. When he warned the reader of *Religio Laici* not to expect 'the Turn of Heroique Poetry in this Poem', he described that turn as follows: 'The Florid, Elevated, and Figurative way is for the Passions; for Love and Hatred, Fear and Anger, are begotten in the Soul by shewing their Objects out of their true proportion; either greater than the Life, or less.' Just as the Heroic became a very inclusive genre for him, so it became the chief factor in his poetic development; and here Milton may have been an important teacher.

In his preface to *The Rival Ladies* Dryden had already defended rhymed couplets against blank verse in drama, and had described the new verse of Waller and Denham. This follows the conversa-tional order or 'the negligence of prose', but has acquired both ease and polish in its articulation. Thus it is appropriate to drama. Waller is its maker, but his sweetness is more suitable to the lyric; he was 'followed in the epic by Sir John Denham, in his *Cooper's Hill*, a poem which . . . for the majesty of the style is, and ever will be, the exact standard of good writing'. Here, then, is the model for heroic style in the couplet. In arguing that rhymed verse can be made to sound as natural as 'ordinary speaking' Dryden admits that inversion cannot always be avoided, but it can be minimized by competence. He mentions, however, another reason for departures from conversational syntax: 'I know some, who, if they were to write in blank verse, *Sir, I ask your pardon*, would think it sounded more heroically to write, *Sir, I your pardon ask.*' Here standards of the natural and of the heroic diverge, and suggest a way to rise above ordinary speaking. Now Dryden associates 'inverting the order of their words' with writing Latin, and thus indicates a common way of elevating English style.

To these masters of the new verse Dryden adds two other poets in *An Essay of Dramatic Poesy*. To the lyric Waller he adds Suckling: the last age 'can produce nothing so courtly writ, or which expresses so much the conversation of a gentleman, as Sir

John Suckling'. To the epic Denham he adds Cowley: 'nothing so elevated, so copious, and full of spirit, as Mr Cowley'. He still defends rhyme in drama by citing unnatural syntax in blank verse: 'Is there any thing in rhyme more constrained than this line in blank verse, *I heaven invoke, and strong resistance make?* where you see both the clauses are placed unnaturally, that is, contrary to the common way of speaking, and that without the excuse of a rhyme to cause it.' Now he says it is enough if the poet makes this order his general rule; 'for I deny not but sometimes there may be a greatness in placing the words otherwise; and sometimes they may sound better, sometimes also the variety itself is excuse enough'. The heroic play has made greater demands upon majesty in verse, which suffers when the poet is obliged to shut the door in rhyme. But Dryden argues that it is a fault of diction, not of rhyme, for Seneca could 'unlock the door' with dignity. His translation of Seneca's Latin, however, does not express 'ordinary things' in 'ordinary speaking', but elevates 'reserate' to 'set wide the palace gates'. Yet he thinks that Ben Jonson perhaps 'did a little too much romanize our tongue'. Poetry as the imitation of nature begins to present problems to Dryden, and largely because the requirements of the heroic became more demanding in his theory.

I

He first stated the problem of the supernatural in his prologue to *The Tempest* (1670). This he wrote with Davenant, whose preface to *Gondibert* started the argument to which Dryden alludes:

> *I must confess 'twas bold, nor would you now*
> *That Liberty to vulgar Wits allow,*
> *Which works by Magick supernatural Things:*
> *But Shakspear's Pow'r is Sacred as a King's.*
> *Those Legends from old Priesthood were receiv'd,*
> *And he then writ, as People then believ'd.*

Thus the supernatural is sanctioned by Shakespeare, and the last couplet anticipates a later argument for this liberty. Dryden's conception of *The Tempest* is later revealed in his *Preface to Albion and Albanius* (1685), where he relates his opera to that play: 'It was originally intended only for a prologue to a play of the nature of

The Tempest; which is a tragedy mixed with opera, or a drama written in blank verse, adorned with scenes, machines, songs, and dances . . . It cannot properly be called a play, because the action of it is supposed to be conducted sometimes by supernatural means, or magic; nor an opera, because the story of it is not sung.' This is why *The Tempest* is not a proper drama but a hybrid form related to the opera, and to the masque as well; proper drama has a different kind of probability, which is violated by magic.

The supernatural is related to the epic in Dryden's essay *Of Heroic Plays* in 1672. There he defends in the heroic poets from Homer to Spenser 'those enthusiastic parts of poetry which com-pose the most noble parts of all their writings'. He then expanded the argument implied in the earlier Prologue: 'And if any man object the improbabilities of a spirit appearing or of a palace raised by magic, I boldly answer him that an heroic poet is not tied to a bare representation of what is true, or exceeding probable: but that he may let himself loose to visionary objects, and to the representation of such things as depending not on sense, and there-fore not to be comprehended by knowledge, may give him a freer scope for imagination. 'Tis enough that in all ages and religions the greatest part of mankind have believed the power of magic, and that there are spirits or spectres which have appeared. This, I say, is foundation enough for poetry.' This is Dryden's willing suspension of disbelief, because it goes beyond Hobbes's 'con-ceived possibility of nature', and asserts that whatever 'for aught we know . . . may be, is not properly unnatural'. He also rejects the verdict of an heroic model: 'Neither am I much concerned at Mr Cowley's verses before *Gondibert* (though his authority is almost sacred to me): 'tis true, he has resembled the old epic poetry to a fantastic fairy land; but he has contradicted himself by his own example.' In 1674 Rymer's *Preface to Rapin* brought this charge against Spenser: 'All is fanciful and chimerical, without any uniformity, without any foundation in truth; his Poem is perfect *Fairy-land*.' Where Davenant argued to reject the enthusias-tic element in the epic, Dryden argued to introduce it into drama. Despite its consequences for his drama, Dryden's esteem for the heroic prepared him to defend both Shakespeare and Milton against critics like Rymer.

At the same time Dryden related the heroic play to the laws of an heroic poem as well as to its use of magic and supernatural agents. Although 'an heroic play ought to be an imitation, in little, of an heroic poem', it was not unlimited: 'The laws of an heroic poem did not dispense with those of the other, but raised them to a greater height, and indulged him in a further liberty of fancy, and of drawing all things as far above the ordinary propor⁄ tion of the stage as that is beyond the common words and actions of human life.' But this meant elevation in fiction as well as in style, and the introduction of 'supernatural means or magic' could loosen probability still further. Here the limit is found in Dryden's definition of an opera in the *Preface to Albion and Albanius*: 'An opera is a poetical tale, or fiction, represented by vocal and instru⁄ mental music, adorned with scenes, machines, and dancing. The supposed persons of this musical drama are generally supernatural, as gods, and goddesses, and heroes, which at least are descended from them, and are in due time to be adopted into their number. The subject, therefore, being extended beyond the limits of human nature, admits of that sort of marvellous and surprising conduct which is rejected in other plays. Human impossibilities are to be received as they are in faith; because, where gods are introduced, a supreme power is to be understood, and second causes are out of doors. Yet propriety is to be observed even here. The gods are all to manage their peculiar provinces; and what was attributed by the heathens to one power ought not to be performed by any other ... To conclude, they must all act according to their distinct and peculiar characters.' It is clear that as drama Dryden is assimilating opera to the heroic poem, and that causation becomes less and less necessary as he moves from dramatic to heroic to operatic probability. And now we see why he begins by recalling his definition of wit in terms of propriety so as to assert its applica⁄ tion to opera, and why it is natural that he should introduce *The State of Innocence and Fall of Man* by an 'Apology for Heroic Poetry and Poetic Licence'.

Dryden's operatic version of *Paradise Lost* raised again both the question of heroic style and the question of the supernatural. If the old poet gave Dryden 'leave to tag his verses', he must have had a better motive than the implied condescension. Certainly Dryden treated him with the respect he gave to Shakespeare in revising *The Tempest*. Indeed, his salute to Milton in 1677 was unparalleled: 'After this, I cannot, without injury to the deceased author of *Paradise Lost*, but acknowledge that this poem has received its entire foundation, part of the design, and many of the ornaments, from him. What I have borrowed will be so easily discerned from my mean productions, that I shall not need to point the reader to the places: and truly I should be sorry, for my own sake, that any one should take the pains to compare them together; the original being undoubtedly one of the greatest, most noble, and most sub-lime poems which either this age or nation has produced.' Ob-viously Dryden has found another model of the heroic, and his feeling cannot have been unknown to the old poet, whose conver-sation he recalls in the *Preface to the Fables*. And Dryden has found in Longinus a new apologist for heroic style, who prefers 'the sublime genius that sometimes errs to the middling or indifferent one which makes few faults'. We may recall the extremes of style that are described by the opponents of the English in the opening of *An Essay of Dramatic Poesy*: the Clevelandism that led to extravagance, and the Levelling that led to flatness. Once again Dryden defends the 'lively' against the merely 'just' and hence favours Clevelandism over Levelling.

Dryden found it difficult to control his enthusiasm for the heroic, which motivated his greatest successes as well as his greatest failures. Now he would be fair: 'I do not dispute the preference of tragedy; let every man enjoy his taste: but 'tis unjust that they who have not the least notion of heroic writing should therefore condemn the pleasure which others receive from it, be-cause they cannot comprehend it.' It is also unreasonable: 'Are all the flights of heroic poetry to be concluded bombast, unnatural, and mere madness, because they are not affected with their excel-lencies?' Moreover, it is immodest: 'Ought they not rather, in modesty, to doubt of their own judgments, when they think this or that expression in Homer, Virgil, Tasso, or Milton's *Paradise* to be too far strained, than positively to conclude that 'tis all fustian, and mere nonsense?' Dryden admits that 'there are limits to be set betwixt the boldness and rashness of a poet'; and hence 'a standing measure' is required as in the *Essay of Dramatic Poesy*, and this finally leads to his definition of wit at the close of the preface.

Dryden accuses his adversaries of reducing imitation to flatness: 'all that is dull, insipid, languishing, and without sinews, in a poem, they call an imitation of nature'. Dryden would call it the product of observation, because the 'height and life of poetry' comes from imagination. Of *A Small Poet* Samuel Butler said:

'Observation and Fancy, the Matter and Form of just Wit, are above his Philosophy.' Here poetry as imitation leads Dryden into the problem of the supernatural, or into poetic licence. This is how he puts it: 'But how are poetical fictions, how are hippo-centaurs and chimeras, or how are angels and immaterial sub-stances to be imaged; which, some of them, are things quite out of nature; others, such whereof we can have no notion? This is the last refuge of our adversaries; and more than any of them have yet had the wit to object against us.' Dryden replies: 'The answer is easy to the first part of it. The fiction of some beings which are not in nature (second notions, as the logicians call them) has been founded on the conjunction of two natures which have a real separate being. So hippocentaurs were imagined by joining the natures of a man and horse together.' For this idea Dryden gives the authority of Lucretius, although he might have cited Hobbes's *Leviathan* (I, ii).

When imitation is founded upon empirical nature, this is poetic licence: 'And poets may be allowed the like liberty for describing things which really exist not, if they are founded on popular belief. Of this nature are fairies, pigmies, and the extra-ordinary effects of magic; for 'tis still an imitation, though of other men's fancies: and thus are Shakespeare's *Tempest*, his *Midsummer Night's Dream*, and Ben Jonson's *Masque of Witches* to be defended.' But how do we image things 'whereof we can have no notion'? Dryden answers: 'For immaterial substances, we are authorized by Scripture in their description: and herein the text accommodates itself to vulgar apprehension, in giving angels the likeness of beautiful young men. Thus, after the pagan divinity, has Homer drawn his gods with human faces: and thus we have notions of things above us, by describing them like other beings more within our knowledge.' Thus the supernatural brought Dryden into conflict with the current doctrine of poetry as the imitation of nature, from which the only escape was by way of poetic licence. Later Dryden set limits to this licence in the heroic poem.

Now Dryden ventures to illustrate such imaging from his *State of Innocence*, and by lines that have been sufficiently beaten by his censors:

> *Seraph and Cherub, careless of their Charge,*
> *And wanton, in full Ease now live at large;*

Unguarded leave the Passes of the Sky,
And all dissolved in Hallelujahs lie.

'I have heard (says one of them) of Anchovies dissolved in Sauce;
but never of an Angel in Hallelujahs. A mighty *Wittycism* (if you
will pardon a new Word!) but there is some Difference between a
Laugher and a Critick.' Thus Dryden was burlesqued by bring'
ing his 'beings more within our knowledge', and making us
laughers rather than critics. For in his play Sathan in Hell is
mocking their foes in Heaven made secure by success, and to have
them dissolved in anything but hallelujahs would ruin the effect.
This is the Dryden we admire, not deplore. Our mistake in
judgment supports his insistence on the criterion of propriety.

Poetic licence, says Dryden, is the liberty that poetry has over
prose: 'This, as to what regards the thought or imagination of a
poet, consists in fiction': and, as to expression, 'if this licence be
included in a single word, it admits of tropes; if in a sentence or
proposition, of figures; both which are of a much larger extent,
and more forcibly to be used in verse than prose'. Speaking of this
licence, Horace 'restrains it so far that thoughts of an unlike nature
ought not to be joined together'. Although this would reject
catachresis and other forms of contemporary wit, Dryden relates
it to Milton's fiction: 'neither, had he now lived, would he have
taxed Milton, as our false critics have presumed to do, for his
choice of a supernatural argument: but he would have blamed my
author, who was a Christian, had he introduced into his poem
heathen deities, as Tasso is condemned by Rapin on the like
occasion'. Thus propriety limits the supernatural, but does not
eliminate it.

The supernatural may even depress heroic style. In his *Preface to
Sylvae* Dryden remarks in 1685: 'Imitation is a nice point, and
there are few poets who deserve to be models in all they write.
Milton's *Paradise Lost* is admirable; but am I therefore bound to
maintain that there are no flats amongst his elevations, when 'tis
evident he creeps along sometimes for above an hundred lines
together?' In his *Discourse concerning Satire* (1693) we get the reason
for this lapse: ' 'Tis true, he runs into a flat of thought, sometimes
for a hundred lines together, but 'tis when he is got into a track of
Scripture.' In the *Preface to Sylvae* Dryden continues: 'Cannot I
admire the height of his invention, and the strength of his expres'

sion, without defending his antiquated words, and the perpetual harshness of their sound?' In the *Discourse concerning Satire* he is more judicious: he thinks Milton went 'too far, in the frequent use of them; yet in my opinion, obsolete words may then be laudably revived, when either they are more sounding, or more significant than those in practice'. He had already defended, by Milton's example and with the same qualification, his own use of old words in *Don Sebastian* (1690).

II

In the *Discourse concerning Satire*, addressed to the patron of his *Essay of Dramatic Poesy*, Dryden finds the Moderns inferior to the Ancients as epic poets. This is not a digression from his subject but an extension of the heroic genre as he has come to view it. He criticizes Tasso especially for his unheroic style: 'he is too flatulent sometimes, and sometimes too dry; many times unequal, and almost always forced; and besides, is full of conceits, points of epigram, and witticisms; all which are not only below the dignity of heroic verse, but contrary to its nature'. The English have only Spenser and Milton, 'who neither of them wanted either genius or learning to have been perfect poets; and yet both of them are liable to many censures'. He then proceeds to the shortcomings of Spen-ser. But his verse, despite 'the ill choice of his stanza', is important to Dryden: 'he is the more to be admired, that labouring under such a difficulty, his verses are so numerous, so various, and so harmonious', that only Waller has surpassed him among the English. It should not be forgotten, however, that Dryden re-garded Milton, not Waller, as 'the poetical son of Spenser'.

After Dryden's salute to Milton in 1677, Thomas Rymer had added a threat to *The Tragedies of the Last Age* (1678): 'With the remaining *Tragedies* I shall also send you some reflections on that *Paradise Lost* of Milton's which some are pleased to call a Poem; and assert Rhyme against the slender Sophistry wherewith he attacks it.' Whatever Dryden's respect for Rymer, it could not have been based on his originality, since he commonly took his cue from Dryden. In effect Dryden now writes another answer to this work of Rymer's besides his *Preface to Troilus and Cressida*: 'As for Mr Milton, whom we all admire with so much justice, his subject is not that of an heroic poem, properly so called. His design is the losing of our happiness; his event is not prosperous, like that of all other epic works; his heavenly machines are many, and his human persons are but two. But I will not take Mr Rymer's work out of his hands. He has promised the world a critique on that author; wherein, tho' he will not allow his poem for heroic, I hope he will grant us that his thoughts are elevated, his words sounding, and that no man has so happily copied the manner of Homer; or so copiously translated his Grecisms, and the Latin elegancies of Virgil.' The last achievements were the latest ambitions of Dryden, and they leave Milton superior to the other Moderns. Dryden then concedes the flats of Scripture and the excessive archaism that we have already noticed. 'Neither will I', says Dryden, 'justify Milton for his blank verse, tho' I may excuse him by the example of Hannibal Caro', whose translation of Virgil he had found best in his *Preface to Sylvae*. Dryden, who held the view of Samuel Daniel, believed that Milton's real reason for rejecting rhyme in his epic was simply that rhyme was not his talent: 'he had neither the ease of doing it, nor the graces of it; which is manifest in his juvenilia, or verses written in his youth, where his rhyme is always constrained and forced, and comes hardly from him, at an age when the soul is most pliant, and the passion of love makes almost every man a rhymer, tho' not a poet'. In short, Milton's rhymed verse had the faults that Dryden had castigated. Why his subject is not properly heroic appears in what follows.

Another reason given for the failure of the Moderns to equal the Ancients in the epic, says Dryden, is our religion: 'they say that Christianity is not capable of those embellishments which are afforded in the belief of those ancient heathens'. Here Dryden faces another problem presented by the supernatural, and one no doubt complicated by his conversion: 'And 'tis true that, in the severe notions of our faith, the fortitude of a Christian consists in patience, and suffering for the love of God, whatever hardships can befall him in the world; not in any great attempt, or in per formance of those enterprises which the poets call heroic, and which are commonly the effects of interest, ostentation, pride, and worldly honour; that humility and resignation are our prime virtues; and that these include no action but that of the soul: when as, on the contrary, an heroic poem requires to its necessary design, and as its last perfection, some great action of war, the accomplish-ment of some extraordinary undertaking, which requires the strength and vigour of the body, the duty of a soldier, the capacity and prudence of a general and, in short, as much, or more, of the active virtue than the suffering.' Thus Dryden poses the question, raised by Milton's critics, whether his supernatural argument can produce a proper heroic poem.

This is the problem of Christian heroism that Milton faced, but Dryden finds a different answer. First he distinguishes private Christian virtues from the virtues of public office: 'But to this the answer is very obvious. God has placed us in our several stations; the virtues of a private Christian are patience, obedience, sub-mission, and the like; but those of a magistrate, or general, or a king, are prudence, counsel, active fortitude, coercive power, awful command, and the exercise of magnanimity, as well as justice.' For the chief role in *Paradise Lost* this distinction tips the balance from Adam to Satan. Then he gives an answer that favours Tasso: 'So that this objection hinders not but that an epic poem, or the heroic action of some great commander, enterprised for the com-mon good, and honour of the Christian cause, and executed happily, may be as well written now as it was of old by the heathens, provided the poet be endued with the same talents; and the language, though not of equal dignity, yet as near approaching to it as our modern barbarism will allow.' Although he has met the Christian threat to heroic action, he finds the objection to Christian machines in the epic more difficult to answer. Virgil is more discreet than Homer in his use of supernatural agents. But Christian machines threaten to destroy suspense; sometimes the only satisfaction for Christians in a modern epic is to 'have gotten God on our side'.

The only acceptable Christian machines are angels; the Old Testament and Christianized Platonism 'have made the ministry of angels as strong an engine for the working up heroic poetry, in our religion, as that of the Ancients has been to raise theirs by all the fables of their gods'. For angels do not destroy suspense: 'But 'tis an undoubted truth that, for ends best known to the Almighty Majesty of Heaven, his providential designs for the benefit of his creatures, for the debasing and punishing of some nations, and the exaltation and temporal reward of others, were not wholly known to these his ministers; else why those factious quarrels, controversies, and battles amongst themselves, when they were all united in the same design, the service and honour of their common master?' Another part of these machines is wanting until we have evil spirits able to deceive by fraud and cunning, for which we have the authority of the Bible and the example of Milton. Thus Christian machinery may be completed and made acceptable in heroic poetry.

To these reflections on the heroic poem Dryden now adds his ambition to write a national epic: 'Of two subjects, both relating to it, I was doubtful whether I should choose that of King Arthur conquering the Saxons . . . or that of Edward, the Black Prince, in subduing Spain.' Like the young Milton, he had romantic notions of the epic; but now that it was too late and he felt like Milton, he did not turn, except in an occasional aside, to Christian heroism, Milton's theme:

> *higher Argument*
> *Remaines, sufficient of it self to raise*
> *That name, unless an age too late, or cold*
> *Climat, or Years damp my intended wing . . .*

Instead, he had to earn an 'Heroic name' by the translation of an Ancient.

Dryden concludes his *Discourse concerning Satire* with some remarks on style relating to his early models: 'Had I time, I could enlarge on the beautiful turns of words and thoughts, which are as requisite in this, as in heroic poetry itself, of which the satire is undoubtedly a species.' Sir George Mackenzie had called his attention to these turns in Waller and Denham about twenty years ago: 'But this hint, thus seasonably given me, first made me sensible of my own wants, and brought me afterwards to seek for the supply of them in other English authors. I looked over the darling of my youth, the famous Cowley; there I found, instead of them, the points of wit, and quirks of epigram, even in the *Davideis*, an heroic poem, which is of an opposite nature to those puerilities; but no elegant turns either on the word or on the thought.' Earlier in this essay he condemned the style of Tasso for the same reasons. Dryden then continues: 'Then I consulted a greater genius (without offence to the *Manes* of that noble author), I mean Milton. But as he endeavours everywhere to express Homer, whose age had not arrived to that fineness, I found in him a true sublimity, lofty thoughts, which were clothed with admirable Grecisms, and ancient words, which he had been digging from the mines of Chaucer and of Spenser, and which, with all their rusticity, had somewhat of venerable in them.' But he found no turns, and by the time he wrote the *Preface to the Fables* his own sympathies were on the side of Homer and Chaucer, and against turns in the heroic poem. Although Dryden found turns in Spenser, it was Milton who revealed to him the shortcomings of Cowley in the heroic style.

In the hybrid satire which mixed the majesty of the heroic with the venom of satire, however, turns had their place and function as a mode of wit. Turns may be defined as the significant repetition of words or ideas in altered form or sense; they may be illustrated by the figure of antimetabole used in the opening of *Cooper's Hill*. They had a tendency to epigram that finally disqualified them for epic. Milton's kind of verbal repetition evidently did not strike Dryden as a species of turn, even approaching the epigrammatic at times: 'Not to know mee argues your selves unknown.' But he took it over for his Lucifer in *The State of Innocence* (III, i): 'Not to know me, argues thy self unknown.' And other turns find their way into its dramatic speech; as when Eve approaches the fatal Tree and its attack upon her senses (IV, i):

> *Thus far, at least, with Leave; nor can it be*
> *A Sin to look on this celestial Tree:*
> *I would not more; to touch, a Crime, may prove:*
> *Touching is a remoter Taste in Love.*
> *Death may be there, or Poison in the Smell,*
> *If Death in any thing so fair can dwell:*
> *But Heav'n forbids: I could be satisfy'd*
> *Were every Tree but this, but this deny'd.*

Even Miltonic syntax occasionally puts Lucifer out of his neoclassical pace:

> *Not wishing then, and thoughtless to obtain*
> *So great a Bliss; but, led by Sense of good,*
> *Inborn to all, I sought my needful Food:*
> *Then, on that Heav'nly Tree, my Sight I cast:*
> *The Colour urg'd my Eye, the Scent my Taste.*
> *Not to detain thee long; I took, did eat:*
> *Scarce had my Palate touch'd th' immortal Meat,*

But on a sudden, turn'd to what I am:
God-like, and, next to thee, I fair became:
Thought, spake, and reason'd; and, by Reason found
Thee, Nature's Queen, with all her Graces crown'd.

As he became a courtier by following his sense of good, so he acquired the grace of speech proper to his transformation. Soon his turns on this sense of good become enough to bewilder Eve:

Severe, indeed: ev'n to Injustice hard;
If Death, for knowing more, be your Reward:
Knowledge of good, is good; and therefore fit;
And to know ill, is good; for shunning it.

Thus Dryden made his turns run from pathos to sophistry; but, unlike Milton's, they were often infected with points of wit.

Dryden offers his most considered treatment of the heroic poem in his *Dedication of the Aeneis* (1697), where he allows only the claims of Homer, Virgil, and Tasso to a place in the short file of heroic poets. Modern contenders for the epic crown are shuffled off with dispatch, except for the English: 'Spenser has a better plea for his *Fairy Queen*, had his action been finished, or had been one. And Milton, if the Devil had not been his hero, instead of Adam; if the giant had not foiled the knight, and driven him out of his stronghold, to wander through the world with his lady errant; and if there had not been more machining persons than human in his poem. After these, the rest of our English poets shall not be mentioned.' In his view the others were not real contenders. Here Dryden not only repeats himself but criticizes Milton in terms appropriate to Spenser, and thus exposes his romantic view of the epic.

For this criticism Dr Johnson rebuked him: 'Dryden, petulantly and indecently, denies the heroism of Adam, because he was overcome; but there is no reason why the hero should not be unfortunate, except established practice, since success and virtue do not necessarily go together.' Both of Dr Johnson's adverbs are wrong, and his reasons fit the view neither of Milton nor of Dryden. The action of the romantic epic, to which Milton opposed *Paradise Lost*, required success both for its meaning and for the virtue of its hero. But Milton's Christian heroism found its action and meaning in suffering, its virtue in patience. Only in Christian terms do those who lose their lives save them, or find victory in defeat; and in the epic, only when the poet rejects conflicting heroic conventions, which Spenser did not. Dryden was not revising his analysis of *Paradise Lost*; he was merely drawing conclusions from his distinction between Milton's epic and the traditional epic. This distinction also appears in the fault that Milton has 'more machining persons than human in his poem', for this excess magnifies the problem of the supernatural which Dryden had already examined.

In style Dryden now finds Virgil more restrictive in his use of turns in heroic poetry, and he also introduces a new affiliation for Milton: 'Spenser and Milton are, in English, what Virgil and Horace are in Latin; and I have endeavoured to form my style by imitating their masters.' The relation of Horace both to Milton and to a translation of Virgil suggests the influence of his *Odes*. If Dryden found Milton's *Paradise Lost* open to question as an epic poem, he never discounted its heroic quality or true sublimity, and in English he never found a better model for 'the majesty of the heroic'. But his objections to *Paradise Lost* show that, despite his romantic taste, he was in some respects more classical than Milton.

III

We may now ask whether Dryden's revision of *Paradise Lost* reflects his subsequent criticism. Certainly he avoided its alleged stylistic defects: Scriptural flats of theological exposition, archaism, and blank verse. But the proper epic had certain requirements that Milton had violated. In subject they were these: the hero must have public virtues, not private Christian virtues; the action must exhibit such virtues; a prosperous outcome is necessary to beget heroic admiration. These requirements seemed to make Satan the hero. Milton's epic machinery was also defective: 'more machining persons than human in his poem' threatened 'concernment'; omniscient and omnipotent machines destroyed suspense; hence they must be limited to angels. In *The State of Innocence* Dryden stuck to the angelic level in his machines and eliminated Christ and God. But in other respects he could only try to minimize the defects he later asserted.

What Dryden produced might be called another *All for Love*, but not 'The World Well Lost'. The roles of 'machining persons' are reduced and those of human persons expanded, especially Eve's. Lucifer's envy of Adam and Eve as lovers is not more sensual than Satan's, but it takes a more Restoration form (III, i):

> *Why have not I like these, a Body too,*
> *Form'd for the same Delights which they pursue?*
> *I could (so variously my Passions move)*
> *Enjoy and blast her, in the Act of Love.*

Rather, the sensuality is found in Milton's description of Eve (IV, 492 ff.):

> *half imbracing leand*
> *On our first Father, half her swelling Breast*
> *Naked met his under the flowing Gold*
> *Of her loose tresses hid . . .*

Satan envies them 'Imparadis't in one anothers arms', because not the least of Hell's torments is fierce but unfulfilled desire. When Dryden's Adam is warned by the Angels (IV, i) he argues against free will and concludes with a complaint against Providence:

> *Hard State of Life! since Heav'n fore-knows my Will,*
> *Why am I not ty'd up from doing Ill?*
> *Why am I trusted with my self at large,*
> *When he's more able to sustain the Charge?*
> *Since Angels fell, whose Strength was more than mine,*
> *'Twould show more Grace my Frailty to confine.*
> *Fore-knowing the Success, to leave me free,*
> *Excuses him, and yet supports not me.*

Although Dryden minimizes theology, his Adam is more obstinate on this theological dilemma, inverting Milton's intention in the last couplet. To the conflict in Adam, Dryden also gives the turn of Restoration heroics (IV, i):

> *In Love, what use of Prudence can there be?*
> *More perfect I, and yet more pow'rful she.*
> *Blame me not, Heav'n, if thou Love's Pow'r had'st try'd,*
> *What could be so unjust to be deny'd?*
> *One Look of hers my Resolution breaks;*
> *Reason it self turns Folly when she speaks:*

> *And aw'd by her whom it was made to sway,*
> *Flatters her Pow'r, and does its own betray.*

This sacrifices Milton's ethics to the conventions of romance. And the provocation to wit is allowed to infect Eve when she plucks the apple: 'Perhaps, far hid in Heav'n, he does not spy, / And none of all his Hymning Guards are nigh.'

All for love reaches its climax when Adam protests (V, i):

> *Y'have shown how much you my Content design:*
> *Yet, ah! would Heav'n's Displeasure pass like mine.*
> *Must I without you, then, in wild Woods dwell?*
> *Think, and but think of what I lov'd so well?*
> *Condemn'd to live with Subjects ever mute;*
> *A Salvage Prince, unpleas'd, though absolute . . .*
> *Cheat not your self, with Dreams of Deity;*
> *Too well, but yet too late, your Crime I see . . .*
> *Not cozen'd, I with choice, my Life resign:*
> *Imprudence was your Fault, but Love was mine.*

And Eve is not to be outdone in heroic love:

> *O wond'rous Pow'r of matchless Love exprest:*
> *Why was this tryal thine, of loving best?*
> *I envy thee that Lot; and could it be,*
> *Would venture something more than Death, for thee.*
> *Not that I fear, that Death th' Event can prove;*
> *W'are both immortal, while so well we love.*

Of course this is not an immortality within the compass of *Paradise Lost*. But it is not unexpected, for when fair angels sang their Bridal Hymn above,

> *Th' Eternal, nodding, shook the Firmament,*
> *And conscious Nature gave her glad Consent.*

And this happened again only to David at the end of *Absalom and Achitophel*:

> *He said. Th' Almighty, nodding, gave consent;*
> *And peals of Thunder shook the Firmament.*

This thunder interrupts the triumphant boast of Lucifer when ' 'Tis done' (V, i):

> *How far more mighty than Heav'n's Love, Hell's Hate!*
> *His Project ruin'd, and his King of Clay:*
> *He form'd an Empire for his Foe to sway.*
> *Heav'n let him Rule, which by his Arms he got;*
> *I'm pleas'd to have obtain'd the second Lot.*
> *This Earth is mine; whose Lord I made my Thrall;*
> *Annexing to my Crown, his conquer'd Ball.*
> *Loos'd from the Lakes, my Legions I will lead,*
> *And, o'er the darken'd Air, black Banners spread.*

This is the proper hero of an heroic poem, and his contempt betrays satiric power. Dryden does not humiliate him as in *Paradise Lost*, but allows God's thunder to reduce his boast:

> *I'll dive below his Wrath, into the Deep,*
> *And waste that Empire, which I cannot keep.*

Finally, Dryden softened the outcome by stressing the fortunate aspect of the Fall. Thus Raphael turns from death to life:

> *Death you have seen: Now see your Race revive,*
> *How happy they in deathless Pleasures live.*
> *Far more than I can show, or you can see,*
> *Shall crown the Blest with Immortality.*

After a scene or vision of the blessed, Adam and Eve are dismissed with these final words:

> *But, part you hence in Peace, and having mourn'd your Sin,*
> *For outward* Eden *lost, find* Paradise *within.*

Even if the ethos of opera were not different from that of epic, Dryden could not sound the depth of religious feeling until after his conversion.

We have seen that Dryden's operatic form is related both to the heroic poem and to the masque; *The State of Innocence* is no exception, and some of the alterations might be explained by the requirements of opera rather than by Dryden's criticism of *Paradise Lost*. If we look at the alterations from this point of view, it is instructive to recall Milton's plans, in his Cambridge Manuscript, for the dramatic treatment of this subject. First of all, he omits God and Christ, and makes large use of personifications, of which vestiges remain in the epic. In the scenario of 'Paradise Lost' he makes greater use of personifications, and in the argument of

'Adam Unparadized' greater use of angels; in both there is a chorus of angels. In the scenario, Justice, Mercy, and Wisdom present the exposition; after the fall 'Conscience cites them to God's examination'; at the end 'Faith, Hope, Charity, comfort and instruct him.' In 'Adam Unparadized' angels assist the chorus, and personifications have less to do. Conscience accuses man, Justice cites him, and finally convinces him. At the end 'Mercy comforts him, promises him the Messiah; then calls in Faith, Hope, Charity; instructs him.' In both plans Milton uses a device which he translated into the epic. In the scenario it is described as follows: 'Adam and Eve, driven out of Paradise, presented by an Angel with Labour, Grief, Hatred, Envy, War, Famine, Pestilence, Sickness, Discontent, Ignorance, Fear, Death —Mutes.' In 'Adam Unparadized' it is stated thus: 'The Angel is sent to banish them out of Paradise; but, before, causes to pass before his eyes, in shapes, a masque of all the evils of this life and world.'

Certainly the dramatic form that Milton envisaged for *Paradise Lost* is a curious mixture of masque, morality, and classical elements; at least as great a hybrid as Dryden's, and weakened by its personifications. It could have been less dramatic, less human, than either Dryden's version or his own *Comus*, but it might not have lost the ethos that Dryden's form abandoned. In becoming dramatic, however, *Paradise Lost* must inevitably have sacrificed the heroic dimension to the safer limits of the theatre.

7

BIAS IN MARVELL'S *HORATIAN ODE*

WHEN Marvell's *Horatian Ode upon Cromwell's Return from Ireland* was cancelled in his *Miscellaneous Poems* of 1681, his attitude towards Cromwell must have seemed more palpable than modern critics have found it. The other cancelled poems on Cromwell's government and death amplify themes of the *Ode* in a less ambiguous fashion. Apparently Marvell became less ambivalent as he became more convinced that Cromwell's rise to power was the result of Providence and personal merit. Actually he seems, like Dryden, to have been just as wary of the tyranny of the many as of the one; or as he put it in *The First Anniversary of the Government under O. C.*:

> 'Tis not a Freedome, that where All command; (279)
> Nor Tyranny, where One does them withstand:
> But who of both the Bounders knows to lay
> Him as their Father must the State obey.

Perhaps we should say that Marvell's poise in the *Ode* was more political than poetic, even humanistic. Certainly its effect was to create a balance that gives unusual integrity to divided feelings.

Whether or not Marvell is indebted to Lucan or May for ideas or phrases in his portrait of an emergent Caesar, he does try to fill the poet's office as he makes Ben Jonson define it in *Tom May's Death*. There he condemns May's biased use of Roman parallels:

> And who by Romes *example* England *lay,*
> Those but to Lucan *do continue* May.

And then his apostasy of the King's cause when he missed the laurel:

> Must therefore all the World be set on flame,
> Because a Gazet writer mist his aim?

Finally he gives eloquent purpose to Ben's voice:

> *When the Sword glitters ore the Judges head,*
> *And fear has Coward Churchmen silenced,*
> *Then is the Poets time, 'tis then he drawes,*
> *And single fights forsaken Vertues cause.*
> *He, when the wheel of Empire, whirleth back,*
> *And though the World's disjointed Axel crack,*
> *Sings still of ancient Rights and better Times,*
> *Seeks wretched good, arraigns successful Crimes.*

The voice of the *Horatian Ode* echoes in these lines without the
Horatian compression. Indeed, in this poem the 'Laurel wand' of
Jonson reigns supreme, 'And *Horace* patiently its stroke does take'.

Cowley has spoken of the difficulties of being a poet in these
times. And Marvell begins *An Horatian Ode* by saying that poetry
is not the current way of ambition:

> *The forward Youth that would appear*
> *Must now forsake his* Muses *dear,*
> *Nor in the Shadows sing*
> *His Numbers languishing.*

It is time to leave the arts of peace:

> *'Tis time to leave the Books in dust,*
> *And oyl th'unused Armours rust,*
> *Removing from the Wall*
> *The Corslet of the Hall.*

So destiny and character begin to shape Cromwell's career:

> *So restless* Cromwel *could not cease*
> *In the inglorious Arts of Peace,*
> *But through adventrous War*
> *Urged his active Star.*

This introduces the luminous figure that is to mark his destiny and
that promptly becomes an active luminary:

> *And, like the three fork'd Lightning, first*
> *Breaking the Clouds where it was nurst,*
> *Did thorough his own Side*
> *His fiery way divide.*

Thus his star in a more warlike figure cuts through his own party, because high spirit cannot be contained:

> *For 'tis all one to Courage high*
> *The Emulous or Enemy;*
> > *And with such to inclose*
> > *Is more than to oppose.*

Ambition is harder to restrain than to oppose, and the metaphor gathers force:

> *Then burning through the Air he went,*
> *And Pallaces and Temples rent:*
> > *And Caesars head at last*
> > *Did through his Laurels blast.*

Thus the destructive force of this 'Courage high' comes to a climax affecting church and state, and emerging through his honours as the head of a Caesar.

The violence of the figure centring in 'blast' expresses Marvell's feeling and provokes anxiety. What can be done?

> *'Tis Madness to resist or blame*
> *The force of angry Heavens flame:*
> > *And, if we would speak true,*
> > *Much to the Man is due.*

This is the work of Providence, and if we would be candid, we must give credit to the man. He owes his place to virtue as well as to destiny:

> *Who, from his private Gardens, where*
> *He liv'd reserved and austere,*
> > *As if his highest plot*
> > *To plant the Bergamot,*
> *Could by industrious Valour climbe*
> *To ruine the great Work of Time,*
> > *And cast the Kingdome old*
> > *Into another Mold.*

But when virtue runs to such extremes, can a poet succeed where Tom May failed?

> *Though Justice against Fate complain,*
> *And plead the antient Rights in vain:*
> > *But those do hold or break*
> > *As Men are strong or weak.*

If Justice without strength is powerless against Fate, then rights depend upon power. But the poet can at least call things by their right names: events may become necessary without being right. The order of nature depends upon such necessity; it belongs to what he later calls the 'several families of the necessities':

> *Nature that hateth emptiness,*
> *Allows of penetration less:*
> > *And therefore must make room*
> > *Where greater Spirits come.*

Men are subject to the same necessity; the weak must give way to the strong, especially in war.

> *What Field of all the Civil Wars,*
> *Where his were not the deepest Scars?*
> > *And* Hampton *shows what part*
> > *He had of wiser Art.*

The rumour of Cromwell's connivance at Charles's escape is used to show that Cromwell also possessed the politic art to achieve his ends without force.

> *Where, twining subtile fears with hope,*
> *He wove a Net of such a scope,*
> > *That* Charles *himself might chase*
> > *To* Caresbrooks *narrow case.*

Thus Charles was made to trap himself and to play a tragic role.

> *That thence the* Royal Actor *born*
> *The* Tragick Scaffold *might adorn:*
> > *While round the armed Bands*
> > *Did clap their bloody hands.*

Nowhere in the poem are the rhymes more charged with implica⁄ tion, or then expanded with such force. Charles was born to royalty, not to the scaffold.

> *He nothing common did or mean*
> *Upon that memorable Scene:*
> > *But with his keener Eye*
> > *The* Axes *edge did try:*
> *Nor call'd the* Gods *with vulgar spight*
> *To vindicate his helpless Right,*

> *But bow'd his comely Head,*
> *Down as upon a Bed.*

He played his part with regal decorum; there was nothing vulgar in his conduct to match the 'bloody hands'. He accepted fate with dignity, did not cry for justice with 'vulgar spite' to defend his 'helpless Right'. Indeed, he accepted defeat as Marvell has said Cromwell must be accepted. No failure in poetic power leads Marvell to repeat 'memorable'.

> *This was that memorable Hour*
> *Which first assur'd the forced Pow'r.*
> *So when they did design*
> *The Capitols first Line,*
> *A bleeding Head where they begun,*
> *Did fright the Architects to run;*
> *And yet in that the* State
> *Foresaw it's happy Fate.*

This act insured Cromwell's power; in context 'forced' makes it the result both of force and of fate. The Roman parallel conveys the mixed feelings of the architects of the new state.

The 'happy Fate', which issued from blood, has been attested by the occasion of the *Ode*:

> *And now the* Irish *are asham'd*
> *To see themselves in one* Year *tam'd:*
> *So much one Man can do,*
> *That does both act and know.*

Fate becomes auspicious by the prowess of its instrument, and also by his virtue.

> *They can affirm his Praises best,*
> *And have, though overcome, confest*
> *How good he is, how just,*
> *And fit for highest Trust.*

This fitness has a more important aspect:

> *Nor yet grown stiffer with Command,*
> *But still in the* Republick's *hand:*
> *How fit he is to sway*
> *That can so well obey.*

He has not been corrupted by power, but is still obedient to the new state. To it he presents both his tribute and, as far as possible, his fame:

> *He to the* Commons Feet *presents*
> *A* Kingdome, *for his first years rents:*
> *And, what he may, forbears*
> *His Fame to make it theirs.*

This servant of the Commons is then given a new similitude, or rather one that resumes the opening figure of power related to the sky.

> *And has his Sword and Spoyls ungirt,*
> *To lay them at the Publick's skirt.*
> *So when the Falcon high*
> *Falls heavy from the Sky,*
> *She, having kill'd, no more does search,*
> *But on the next green Bow to pearch;*
> *Where, when he first does lure,*
> *The Falckner has her sure.*

To the fiery figure of heaven Marvell now adds the element of control, and we get the falcon obedient to the falconer. Thus Cromwell may be directed to enhance national prestige:

> *What may not then our* Isle *presume*
> *While* Victory *his* Crest *does plume!*
> *What may not others fear*
> *If thus he crown each* Year!

But a greater cause is involved in his triumphs:

> *A* Caesar *he ere long to* Gaul,
> *To* Italy *an* Hannibal,
> *And to all States not free*
> *Shall* Clymacterick *be.*

Now the Scots shall be forced to show their true colours, not allowed to hide under a mind and plaid that derive from a Latin meaning of Pict:

> *The* Pict *no shelter now shall find*
> *Within his party-colour'd Mind;*
> *But from this Valour sad*
> *Shrink underneath the Plad.*

Driven from equivocation by this grave valour, he will cower underneath his plaid. Indeed, he will be happy if he escapes detection in the hunt:

> *Happy if in the tufted brake*
> *The* English Hunter *him mistake;*
> *Nor lay his Hounds in near*
> *The* Caledonian *Deer.*

This is the ignominy to which the Scots are to be reduced.

But Marvell cannot leave Cromwell without a word of admonition mixed with praise:

> *But thou the Wars and Fortunes Son*
> *March indefatigably on:*
> *And for the last effect*
> *Still keep thy Sword erect . . .*

Because he owes his power to war and fortune, he must keep his means to power upright until the end. And the reason is more than magical:

> *Besides the force it has to fright*
> *The Spirits of the shady Night,*
> *The same* Arts *that did* gain
> *A* Pow'r *must it* maintain.

To retain his power he must continue to practise the arts by which he rose, his virtues must maintain his destiny. The danger of power—or as Marvell put it, 'Nor yet grown stiffer with Command'—is the danger of tyranny. Aside from Providence and the greatness of Cromwell, Marvell's chief argument for Cromwell is that power has not corrupted him. Though his government is founded in blood, it is supported by character and must be preserved by character.

Apparently Cromwell did not fail Marvell. In *A Poem upon the Death of O. C.* he wrote large and unambiguously the roles of Providence and virtue in Cromwell's career. And into unqualified eulogy he infused undiluted elegiac feeling:

> *I saw him dead, a leaden slumber lyes,*
> *And mortal sleep over those wakefull eyes:*
> *Those gentle Rays under the lids were fled,*
> *Which through his looks that piercing sweetnesse shed;*

> *That port which so Majestique was and strong,*
> *Loose and depriv'd of vigour, stretch'd along:*
> *All wither'd, all discolour'd, pale and wan,*
> *How much another thing, no more that man?*
> *Oh humaine glory, vaine, Oh death, oh wings,*
> *Oh worthlesse world, oh transitory things!*
> *Yet dwelt that greatnesse in his shape decay'd*
> *That still though dead, greater than death he lay'd;*
> *And in his alter'd face you something faigne,*
> *That threatens death, he yet will live againe.*

Over his restless soul death shall have no dominion. Thus to Cromwell, as to Charles, he brought the homage of appropriate feeling for virtue.

II

Milton also saluted Cromwell before he became Protector in a sonnet *To the Lord General Cromwell.* And this poem was also suppressed in the 1673 edition of his *Poems.* This sonnet not only recalls *Lycidas* but is a plea against a new threat of Church Establishment. Like Marvell's *Ode,* it celebrates actions that brought peace to the realm; for, as Dryden put it in his *Heroick Stanza's*:

> *He fought to end our Fighting, and assay'd*
> *To stanch the Blood by breathing of the Vein.*

Milton addresses Cromwell as one who

> *Guided by faith and matchless Fortitude,*
> *To peace and truth thy glorious way has plough'd,*
> *And on the neck of crowned Fortune proud*
> *Hast rear'd God's Trophies and his work pursu'd ...*

Here Royalist Fortune is defeated by Divine Providence, and Cromwell is qualified for Milton's appeal:

> *yet much remains*
> *To conquer still; peace hath her victories*
> *No less renown'd than war, new foes arise*
> *Threat'ning to bind our souls with secular chains.*

In this general conviction Milton grew increasingly vehement, but he never learnt the possible cost of peace more bitterly than in his *History of Britain*. Thus Milton begins to sketch the character of Cromwell as the champion of Providence and the defender of liberty. He completes this sketch in the famous eulogium of his *Second Defence of the English People* after Cromwell has become Protector.

When Milton answered the *Eikon Basilike* for the Government, he was already an historian of his country, who could later assert in his *Second Defence*: 'I did not insult over fallen majesty, as is pretended; I only preferred queen Truth to king Charles.' This is the queen to whom he had recently dedicated Cromwell. But what aspects of Cromwell did Milton now salute?

He starts at the same point as Marvell, but presents Cromwell's rise to power in less colourful or definitive terms: 'In the vigour and maturity of his life, which he passed in retirement, he was conspicuous for nothing more than for the strictness of his religious habits, and the innocence of his life.' Cromwell began his rise prosaically enough: 'In the last parliament which was called by the king, he was elected to represent his native town, when he soon became distinguished by the justness of his opinions, and the vigour and decision of his counsels.' Now Marvell's figure begins to appear, but with religious colours: 'When the sword was drawn, he offered his services, and was appointed to a troop of horse, whose numbers were soon increased by the pious and the good, who flocked from all quarters to his standard; and in a short time he almost surpassed the greatest generals in the magnitude and the rapidity of his achievements.' Then Milton translates into moral terms some of the elements that are implicit in Marvell's figure: 'Nor is this surprising; for he was a soldier disciplined to perfection in the knowledge of himself. He had either extinguished, or by habit had learned to subdue, the whole host of vain hopes, fears, and passions, which infest the soul. He first acquired the government of himself, and over himself acquired the most signal victories; so that on the first day he took the field against the external enemy, he was a veteran in arms, consummately practised in the toils and exigencies of war.' What emerges here is the 'true warfaring Christian' of *Areopagitica*, or Milton's moral soldier. Indeed, it is the very form of Cromwell's greatness: 'This alone seems to be a sufficient proof of his extraordinary and almost supernatural virtue, that by the vigour of his genius, or the excellence of his discipline, adapted not more to

the necessities of war than to the precepts of Christianity, the good
and the brave were from all quarters attracted to his camp, not
only as to the best school of military talents, but of piety and
virtue.' By such discipline, says Milton ('and the regularity of his
pay'), Cromwell kept the obedience of his troops.

In his passing tribute to Fairfax, Milton remarks 'the spotless
innocence of whose life seemed to point him out as the peculiar
favourite of Heaven'. And he excuses Fairfax's retirement with
another tribute to Cromwell: 'I am convinced, that nothing could
have induced you to relinquish the service of your country, if you
had not known that in your successor liberty would meet with a
protector, and England with a stay to its safety, and a pillar to its
glory. For, while you, O Cromwell, are left among us, he hardly
shews a proper confidence in the Supreme, who distrusts the
security of England; when he sees that you are in so special a
manner the favoured object of the divine regard.' For Milton, as
for Marvell, Cromwell is sanctioned by Providence, and his subjection of the Scots is climactic: 'A profound peace ensued; when
we found, though indeed not then for the first time, that you were
as wise in the cabinet as valiant in the field.' For Milton, however,
wisdom is shown by Cromwell's dealings with Parliament, whose
incapacity brought him to the head of the state: 'In this state of
desolation, to which we were reduced, you, O Cromwell! alone
remained to conduct the government, and to save the country.
We all willingly yield the palm of sovereignty to your unrivalled
ability and virtue . . .' Except, he adds, the few among us who
are ambitious or envious or ignorant 'that the supreme power
should be vested in the best and the wisest of men'. He praises
Cromwell for refusing the title of king, because it meant keeping
his virtue: 'For if you had been captivated by a name over which,
as a private man, you had so completely triumphed and crumbled
into dust, you would have been doing the same thing as if, after
having subdued some idolatrous nation by the help of the true
God, you should afterwards fall down and worship the gods
which you had vanquished.' This is the bitter lesson of his
History of Britain, how the victor was vanquished by the defeated.

Like Marvell in his *Ode*, Milton concludes with a plea to Cromwell to preserve his character: 'Do you then, sir, continue your
course with the same unrivalled magnanimity'; a course by which
he has 'not only eclipsed the achievements of all our kings, but

even those which have been fabled of our heroes'. Milton then lectures Cromwell on how to sustain this character: he must revere liberty, the hopes of his country, his companions in arms, the martyred dead, the hopes of foreign states, and his own integrity. Indeed, the trials of peace 'will evince whether you really possess those great qualities of piety, fidelity, justice, and self-denial, which made us believe that you were elevated by the special direction of the Deity to the highest pinnacle of power'. Among these trials Milton does not forget 'the blandishments of pleasure and pomp of power'; altogether 'these are exertions compared with which the labour of war is mere pastime'.

It is obvious that Milton brings his own inflection to themes he shares with Marvell, and that this inflection expresses his fervid commitment to a cause. He is most at odds with Marvell when he cites this pledge of the justice of Cromwell's associates: 'of their justice in this, that they even brought the king to trial, and when his guilt was proved, refused to save his life'. And it is worth adding that Dryden's *Heroick Stanza's* on Cromwell share various themes with Marvell and Milton, including Divine sanction, but without Marvell's respect for 'ancient Rights' or Milton's commitment to a cause. The bias of all three might be defined by their attitude towards the role of Providence in history.

III

Marvell's bias in the *Horatian Ode* may also be estimated by his attitude towards its subject twenty years later. This is most fully expressed in *The Rehearsal Transprosed*, the first part of which appeared in 1672 without Marvell's name, and the second part in 1673 with Marvell's name. Milton published a revised edition of his *Poems* in 1673, but without the Cromwell sonnet, which did not appear until 1694. Marvell might also be expected not to exhibit any evidence of republican sympathies, and even to cancel one bias by another. Thus we may think it useless to ask whether this controversial work revises or extends the attitude of the *Horatian Ode*.

Although writing anonymously, this is how Marvell spoke of the Restoration: 'For, whereas among all the decent circumstances of his welcome return, the providence of God had so cooperated with the duty of his subjects, that so glorious an action should neither be soiled with the blood of victory, nor lessened by any capitulations of treaty, so not to be wanting on his part in cour- tesy, as I may say, to so happy a conjuncture, he imposed upon himself an oblivion of former offences, and his indulgence in ecclesiastical affairs' (ed. Thompson, II, 67). Again Providence is involved, but this time it co-operated with the duty of the subject. Perhaps most revealing is the stress on decency, the decencies expected of king and subject, or the moral courtesy of both parties.

Still anonymously Marvell expresses his attitude towards the late war and the 'bloody hands' of the *Horatian Ode*: 'But as to that, Mr Bayes, which you still inculcate of the late war, and its horrid catastrophe, which you will needs have to be upon a religious account: 'tis four and twenty years ago, and after an Act of Oblivion; and for ought I can see, it had been as seasonable to have shown Caesar's bloody coat, or Thomas à Becket's bloody rochet. The chief of the offenders have long since made satisfaction to justice; and the whole nation hath been swept sufficiently of late years by those terrible scourges of heaven: so that methinks, you might in all this while have satiated your mischievous appetite. Whatsoever you suffered in those times, his Majesty, who had much the greater loss, knowing that the memory of his glorious father will alwayes be preserved, is the best judge how long the revenge ought to be pursued' (ed. Thompson, II, 176). No longer must 'Justice against Fate complain, / And plead the antient Rights in vain'; rather the balance has turned and decency has other duties, for the king is to be followed.

Among the causes of the late war Marvell blames Arminianism and Bishop Laud, but chiefly for their political consequences: 'Neither yet do I speak of these things with passion, considering at more distance how natural it is for men to desire to be in office; and no less natural to grow proud and intractable in office; and the less a clergyman is so, the more he deserves to be commended. But these things before mentioned, grew yet higher, after that Bishop Laud was once not only exalted to the See of Canterbury, but to be chief Minister. Happy had it been for the King, happy for the nation, and happy for himself, had he never climbed that pinnacle' (ed. Thompson, II, 210). Laud fell a victim to the natural man and by his Arminianism 'deformed the whole reign

133

of the best prince that ever wielded the English scepter'. Then Marvell helps to define his tribute to Charles in the *Horatian Ode*: 'For his late Majesty being a prince truly pious and religious, was thereby the more inclined to esteem and favour the clergy. And thence, though himself of a most exquisite understanding, yet he could not trust it better than in their keeping. Whereas every man is best in his own post, and so the preacher in the pulpit. But he that will do the clergyes drudgery, must look for his reward in another world. For they having gained this ascendent upon him, resolved, whatever became on't, to make their best of him; and having made the whole business of state their Arminian jangles, and the persecution for ceremonies, did for recompence assign him that imaginary absolute government, upon which rock we all ruined' (ed. Thompson, II, 211). Later Marvell accuses Parker of deriving this kind of government from necessity—the original necessity 'that was pre-eternal to all things, and exercised dominion not only over all humane things, but over Jupiter himself and the rest of the Deities, and drove the great iron nail thorough the axletree of nature' (ibid., II, 364). This recalls, but does not repeat, the striking crack of the world's axle in my citation from *Tom May's Death*.

Finally Marvell expresses the view that is commonly quoted: 'Whether it be a war of religion, or of liberty, is not worth the labour to enquire. Which soever was at the top, the other was at the bottome; but upon considering all, I think the cause was too good to have been fought for. Men ought to have trusted God; they ought and might have trusted the King with that whole matter.' But the reasons for this judgment are commonly omitted: 'The arms of the church are prayers and tears, the arms of the subjects are patience and petitions. The King himself being of so accurate and piercing a judgement, would soon have felt where it stuck. For men may spare their pains where nature is at work, and the world will not go the faster for our driving. Even as his present Majesties happy restauration did itself, so all things happen in their best and proper time, without any need of our officiousness' (ibid., II, 212). Just as the wrong arms were used, so the work of Providence cannot be rushed by the officiousness of man. Later Marvell describes the necessity of God: 'beside all other the in-numerable calamities to which human life is exposed, he has in like manner distinguished the government of the world by the intermitting seasons of discord, war, and public disturbance. Neither has he so ordered it only (as men endeavour to express it) by meer permission, but sometimes out of complacency' (ibid., II, 367). This is why the 'good old cause' was beyond war, or rather could not be won by a war. For the dangers of office that beset Laud and beguiled Charles are also related to Cromwell in the *Horatian Ode*. In a world governed by different kinds of necessity, Marvell became a stickler for the decencies.

When Marvell continued *The Rehearsal Transprosed* under his own name, he could be expected to find discretion the better part of valour. Moreover, Samuel Parker became his target very much as Salmasius became Milton's. The result, however, was no less candid a revelation of the man. Although controversy exaggerates bias, it also tries the temper of a man.

Now Marvell cautions the reader not 'to impute any errors or weakness of mine to the Nonconformists, nor mistake me for one of them, (not that I fly it as a reproach, but rather honour the most scrupulous:) for I write only what I think befits all men in humanity, Christianity, and prudence toward Dissenters' (ed. Thompson, II, 291). Whether this is ambiguity or definition, principle or prudence, on Marvell's part, it names the standards of decency that always seemed to guide him. In reply to a personal insinuation by Parker, he defines his relation to the government of Cromwell's time: 'This therefore is a greater errour in chronology than your former; for as to myself I never had any, not the remotest relation to publick matters, nor correspondence with the persons then predominant, until the year 1657, when indeed I entered into an imployment, for which I was not altogether improper, and which I considered to be the most innocent and inoffensive toward his Majesties affairs of any in that usurped and irregular government, to which all men were then exposed' (ed. Thompson, II, 320). Certainly this is the government he described in his *Horatian Ode*, and certainly his loyalty to the king is not a change of attitude.

Samuel Parker's chronology, however, was still in error in the later *History of His Own Time* when he attacked *The First Anniversary*, which Marvell had published anonymously in 1655. Thus Parker: 'At length, by the interest of *Milton*, to whom he was somewhat agreeable for his ill-natur'd wit, he was made Under-secretary to *Cromwell's* Secretary. Pleas'd with which honour, he publish'd a congratulatory poem in praise of the Tyrant; but when he had a long time labour'd to squeeze out a panegyrick he brought forth a satyr upon all rightfull Kings; saying that *Cromwell* was the sun, but other Monarchs were slow bodies, slower than *Saturn* in their revolutions, and darting more hurtful rays upon the earth . . .' This seems damaging enough, but Marvell was not thinking of the martyred Charles but rather of foreign kings:

> While by his Beams observing Princes steer,   (103)
> And wisely court the Influence they fear;
> O would they rather by his Pattern won,
> Kiss the approaching, nor yet angry Son;
> And in their numbered Footsteps humbly tread
> The path where holy Oracles do lead . . .

This path had led Marvell to a more enthusiastic but still provi-dential view of Cromwell:

> Hence oft I think, if in some happy Hour   (131)
> High Grace should meet in one with highest Pow'r,
> And then a seasonable People still
> Should bend to his, as he to Heavens will,
> What we might hope, what wonderful Effect
> From such a wish'd Conjuncture might reflect.

Yet the future was nevertheless beyond mortal vision:

> But a thick Cloud about that Morning lyes,   (141)
> And intercepts the Beams of Mortal eyes,
> That 'tis the most which we determine can,
> If these the Times, then this must be the Man.

And this is what Marvell's poem proceeds to argue, then more doubtful of the times than of the man.

But in *The Rehearsal Transprosed* Marvell adds this evidence of his loyalty: 'And this I accordingly discharged without dis-obliging any one person, there having been opportunity and endeavours, since his Majesties happy return, to have discovered had it been otherwise.' As we have seen, Marvell never blamed the king for what came to pass, which he could not describe in lesser terms than

To ruine the great Work of Time,
And cast the Kingdome old
Into another Mold.

He was what he now says his father was: 'a conformist to the established rites of the Church of England, though I confess none of the most over-running or eager in them'. Marvell resembled Lord Falkland, whom he cites, and Milton benefited from his moderation.

Marvell's commonest appeals are to standards of humanity. He invokes them against Parker's persecution of the Nonconformists. First, he challenges Parker: 'Pray, Sir, who are these Fanaticks? Most of 'em, I assure you, better men than yourself, of truer principles than you are, and more conformable to the doctrine of the church of England.' And then he rebukes him: 'There is not any more visible token of a mean spirit, than to taunt and scoff at those in affliction; and for a man by virulent jeers to exasperate and impoyson the wounds of his own giving . . . There is a certain civility due to such as suffer, and to bruise a broken reed is inhumane' (ed. Thompson, II, 450). Never does the temper of the man appear more clearly, and this rebuke came from a man who knew all the temptations of wit.

Nowhere does Marvell's bias, or balance, appear more strongly than in his defence of Milton: 'You do three times at least in your *Reproof,* and in your *Transproser Rehearsed* well nigh half the book thorow, run upon an author J. M. which does not a little offend me. For why should any other man's reputation suffer in a contest betwixt you and me? But it is because you resolved to suspect that he had an hand in my former book, wherein whether you deceive yourself or no, you deceive others extreamly. For by chance I had not seen him of two years before; but after I undertook writing, I did more carefully avoid either visiting or sending to him, lest I should any way involve him in my consequences. And you might have understood, or I am sure your friend the author of the *Common Places* could have told you, (he too had a slash at J. M. upon my account) that had he took you in hand, you would have had cause to repent the occasion, and not escaped so easily as you did under my *Transprosal*' (ed. Thompson, II, 496). Moreover, he is annoyed that Parker should think him incapable of 'such a simple book', and calls that doubt a sign

137

that Parker really did not know him very well. The presumption of friendship provokes Marvell even more: 'But because in your 115 p. you are so particular "you know a friend of ours, &c." intending that J. M. and his answer to Salmasius, I think it here seasonable to acquit my promise to you in giving the reader a short trouble concerning my first acquaintance with you. J. M. was, and is, a man of great learning and sharpness of wit as any man. It was his misfortune, living in a tumultuous time, to be tossed on the wrong side, and he writ *flagrante bello* certain dan⁄gerous treatises. His books of *Divorce* I know not whether you may have use of; but those upon which you take him at advantage were of no other nature than that which I mentioned to you, writ by your own father; only with this difference, that your father's, which I have by me, was written with the same design, but with much less wit or judgement, for which there was no remedy: unless you will supply his judgment with his high court of justice. At his Majesties happy return, J. M. did partake, even as you yourself did for all your huffing, of his regal clemency, and has ever since expiated himself in a retired silence' (ibid., II, 497). If this apology was expressed with tact, it nevertheless did not make Marvell a turncoat. If Milton heard of it, he must have shuddered at the phrasing of his misfortune, 'to be tossed on the wrong side', and he would have interpreted the phrase '*flagrante bello*' rather differently from Marvell. But it would appear that Marvell felt himself less obligated to silence than either Parker or Milton.

Finally Marvell expresses his contempt for Parker in his strongest language: 'It was after that, I well remember it, that being one day at his house, I there first met you and accidentally. Since that I have been scarce four or five times in your company, but, whether it were my foresight or my good fortune, I never contracted any friendship or confidence with you. But then it was, when you, as I told you, wandered up and down Moor⁄fields astrologizing upon the duration of his Majesties government, that you frequented J. M. incessantly and haunted his house day by day. What dis⁄courses you there used he is too generous to remember. But he never having in the least provoked you, for you to insult thus over his old age, to traduce him by your *Scaramuccios*, and in your own person, as a school⁄master, who was born and hath lived much more ingenuously and liberally than yourself; to have done all this, and lay at last my simple book to his charge, without ever taking care to inform yourself better, which you had so easie opportunity to do; nay, when you yourself too have said, to my knowledge, that you saw no such great matter in it but that I might be the author: it is inhumanely and inhospitably done, and will I hope be a warning to all others, as it is to me, to avoid (I will not say such a Judas,) but a man that creeps into all com-panies, to jeer, trepan, and betray them' (ibid., II, 498). If Marvell ascribes too much to Parker, as Milton did to Salmasius, he obviously regards Parker as a turncoat who is unworthy of the generosity that Milton has earned. But it is the personal betrayal that he cannot forgive because it offends the deepest instincts of his character.

Neither Cromwell nor Milton ever changed his moral decorum, and this is the kind of integrity that Marvell respected. But man is constrained to submit to Providence, and yet the poet in his public office must defend virtue's cause:

> *He, when the wheel of Empire, whirleth back,*
> *And though the World's disjointed Axel crack,*
> *Sings still of ancient Rights and better Times,*
> *Seeks wretched good, arraigns successful Crimes.*

Nevertheless, by humanistic standards, Marvell felt obliged to observe decorum with urbanity as well as candour, or what Dryden called 'candour and civility'. Hence we get the mixed feelings of *An Horatian Ode*.

8

MARVELL'S 'HORTUS' AND 'GARDEN'

THESE poems lose their difference when they are detached from the context of their original. This context is rightly approached through Cowley, although it is often identified with foreign in-fluence. When Thomas Sprat wrote his *Life of Cowley* (1668) he observed that Cowley's *Essays* were 'upon some of the gravest subjects that concern the Contentment of a Virtuous Mind. These he intended as a real Character of his own thoughts upon the point of his Retirement.' They were intended to be 'a kind of Apology for having left humane Affairs, in the strength of his Age, while he might still have been serviceable to his Country'. In this respect they resemble Sir William Temple's essay 'Upon the Gardens of Epicurus' (1685) and more generally 'The Great Prerogative of a Private Life', which was translated from La Mothe le Vayer in 1678.

I

But this theme, as Cowley reminds us, had found early expression in his verse. It first appeared in 'A Vote', published in *Sylva* in 1636, where Cowley voted to be like Horace on his Sabine farm. He would not be a Puritan, School-master, Justice of Peace, Courtier, et cetera. And he would be preserved 'from your Court-Madams beauty'. In 'The Wish', published in *The Mis-tress* in 1647, he again votes for the Horatian retreat, but he now adds an amatory element, no doubt because of the nature of his book, though possibly because of Horace's second Epode. He returned to the theme of retirement in the Preface to his *Poems* of 1656.

In his last essay, 'Of My self', published in the *Works* of 1668, he fills in the story of this vote in order to explain his preceding essays: 'As far as my Memory can return back into my past Life, before I knew, or was capable of guessing what the world, or glories, or business of it were, the natural affections of my soul gave me a secret bent of aversion from them, as some Plants are said to turn away from others, by an Antipathy imperceptible to themselves, and inscrutable to mans understanding. Even when I was a very young Boy at School, instead of running about on Holy-daies and playing with my fellows; I was wont to steal from them, and walk into the fields, either alone with a Book, or with some one Companion, if I could find any of the same temper . . . That I was then of the same mind as I am now (which I confess, I wonder at my self) may appear by the latter end of an Ode, which I made when I was but thirteen years old, and which was then printed with many other Verses. The Beginning of it is Boyish, but of this part which I here set down (if a very little were corrected) I should hardly now be much ashamed.'

Cowley quotes the last three stanzas of 'A Vote'. And then he comments: 'You may see by it, I was even then acquainted with the Poets (for the Conclusion is taken out of *Horace*;) and perhaps it was the immature and immoderate love of them which stampt first, or rather engraved these Characters in me: They were like Letters cut into the Bark of a young Tree, which with the Tree still grow proportionably.' His essay 'Of Agriculture' draws largely on these poets, but here he proceeds to describe his worldly 'condition in banishment and publick distresses' before adding, 'yet I could not abstain from renewing my old School-boys Wish in a Copy of Verses to the same effect'. Then he quotes the first two lines of 'The Wish'.

This passion had another consequence. John Evelyn's *Kalen-darium Hortense*, first published in 1664, was dedicated to Cowley in its second edition (1666): 'This *Hortulan Kalendar* is yours, mindful of the honour once conferr'd on it, when you were pleas'd to suspend your nobler raptures, and think it worthy your tran-scribing. It appears now with some advantages which it then wanted; because it had not that of publishing to the world, how infinitely I magnifie your contempt of (not to say revenge upon) it; whilst you still continue in the possession of your self, and of that repose which few men understand, in exchange for those pretty miseries you have essay'd . . . and as the philosopher in Seneca desir'd only bread and herbs to dispute felicity with

Jupiter, you vie happiness in a thousand easy and sweet diversions; not forgetting the innocent toils which you cultivate, the leisure and the liberty, the books, the meditations, and, above all, the learned and choice friendships that you enjoy. Who would not, like you, *cacher sa vie*? 'Twas the wise impress of Balzac, and of Plutarch before him; you give it lustre and interpretation. I assure you, Sir, it is what in the world I most inwardly breathe after and pursue.' Thus Evelyn places Cowley in the European tradition of libertine philosophy that justified retirement.

Cowley returned the compliment by dedicating his essay on 'The Garden' to Evelyn, where he again touched upon his favourite theme: 'I never had any other desire so strong, and so like to Covetousness as that one which I have had always, that I might be master at last of a small house and large garden, with very moderate conveniencies joyned to them, and there dedicate the remainder of my life only to the culture of them and study of Nature . . . But several accidents of my ill fortune have disap-pointed me hitherto, and do still, of that felicity; for though I have made the first and hardest step to it, by abandoning all ambitions and hopes in this World, and by retiring from the noise of all business and almost company, yet I stick still in the Inn of a hired House and Garden, among Weeds and Rubbish; and without that pleasantest work of Human Industry, the Improvement of something which we call (not very properly, but yet we call) Our Own.'

Evelyn had quoted Cowley's 'Wish' in his dedication of the *Hortulan Kalendar,* and Cowley concluded his essay 'Of My self' with these words about his garden life: 'Nothing shall separate me from a Mistress, which I have loved so long, and have now at last married; though she neither has brought me a rich Portion, nor lived yet so quietly with me as I hoped from Her.' By this time Cowley had confessed in his essay 'Of Greatness', as evi-dence of his moderation, that 'if I were ever to fall in love again (which is a great Passion, and therefore, I hope, I have done with it) it would be, I think, with Prettiness, rather than with Majesti-cal Beauty'.

The verses in 'The Garden' elaborate the conditions of life desired in 'The Wish' until they approach the ambitious *Elysium Brittannicum* which Evelyn had outlined to Sir Thomas Browne on 28 January 1657-8. This glorification of gardens envisaged 'a

society of the *paradisi cultores*, persons of antient simplicity, Paradisean and Hortulan saints'. One of its gardens was the subject
of Browne's *Garden of Cyrus*, published in the same year. But
only one chapter of Evelyn's work was ever published: *Acetaria,
a Discourse of Sallets*, in 1699. In this discourse he quotes Cowley's
'Garden', stanza 8 and stanza 6, and *Plantarum*, the opening of
Book IV; he also quotes garden passages from Milton's *Paradise
Lost* (Book V): 'As our Paradisian Bard introduces Eve, dressing
of a sallet for her angelical guest'; and again, 'so in the most
blissful place and innocent state of nature, see how the first empress
of the world regales her celestial guest'.

The advantages of the garden life were continued by Temple,
'Upon the Gardens of Epicurus': 'If we believe the Scripture, we
must allow that God Almighty esteemed the life of a man in a
garden the happiest he could give him, or else he would not have
placed Adam in that of Eden; that it was the state of innocence
and pleasure; and that the life of husbandry and cities came in
after the fall, with guilt and with labor.' But Cowley's verses in
'The Garden' offer a compendium of common garden themes,
even to that of Marvell's 'Mower against Gardens' on grafting
the cherry.

In 1665 the theme of retirement had found another advocate
when Sir George Mackenzie published his essay of *Solitude
preferred to Public Employment*. This provoked an answer from
Evelyn in 1667, entitled *Public Employment preferred to Solitude*. In
a letter to Cowley, 12 March 1667, Evelyn admits that Cowley
'had reason to be astonished' and explains that he wrote by way
of paradox, 'as those who praised dirt, a flea, and the gout'. He
conjures Cowley to believe that he is still of the same mind, 'and
that there is no person alive who does more honour and breathe
after the life and repose you so happily cultivate and adorn by
your example'. In his reply of 13 May 1667 Cowley asks to
borrow Mackenzie's essay and explains: 'I have sent all about the
town in vain to get the author, having very much affection for the
subject, which is one of the noblest controversies both modern
and ancient.' This was written not long before his death.

II

We may now return to 'The Wish', which was certainly earlier than Marvell's two poems. It will help to quote it in full.

i

Well then, I now do plainly see
This busie World and I shall ne'er agree;
The very Honey of all earthly joy
  Does of all meats the soonest cloy.
  And they (methinks) deserve my pity,
Who for it can endure the stings,
The Croud, and Buz, and Murmurings
  Of this great Hive, the City.

ii

Ah, yet, e'er I descend to th' Grave,
May I a small House, and large Garden have!
And a few Friends, and many Books, both true,
  Both wise, and both delightful too!
  And since Love ne'er will from me flee,
A Mistress moderately fair,
And good as Guardian-Angels are,
  Only belov'd, and loving me!

iii

Oh, Fountains, when in you shall I
My self, eas'd of unpeaceful thoughts, espy?
Oh Fields! Oh Woods! when, when shall I be made
  The happy Tenant of your Shade?
  Here's the Spring-head of Pleasure's flood;
Here's wealthy Nature's Treasury,
Where all the Riches lye, that she
  Has coin'd and stamp'd for good.

iv

> *Pride and Ambition here,*
> *Only in far-fetch'd Metaphors appear;*
> *Here nought but Winds can hurtful Murmurs scatter,*
> *And nought but Eccho flatter.*
>   *The Gods, when they descended, hither*
> *From Heav'n, did always chuse their way;*
> *And therefore we may boldly say,*
>   *That 'tis the Way too thither.*

v

> *How happy here should I,*
> *And one dear She live, and embracing die?*
> *She who is all the world, and can exclude*
>   *In desarts Solitude,*
> *I should have then this only fear,*
> *Lest men, when they my pleasures see,*
> *Should hither throng to live like me,*
>   *And so make a City here.*

Cowley's 'Wish', which is most like Horace's Satire II, vi, sets town and country in opposition. His wish does not exclude woman or seek solitude. Marvell, however, opposes woman to nature in 'Hortus', and in 'The Garden' makes woman an enemy to solitude as well as to the love of nature. For Cowley, as for Marvell in 'The Garden', nature offers (iii) the innocent pleasures and (iv) the way to Heaven. For Cowley the honey of the city is not worth its price; but, ironically, envy of his pleasures may turn his retreat into a city. Both ambition and woman are threats to Marvell's paradise.

It is the use of the amatory element that distinguishes 'The Wish' most sharply from 'Hortus'. In the former, love will not flee from him, but in the latter all flee from the love of woman to the love of nature. In 'Hortus' Cupid himself is conquered by nature, and the gods rejoice 'to see his lessening rage' as they turn from women to trees—from Neaera, Chloe, Faustina, Corynna to Elm, Poplar, Cypress, Plane; not to mention the Oak, Beech,

Laurel, Reed versus Juno, Venus, Daphne, Syrinx. Thus the gods ran 'passion's heat'. It is this development that adds three stanzas to the five of 'The Wish'. But when 'The Garden' re-places these three stanzas by another three that develop the con-templative life, it adds a ninth stanza—the penultimate—which exploits the idea of woman's threat to Paradise. Cowley employs this theme in his later poem 'Of Solitude'.

Here are the three stanzas from 'Hortus' in the translation of Edmund Blunden (*T.L.S.*, v. 54, p. 462):

> *A maiden's beauty binds us all in spells,*
> *But I am sure your flourishing green excels,*
> *Her snowy white, her rosy red o'erthrows,*
> *Her locks yield to your leaves, her arms t'your boughs.*
> *Your breezy whisper makes her voice less sweet.*
> *But I have seen (and who could think to see't?)*
> *The cruel lover carve the mistress' name*
> *Upon your finer skin, nor felt it shame*
> *So to inscribe wounds on each sacred stem!*
> *Should I, O trees, should I make bold with them,*
> *Neaera, Chloe, will not there be named;*
> *In her own book each tree shall be acclaimed.*
> *Beloved Elm, Poplar and Cypress, Plane!*
> *Faustina and Corynna we disdain.*
>
> *Love here, those weapons which might once have slain*
> *Dropped, and the nerveless bow and wings even doffed,*
> *Puts slippers on, and saunters byways soft;*
> *He lowers his torch; affrights no lover ever;*
> *He lolls at ease, or dozes on his quiver;*
> *Though Venus called, he will not hear: his dreams,*
> *Now empty, shew no offence of former schemes.*
>
> *The Immortals joy to see his lessening rage,*
> *And though conversant through so many an age*
> *With Nymphs and Goddesses, they all avow*
> *Some tree gives each a better conquest now.*
> *Jove for an old Oak pines and shuns his wife,*
> *No rival so grieved Juno in her life;*
> *No lover now invades poor Vulcan's bed,*
> *The Beech drives Venus out of Mars's head;*

> *Phoebus on lovely Daphne's steps has panted*
> *That she might grow a Laurel, naught else wanted;*
> *And did the goatfoot Pan for Syrinx speed,*
> *'Twas but to own again his tuneful reed.*

Between these and the final stanza in the 1681 text of 'Hortus' are inserted the words 'Desunt multa', evidently in comparison with 'The Garden'. The part of 'Hortus' which differs radically from 'The Garden' runs from the line, 'Should I, O trees, etc.' to the line, 'The Beech drives Venus, etc.'

The substituted stanzas of 'The Garden' are the following:

> *What wond'rous life is this I lead!*
> *Ripe apples drop about my head;*
> *The luscious clusters of the vine*
> *Upon my mouth do crush their wine;*
> *The nectarine and curious peach*
> *Into my hands themselves do reach;*
> *Stumbling on melons as I pass,*
> *Ensnared with flowers, I fall on grass.*

> *Meanwhile the mind from pleasure less*
> *Withdraws into its happiness;*
> *The mind, that ocean where each kind*
> *Does straight its own resemblance find,*
> *Yet it creates, transcending these,*
> *Far other worlds and other seas,*
> *Annihilating all that's made*
> *To a green thought in a green shade.*

> *Here at the fountain's sliding foot,*
> *Or at some fruit tree's mossy root,*
> *Casting the body's vest aside,*
> *My soul into the bough does glide;*
> *There like a bird it sits and sings,*
> *Then whets, then combs its silver wings;*
> *And till prepared for longer flight,*
> *Waves in its plumes the various light.*

In the first stanza his physical needs are provided without effort on his part but with innocence. His satisfactions are reminiscent of 'Bermudas'; and the Fall of man, if present, is innocent. In the next stanza his mind finds its pleasure in creative contemplation, transforming the garden into forms even more ideal. In 'Hortus', instead of reducing all 'To a green thought in a green shade' he seeks and finds Quiet and Simplicity 'Concealed in green plants and like-coloured shade (Celârant plantae virides, et concolor umbra)'. In both instances, however, the garden colours the moral product. Lastly his soul finds in the garden the aspiration that prepares it for longer flight to a higher world. It waves the light in its plumes as the flowers do in the dial of the final stanza. Thus 'that happy garden state' is defined for body, mind, and soul, which can find the sacred plantings of quiet and innocence only among the plants.

Thus what is supposed to be missing in 'Hortus' makes 'The Garden' a different poem. Both poems have similar beginnings and ends, but quite different middles. 'Hortus' is concerned with the opposition of the love of woman and the love of nature, where Cowley had united them. It is centred on the theme of society versus solitude and the love which dominates each .'The Garden' turns this opposition into an active versus contemplative theme; the mythic parallels to the opposition are reduced to the stories of Daphne and Syrinx.

In 'Hortus' the search is for nature's peace and quiet rather than the rewards of retirement or the contemplative life. In 'The Garden' nature becomes the locus of the contemplative life and the means of evaluating it against the active life. Prudence rather than heroics now is measured in terms of garden spoils. The change in major theme explains the different middles and the alterations of beginning and end. In 'Hortus' there is no connection of the garden with Paradise as the prototype of the ideal life; no relation of the ending to this concept, or to an adjudication of the active versus contemplative life, for which Eden before Eve is the perfect archetype.

Hence the play of wit on woman is turned in 'The Garden' with a new propriety:

> *Such was that happy garden-state,*
> *While man there walked without a mate;*
> *After a place so pure and sweet,*
> *What other help could yet be meet!*
> *But 'twas beyond a mortal's share*
> *To wander solitary there;*

> *Two paradises 'twere, in one,*
> *To live in paradise alone.*

Marvell reverses the words of God in Genesis: 'It is not good that the man should be alone; I will make him an help meet for him.' Marvell thinks that it is good for man to be alone, and that the garden is enough of a help in its similitude to the original 'dial'. If the levity of contradicting Scripture on 'help meet' seems flip-pant, it should be recalled that the garden is Marvell's refuge from 'passion's heat', which began when Eve broke the solitude of Eden and destroyed its quiet and innocence.

The final stanza modulates the curse of labour after the Fall (Genesis iii, 19) into its pleasantest form:

> *How well the skillful gard'ner drew*
> *Of flowers and herbs this dial new,*
> *Where, from above, the milder sun*
> *Does through a fragrant zodiac run;*
> *And as it works, th' industrious bee*
> *Computes its time as well as we.*
> *How could such sweet and wholesome hours*
> *Be reckoned but with herbs and flowers?*

But its main point is to instruct us how to compute our time until prepared for longer flight. The 'milder sun' is 'candidior' and the ambiguity of 'thyme' is explicit in the Latin. Here Cowley's bee has left the city, but remains the sign of industry or ambition.

9

THE DESIGN OF DONNE'S
ANNIVERSARIES

BEFORE we conclude that Donne wrote his *Anniversaries* out of the *Spiritual Exercises* of St Ignatius Loyola, perhaps we ought to meditate on some other contexts for these poems. In passing we may recall that at this time Donne pilloried Loyola and mocked the Jesuits in *Ignatius his Conclave*. There when 'Lucifer stuck in a meditation', he was rescued by the sophistry of Ignatius Loyola; there no innovator was found to rival Ignatius as a guide to spiritual error.

Any perusal of Donne's Letters will show that 'meditation' was a general, not a special, term for him. In one letter he applies it to religious verse: 'Since my imprisonment in my bed, I have made a meditation in verse, which I call a Litany; the word you know imports no other than supplication, but all Churches have one forme of supplication, by that name.' Then, although he will not condemn his 'evaporations' of wit, he thanks God for 'his comfort of sadder meditations'. Another such occasion produced his *Devotions upon Emergent Occasions*, but are their formulas Ignatian? Of course Donne knew—after Virgil (*Ecl.* i)—how 'Musam meditari'; or as Milton put it, to 'meditate the thankless Muse'.

In *The Poetry of Meditation* Professor Louis Martz hazards as evidence for his thesis 'the curious "composition of place" with which *The Extasie* opens', without knowing its secular origin, which may be found in my *Seventeenth Century Contexts*. Indeed when is a 'composition of place' absent from a lyric poem involving a dramatic situation? And when Martz (p. 39) relates his methodical meditation to a fundamental tendency of the human mind 'to work from a particular situation, through analysis of that situation, and finally to some sort of resolution of the problems which the situation has presented', he confuses the methods of devotion with those of logic and rhetoric, and lands in the general area of reflective poetry. Of course this description fits 'The Extasie', or any poem that works from a situation to a solution.

However, it was in a satiric ecstasy that Donne's 'little wandring sportful Soule' found, in the words of a friend [Donne], 'how hard a matter it is for a man much conversant in the bookes and Acts of Jesuites, so throughly to cast off the Jesuits, as that he contract nothing of their naturall drosses, which are Petulancy, and Light-nesse'. Are we therefore to conclude not only that Donne failed to cast off their spiritual exercises, but that he made their form of 'mis-devotion' most evident in his *Anniversaries*? It is an obvious question. But it poses a recurrent problem. Various elements of Metaphysical poetry as defined by Grierson and Eliot have since been translated into more fashionable terms: by James Smith into truly metaphysical ideas; by Rosemond Tuve into Ramist logic; and now by Louis Martz into devotional methods.

In the application of numerology to the *Anniversaries* Martz is again on treacherous ground. Relative to the *First Anniversary* he remarks (p. 223): 'Thus the number five becomes associated with the celebration of the Virgin: the five-petaled Rose becomes her flower. This, evidently, is what lies behind Donne's treatment of the five-petaled flower in his poem, "The Primrose".' As for the first application, we may recall Ben Jonson's opinion that 'if it had been written of the Virgin Marie it had been something'. As for 'The Primrose', there is contrary evidence in the author. In the last stanza 'this mysterious number' reveals its climactic wit. Earlier his true Love is defined as something more than 'a mere woman', and hence in terms of his analogy either a four- or a six-petalled flower. But if, he reasons, she were more or less than a woman, she would be either above or below sexual response. If necessary, he would prefer to have her falsified by art rather than by nature.

Hence he is forced to conclude that his true Love must be found in the ordinary primrose of five petals; furthermore the mystery of this number gives scope enough to feminine ambition. Obviously the Virgin's flower by this time would be in a very awkward context. But let us see how the real numerology, which is Pythagorean, develops his wit. First Donne says, as in his *Essays in Divinity* (ed. Simpson, p. 59):

> *Ten is the farthest number; if half ten*
> *Belong unto each woman, then*
> *Each woman may take half us men.*

Another turn on this numerology is found in his *Essays* (p. 46) when he says: 'And from Sarai's name He took a letter, which expressed the number *ten*, and reposed one, which made but *five*; so that she contributed that five which man wanted before, to show a mutual indigence and supplement.' But in the poem, if woman will not be content with this division,

> *Or if this will not serve their turn, since all*
> *Numbers are odd, or even, and they fall*
> *First into this five, women may take us all.*

Chapman used this Pythagorean numerology to describe true marriage in *Hero and Leander* (Sestiad 5), where he explained:

> *And five they hold in most especial prize,*
> *Since 'tis the first odd number that doth rise*
> *From the two foremost numbers' unity,*
> *That odd and even are, which are two and three;*
> *For one no number is, but thence doth flow*
> *The powerful race of number.*

For Donne even a mere woman may turn out to be more than a woman, but hardly the Virgin Mary.

I

When Jonson objected to Donne's *Anniversarie*, it was not as a perversion of the spiritual exercise but as a profane apotheosis, 'full of blasphemies'. No doubt it was a matter of decorum for this erstwhile Catholic. Puttenham's *Arte of English Poesie*, which Jonson possessed, made a point of decorum in such poems: 'Wherefore the Poet in praising the maner of life or death of anie meane person, did it by some litle dittie or Epigram or Epitaph in fewe verses & meane stile conformable to his subject' (I, xx). Loftier forms and styles were reserved for gods, princes, and heroes. Puttenham adds that for the Roman 'orations funerall and commendatorie . . . our *Theologians*, in stead thereof use to make sermons, both teaching the people some good learning, and also saying well of the departed' (I, xxiv).

Obviously Elizabeth Drury was below the dignity of subject required for the proper encomium or funeral oration, and yet Donne's *Anniversaries* fulfilled both functions of the latter. In 'gravitie and majestie' they seemed more befitting the Virgin Mary. But Donne's defence of his encomium was that 'he described the Idea of a Woman, and not as she was'. Dryden likewise recalled the Roman panegyrics when he dedicated his *Eleonora*, but he was so pleased by Donne's *Anniversaries* that he took them for his model. It is significant that the *Anniversaries* seem to have been the same kind of poem for all three poets.

Dryden excused the character of his *Eleonora* thus: 'It was intended as Your Lordship sees in the Title, not for an Elegie, but a Panegyrique. A kind of Apotheosis, indeed; if a Heathen Word may be applied to a Christian use. And on all Occasions of Praise, if we take the Ancients for our Patterns, we are bound by Prescription to employ the magnificence of Words, and the force of Figures, to adorn the sublimity of Thoughts.' He then appeals to the ancient examples of panegyric, and finally relates his poem to the example of Donne's *Anniversaries*: 'However, I have follow'd his Footsteps in the Design of his Panegyrick; which was to raise an Emulation in the Living, to Copy out the Example of the Dead. And therefore it was, that I once intended to have call'd this Poem the Pattern: And though on a second Consideration, I have chang'd the Title into the Name of that Illustrious Person, yet the Design continues, and Eleonora is still the Pattern of Charity, Devotion, and Humility; of the best Wife, the best Mother, and the best of Friends.'

Moreover, to say of Donne 'that he had never seen Mrs Drury', Dryden must have known Donne's defence of the *Anniversaries* in his letter of 14 April 1612 to George Gerrard, published in the *Letters* of 1651. And it could be argued that Dryden had a better excuse to magnify the person than Donne, but Donne also could defend the decorum of his poem when it was related to a Pattern of womanhood. We must not overlook the design which the Catholic Dryden saw in Donne's *Anniversaries*.

If the design of the *Anniversaries* 'was to raise an Emulation in the Living, to Copy out the Example of the Dead', it was achieved by 'both teaching the people some good learning, and also saying well of the departed'. These two functions provide the chief explanation for the two main elements in both poems. But in explaining the elegiac function Puttenham said that the poet must 'play also the Phisitian, and not onely by applying a medi⁄cine to the ordinary sicknes of mankind, but by making the very greef it selfe (in part) cure of the disease'. Irrevocable sorrows must find their sources of consolation not in the Galenist cure by con⁄trary but in the Paracelsian cure by similitude—in the very grief itself. It is most probable that Donne's *Anniversaries* were read from Jonson to Dryden in terms of such principles as these.

II

In terms of Donne's own work, however, they have another im⁄portant context. This is the first of his ambitious poems, the epic satire on original sin, which he left unfinished but 'Consecrated to Endlessness'. Here he first employed the idea of a progress of the soul and its relation to the scale of being. According to Ben Jonson, 'The conceit of Donne's Transformation, or *Metem⁄psychosis* was that he sought the soule of that apple which Eve pulled and thereafter made it the soule of a bitch, then a shee wolf, and so of a woman; his generall purpose was to have brought in all the bodies of the Hereticks from the soule of Cain, and at last left it in the bodie of Calvin.' As in *Ignatius his Conclave*, spiritual innovation was to be the crowning sin of *The Progresse of the Soule*.

But Donne married the idea of progress to the Pythagorean idea of transmigration and explained his device in his Epistle: 'All which I will bid you remember, (For I will have no such Readers as I can teach) is, that the Pithagorian doctrine doth not onely carry one soule from man to man, nor man to beast, but indiffer⁄ently to plants also.' Here we may notice the artful parenthesis which disclaims any ability to teach others. Then Donne con⁄tinues, 'and therefore you must not grudge to finde the same soule in an Emperour, in a Post⁄horse, and in a Mucheron, since no unreadinesse in the soule, but an indisposition in the organs workes this'. For Sir Thomas Browne this was the cause of monsters. Finally, Donne explains his scale of being: 'And there⁄fore though this soule could not move when it was a Melon, yet it may remember, and now tell mee, at what lascivious banquet it was serv'd. And though it could not speake, when it was a spider, yet it can remember, and now tell me, who used it for poyson to attaine dignitie. How ever the bodies have dull'd her other facul-ties, her memory hath ever been her owne, which makes me so seriously deliver you by her relation all her passages from her first making when shee was that apple which Eve eate, to this time when shee is hee, whose life you shall find in the end of this booke.' Here the soul, as in Pythagorean doctrine, is limited by its successive bodies in all but memory, which makes possible Donne's account of its adventures. A popular use of such doc-trine was the fifteenth book of Ovid's *Metamorphoses*; a compre-hensive treatment is found in the seventeenth-century *History of Philosophy* by Thomas Stanley.

Each level in the scale of being—here plant, animal, human—subsumes the level or levels below it. The progress of the soul up the scale of being—vegetal, sensitive, rational—is used to show the proliferation of original sin and to satirize its effects. The idea of metempsychosis is used to dramatize and multiply the shapes of sin. By other means Milton shows Adam the shapes of sin and death in *Paradise Lost* (XI). The apple is of course the traditional symbol of original sin and embodies the vegetable soul. Jonson's explanation (*pace* Calvin) certainly agrees with Donne's Preface, and together they provide our best guide to the poem. Here I accept the traditional view rather than the theory advanced by W. A. Murray (*R.E.S.*, n.s., X, 141–55).

In both the *Metempsychosis* and the *Anniversaries* Donne is con-cerned with central questions of his time about the origin, nature, and powers of the soul—on which Sir John Davies's *Nosce Teipsum* remained a popular treatment. Both it and Burton's *Anatomy of Melancholy* can be used to gloss many of the ideas in these poems. In Davies the origin of the soul, for example, elicited theories like immediate creation by God, traduction from Nature, or the transmigration of original souls. By means of the scale of being Donne often drew 'three souls out of one weaver'; it was a favourite device with him. In his verse letter of August 1614, 'To the Countesse of Salisbury', he uses them in apology:

> *Wee first have soules of growth, and sense, and those,*
> *When our last soule, our soule immortall came,*
> *Were swallowed into it, and have no name . . .*

. . . I owe my first soules thankes, that they
For my last soule did fit and mould my clay.

When Donne begins his satiric epic, 'I sing the progresse of a
deathlesse soule', he involves 'all times before the law / Yoak'd us'
(a favourite theme) and lastly the four ages of the world. In
Stanza II we learn that 'this great Soule' began to be one day
before the sun, and Genesis tells us that on that day God created
life on the vegetal level. Thus, in the scale of being, life begins
with the vegetable soul. All the diverse shapes of life have since
been 'inform'd by this heavenly sparke'. Then Donne prays to
Destiny, 'which God made', that he may understand himself
enough to know something of his span of life. Unless he has thirty
years more, and

> *Except my legend be free from the letts*
> *Of steepe ambition, sleepie povertie,*
> *Spirit-quenching sicknesse, dull captivitie,*
> *Distracting businesse, and from beauties nets,*
> *And all that calls from this, and to others whets,*
> *O let me not launch out, but let mee save*
> *Th'expense of braine and spirit;*

because he owes the grave 'a whole unwasted man'. But if his days
are to be sufficient, he will persist in this endeavour, and his scope
will be from Paradise to the Thames ('I launch at paradise, and I
saile towards home'). However, his fortune was not to be free
from these 'letts' and so he failed to make good his promise:

> *And shall, in sad lone wayes a lively spright,*
> *Make my darke heavy Poëm light, and light.*

The much disputed Stanza VII becomes clear if we relate it to
Stanza III. All the shapes that 'have beene moved' have been
informed by the 'great Soule' that is identified in Stanza II. This
soul now dwells amongst us, 'and moves that hand, and tongue,
and brow, / Which, as the Moone the sea, moves us'. Thus
Elizabeth is now informed by this soul, for by transmigration it
became the soul of innovation, of heresy, of *Ignatius his Conclave*,
'And liv'd when every great change did come'. As the crown of
his song this soul is to take the form of heresy and rule Elizabeth
too.

Later, in *Ignatius his Conclave*, Ignatius is made to say: 'Nor can I call to minde any woman, which either deceived our hope, or scaped our cunning, but *Elizabeth* of *England* . . . And yet this *Elizabeth* was not free from all *Innovation*: For the ancient *Religion* was so much worne out, that to reduce that to the former dignity, and so to renew it, was a kinde of *Innovation*. . . . Neither dare I say, that this was properly an *Innovation*, lest thereby I should confesse that *Luther* and many others which live in banishment in *Heaven* farre from us, might have a title to this place, as such *Innovators*.'

Although this soul 'Had first in paradise, a low, but fatall roome', its ultimate potentiality was to be reached on the Cross, because, as his 'Hymne to God my God' put it, '*Christs* Crosse, and *Adams* tree, stood in one place.'[1] As Milton, opening the story of the Fall, looks forward 'till one greater Man / Restore us', so Donne envisages the story of life. But with both poets the immediate concern is with original sin. Hence Donne introduces the serpent taking the apple, 'which this Soule did enlive', so as to bring about the Fall, and we 'thence die and sweat'. Thus life or the soul was tainted.

Henceforth the soul's progress in the scale of being reveals new powers at every level. Its passage from the vegetal to the sensitive or animal level occurs in Stanza XVIII, but its transitional form is the mandrake, which bought conception for Leah in Genesis (xxx, 15). The power of generation in passing to the animal level acquires new potentialities from sense and movement. The passage from the animal to the rational level comes in Stanza L, but its transitional form is the Ape, who 'the first true lover was'. Stanza LI recalls 'The Funerall' as it creates the brain which enables woman to be a pattern of sin, 'keeping some quality / Of every past shape'. Among these past shapes the poem has included many of the targets of Donne's other satires. Finally, to cap this unfinished poem, the achievements of man are given a closing paradox and principle of relative judgment. But *Ignatius his Conclave* might be regarded as a continuation of this satire.

Donne's *Metempsychosis* introduces the progress of the soul as the formal conceit of his major poems; to this the scale of being is instrumental. In the *Metempsychosis* we see the rise of sin in the scale of being. In the *First Anniversary* we see the descent of sin in

[1] See Arno Esch, *Anglia*, lxxviii, 74–77.

the scale of being from the angels to nature, or the effects of the
Fall which brought death into the world. In the *Second Anniversary*
we see the rise of man on the scale of being to virtue and Heaven,
or lessons of the Fall that concern his progress. Pythagorean change
or mutability as the eternal flux of form has a bearing on all of
these progresses.

III

The titles of the *Anniversaries* indicate that the death of Elizabeth
Drury is only the occasion for the main theme of each poem.
Nevertheless, as a pattern, form, or shape, she has a relation to
these themes. In relation to man or the microcosm, she is a per-
sonification of virtue, the form to which his soul is related from the
beginning. In relation to the macrocosm she is the form or soul of
the world. In relation to the Golden Age she is Astraea. In the
Anniversaries we are reminded that 'world' as a name is related to
'cosmos', meaning order, harmony, system as opposed to chaos.
As a pattern Elizabeth Drury becomes a synonym for world. And
order in both the microcosm and the macrocosm involves the scale
of being as it involves degree in *Troilus and Cressida* (I, iii) or in
Paradise Lost, not least in the faculties of man. These ideological
connections between Elizabeth Drury and both of these worlds
turn into extreme hyperbole on the elegiac side of the poems, but
the occasional ligatures do not destroy the seriousness or importance of the poems as expressions of Donne's poetic thought.

The original title of the *First Anniversary* was *An Anatomie of the
World*, and its subtitle, 'Wherein, By occasion of the untimely
death of Mistris Elizabeth Drury, the frailty and the decay of this
whole World is represented.' Besides being an ambitious title, it
clearly indicates that the death of Elizabeth Drury is the occasion
but not the theme of the poem; the theme is both the frailty and
the decay of the world that is to be analysed. Of course, an
anatomy is appropriate to death, but the title emphasizes a repre-
sentative relation between the two subjects of death.

The poem really deals with the significance of the death of
virtue, both particular and general, elaborated by the evidences of
decay in man and in the world order as revealed by the new
philosophy. Elizabeth Drury is identified with the soul of both
the microcosm and the macrocosm—the essential form: in man,

of virtue; in the world, of order and harmony. Her death represents the death of virtue and leaves the world to corruption.

> *For who is sure he hath a Soule, unlesse*
> *It see, and judge, and follow worthinesse?*

But the world has forgot its name and meaning:

> *Her name defin'd thee, gave thee forme, and frame,*
> *And thou forgett'st to celebrate thy name.*

Then Donne presents the dual aspect of her death:

> *Some moneths she hath beene dead (but being dead,*
> *Measures of times are all determined)*
> *But long she'ath beene away, long, long, yet none*
> *Offers to tell us who it is that's gone.*

Elizabeth Drury died lately, but virtue has long been away.
Although measures of time are ended by death, all are reluctant
to say that virtue is dead. The world that still exists is created by
her memory:

> *. . . the matter and the stuffe of this,*
> *Her vertue, and the forme our practice is.*

Then Donne justifies his anatomy:

> *This new world may be safer, being told*
> *The dangers and diseases of the old:*
> *For with due temper men doe then forgoe,*
> *Or covet things, when they their true worth know.*

Virtue once kept the world from corruption as the soul keeps the
body. Now the corruption is only relieved by the example of
Elizabeth Drury. The verse letter 'To the Countesse of Salisbury'
also praises a woman by making the world a foil to her virtues,
'faire, great, and good'; another 'To the Countesse of Hunting-
don' gives another turn to the death of virtue.

Finally Donne begins to elaborate his lessons by the evidence for
the decay of the world that is found in Ralegh's *History of the
World* and that is examined in Victor Harris's *All Coherence Gone.*
Donne's argument has a threefold pattern: the statement and proof
of a thesis, an elegiac antithesis, and the lesson. The second part
both eulogizes the girl and climaxes the argument. It properly

takes this verbal form: 'But she . . . shee's dead.' The third part
infers the appropriate lesson, and always begins: 'And learn'st
thus much by our Anatomie.' This form is repeated for each thesis
of the argument for the Decay of the World.

The first thesis, however, is made up of subordinate parts that
show the degeneration of man or the microcosm: 'Oh what a
trifle, and poore thing he is!' Then Elizabeth Drury provides a
relevant contrast that crowns the proof, and the lesson for man
follows.

The second thesis begins,

> *Then, as mankinde, so is the worlds whole frame*
> *Quite out of joynt, almost created lame.*

The proof begins by finding the origin of corruption in the Fall
of the Angels, and proceeds to show the 'decay of nature in other
parts', or the effects of original sin on the macrocosm. This thesis
is likewise made up of subordinate parts, but here each part is
followed by an elegiac antithesis. To the 'generall maime' Elizabeth Drury presents a contrasting pattern. Because the world's
beauty is gone, or its colour and proportion, particular attention is
given to the 'disformity of parts', including moral. Elizabeth
Drury is the measure of proportion or harmony; Pythagoras
would have said 'That Harmony was shee'. This allusion emphasizes the Pythagorean order and harmony that have been
destroyed. After a lesson in proportion, the world's loss of colour
is considered. Again Elizabeth Drury provides the true ingredients
of beauty.

The greatest evidence of decay, however, is found in the 'want
of correspondence of heaven and earth':

> *Nor in ought more this worlds decay appeares,*
> *Than that her influence the heav'n forbeares.*

Of course this makes Elizabeth Drury's influence only partially
effective; moreover, living virtue is more efficacious than dead
virtue. Nevertheless she gave some tincture of virtue to many. The
final lesson is that nothing is worth our trouble 'But those rich
joyes, which did possesse her heart', and which will be developed
in the *Second Anniversary*. His conclusion includes, besides reasons
for concluding, an apology for praising Elizabeth Drury in verse,
because it is not indecorous and it will make her memorable. The

First Anniversary concludes by immortalizing her in an earthly context; the *Second* in a heavenly context.

IV

Of the Progresse of the Soule begins its progress at a higher level on the scale of being than the *Metempsychosis*. Again the subtitle points to its main theme: 'Wherein, By occasion of the Religious death of Mistress Elizabeth Drury, the incommodities of the Soule in this life, and her exaltation in the next, are contemplated.' Now the occasion is the 'religious death' rather than the 'untimely death' of the *First Anniversary*. Thus death passes from a mortal context to an immortal context, for a religious death releases the soul from its mortal prison to its immortal home.

If we remember the lesson of the decay of the world, not of man, in the *First Anniversary*,

> *And that thou hast but one way, not t'admit*
> *The worlds infection, to be none of it,*

we are prepared for its rejection in the *Second Anniversary*. And if we recall the concluding turn on death in the *First*,

> *for though the soule of man*
> *Be got when man is made, 'tis borne but then*
> *When man doth die;*

we are ready to follow the progress of the soul as 'death directs it home'. But this release from the body involves some of the apprehension later found in the sickbed of Donne's *Devotions*, and so becomes the most trying step in the progress. Now Pythagorean mutability sounds a plangent music, and the ills that flesh is heir to are treated more intensely. No doubt because this poem is more subjective, for it is Donne's *Nosce Teipsum*, and shares vital topics with the poem by Sir John Davies.

In the same dead world as before, Donne seeks to preserve the memory of virtue until he too is called:

> *All have forgot all good,*
> *Forgetting her, the maine reserve of all.*

On the didactic side this involves the preparation of the soul for 'Gods great *Venite*', which is heard in the famous Holy Sonnet

'At the round earth's imagin'd corners'. First he develops the lesson of the decay of the world originally stated in the *First Anniversary*. On the elegiac side the rejection of the world is supported by the death of a new Astraea, in whom 'Some Figure of the Golden times was hid'. In presenting the soul's relation to both worlds this poem becomes another exploration of the limitations and state of this world—made by comparison with the soul's true health and home.

If death is to direct our soul home, then it becomes a crucial step in the soul's progress. Hence the long persuasion of the soul to accept death cheerfully. On the elegiac side even Elizabeth Drury found that 'Death must usher, and unlocke the door'. Then the disadvantages of the body are to be considered. For the soul, the body is both an infection and a prison.

> *Thinke that it argued some infirmitie,*
> *That those two soules, which then thou foundst in me,*
> *Thou fedst upon, and drewst into thee, both*
> *My second soule of sense, and first of growth.*

This is the scale that was ascended in the *Metempsychosis*. From its prison the soul achieves liberty by death. Henceforth the progress of the soul can be followed only by means of ecstasy: 'So by the Soule doth death string Heaven and Earth.' The assumption of this means is explicitly mentioned at the marginal notation 'Of our company in this life, and in the next.' Ecstasy provides a mode of vision instrumental to a comparison of this life and the next. The same device was employed as a means to vision in 'The Extasie' and *Ignatius his Conclave*. If the passage to heaven must 'thy long-short Progresse bee', the example of Elizabeth Drury serves 'To advance these thoughts'.

Another argument for this progress is that it carries one from ignorance to knowledge. Here the theme of *nosce teipsum*, which Donne mocked in 'Negative Love', leads him into all the limitations that the lower souls of the body impose on the rational soul and that set man's mediate knowledge below the angel's immediate knowledge. Only Elizabeth Drury approached this higher form of knowledge, and her death took away our example.

On our company in this life and the next Donne argues, with a touch of satire, that no station in this life is free from corruption when compared with the virtue and concord of heaven. Elizabeth

Drury provides a further example and incentive to share in the joy of such company.

If Elizabeth Drury shows that accidental joys may exist in Heaven, the soul must consider essential joy in this life and the next. Then he proceeds to show that the 'accessories' of happiness change, only the essentials abide. This he illustrates by the moving passage on the transience of beauty, in which Pythagorean change touches pathos rather than satire. God alone is the centre of essential joy, and Elizabeth Drury embodied such knowledge on earth.

Our accidental joys at best are poor and transitory; only in Heaven 'accidentall things are permanent'. Again Elizabeth Drury is such an example that only Heaven could add to her perfection. But here at least 'mis-devotion' makes Donne stop short of canonization. Obviously the four last things—death, judgment, heaven, and hell—are not regarded as the property of one mode of religious poetry.

The number of basic parts indicated by the marginal captions remain essentially the same in the two *Anniversaries*, but the eulo-gies of Elizabeth Drury are increased by two in the *Second*. For its devotional aspect Martz cites Donne as saying in his *Essays in Divinity* (p. 59) that '*Seven* is ever used to express infinite.' But this remark is parenthetical to a text which makes any 'over-curious' numerology 'too Cabalistick and Pythagorick for a vulgar Christian'. The formal pattern and phrases of the *First Anniversary* are reduced in the *Second* to alternating lesson and example, in-struction and eulogy, or the basic parts of elegy for Puttenham. Both parts are designed to persuade one to follow the progress of the soul. The major antithesis in the *Second Anniversary* is between heaven and earth. Elizabeth Drury is made throughout an attrac-tion towards God, and so her eulogy is integrated into the argu-ment for the progress of the soul from this world to the next. She is the antithesis, however, of the woman with whom the satiric progress of the soul ended.

Donne's original projection of the progress of the soul extended from Paradise to the Thames, but he finally stretched it up the scale of being to Heaven. In the *Metempsychosis* he took a satirical view of original sin; in the *First Anniversary* he explored seriously the consequences of original sin in the world he knew; in the *Second Anniversary* he pondered the Christian answer to these consequences, and completed the journey of the soul from creation to its potential destiny. No doubt he did not anticipate this result of his 'expense of braine and spirit' or this manner of making his 'darke heavy Poëm light, and light'. Nevertheless the persistence of this structural idea reveals a dimension of his thought that led to a definition of his life.

10

STRUCTURE IN VAUGHAN'S POETRY

CRITICS often conclude that Vaughan triumphs in the part at the expense of the whole, being incapable of sustained achieve/ ment. Possibly the splendour of the part sometimes obscures the nature of the whole, but this incongruity is not above suspicion. At least it justifies some inquiry into the contrast. Perhaps the most striking example is found in the poem called *The World*, whose opening lines are thought to be worth the whole poem. No doubt Vaughan would have agreed, but not for the reason often given. His title and poem derive from his Scriptural epigraph, 1 John ii, 16–17:

'All that is in the world, the lust of the flesh, the lust of the Eye, and the pride of life, is not of the Father, but is of the world.

'And the world passeth away, and the lusts thereof; but he that doth the will of God abideth for ever.'

This passage centres in the opposition between the world and God, and so Vaughan constructs his poem upon this opposition. First as the realms of time and eternity, by the splendid antithesis which makes time the shadow of eternity in Plato's *Timaeus*, the Ring of light being translated into shadow by the spheres. These opposites become the poles of being:

> *I saw eternity the other night*
> *Like a great* Ring *of pure and endless light,*
> *All calm, as it was bright;*
> *And round beneath it, Time in hours, days, years,*
> *Driv'n by the spheres*
> *Like a vast shadow mov'd, In which the world*
> *And all her train were hurl'd.*

The epithets of the Ring specify the attractions of eternity as op/ posed to the pressures of time in which the world moves. Vaughan

165

then begins to describe the world's train of lusts, first in the 'doting Lover', as contrast to the conclusion. Appropriately his gaze is not directed towards the Ring: 'while he his eyes did pour / Upon a flowr'.

The lust of the States-man is much heavier and the most devious of all. Here the dark side of the antithesis multiplies its effects:

> *The darksome States-man hung with weights and woe,*
> *Like a thick midnight-fog, mov'd there so slow,*
>   *He did not stay, nor go;*
> *Condemning thoughts like sad Ecclipses scowl*
>   *Upon his soul,*
> *And Clouds of crying witnesses without*
>   *Pursued him with one shout.*
> *Yet digg'd the Mole, and, lest his ways be found,*
>   *Workt under ground ...*

The description dwells upon privations of light and deviousness of movement to characterize this pillar of state. He got his prey, 'but one did see / That policie', while he took churches, perjury, blood and tears in his stride. Vaughan now employs the rhetoric of blame, but he does not exhibit a real decline in power.

Avarice is a more obvious lust, but the miser lives in apparent straits:

> *The fearfull miser on a heap of rust*
> *Sate pining all his life there, did scarce trust*
>   *His own hands with the dust,*
> *Yet would not place one peece above, but lives*
>   *In fear of theeves.*

Other misers hugged their own treasure:

> *The down-right Epicure plac'd heav'n in sense,*
>   *And scorn'd pretence;*
> *While others, slipt into a wide Excesse,*
>   *Said little lesse ...*

Others were more contemptible:

> *The weaker sort slight, triviall wares Inslave,*
>   *Who think them brave,*
> *And poor, despised truth sate Counting by*
>   *Their victory.*

Thus the metaphor of counting levels the values of various lusts.

The last stanza turns from the dark side of the antithesis to the light, or back to the original image:

> *Yet some, who all this while did weep and sing,*
> *And sing and weep, soar'd up into the* Ring;
> > *But most would use no wing.*
> *O fools, said I, thus to prefer dark night*
> > *Before true light!*

But as he rebukes this preference for the dark night of the world, he hears another voice:

> *But as I did their madnes so discusse*
> > *One whisper'd thus,*
> This Ring the Bride⸗groome did for none provide,
> > But for his bride.

And this is the voice of Revelation making the Ring a sign of marriage with the Lamb. Thus the passage from darkness to light, from the world to God, is dependent on both our 'wing' and the 'Bride⸗groome' Christ.

Obviously this poem is an organization of elements from the book of God's works and the book of God's word designed to magnify the opening image of its meaning. And so what critics sometimes regard as evidence of Vaughan's failure becomes evi⸗dence of the poem's success. Vaughan's antithesis derives from the Scriptural passage, and is just as basic to his meaning. Indeed, editors who omit Vaughan's Biblical text not only remove the evidence of his intention but also clues to its achievement. It is, in fact, more mutilating than to omit the motto from an emblem poem. But its omission does help to protect the hasty critic.

The same vision haunts one of Vaughan's finest poems on death:

> *They are all gone into the world of light!*
> > *And I alone sit lingring here!*
> *Their very memory is fair and bright,*
> > *And my sad thoughts doth clear.*

Its attraction beautifies death itself:

> *Dear, beauteous death; the Jewel of the Just!*
> > *Shining no where but in the dark;*
> *What mysteries do lie beyond thy dust,*
> > *Could man outlook that mark!*

Ordinarily death is a jewel only to the just and shines only in the darkness of life. But a feeling of transcendence often produces a sense of frustration in Vaughan, and so he seeks for some re-assurance:

> *If a star were confin'd into a Tomb,*
> *Her captive flames must needs burn there;*
> *But when the hand that lockt her up gives room,*
> *She'll shine through all the sphaere.*

This image connects his soul with his vision, or as he said in *The Bird*,

> *For each inclosed Spirit is a star*
> *Inlightning his own little sphaere,*

and so he ends with a prayer alluding to Romans viii, 21:

> *O Father of eternal life, and all*
> *Created glories under thee!*
> *Resume thy spirit from this world of thrall*
> *Into true liberty!*
>
> *Either disperse these mists, which blot and fill*
> *My perspective still as they pass;*
> *Or else remove me hence unto that hill,*
> *Where I shall need no glass.*

This is the frustrating physical veil that he often laments in his poetry, but it is a limitation that he discovers in the book of God's works. Like *The World*, this poem really sustains its power and builds to a conclusion appropriate to his feeling about death.

The Incarnation, and Passion plays upon the paradoxical union of opposites implicit in these religious events. The union of divine and human nature looks at once to its no less paradoxical end:

> *Lord! when thou didst thyselfe undresse,*
> *Laying by thy robes of glory,*
> *To make us more thou wouldst be lesse,*
> *And becam'st a wofull story.*

Two stanzas then magnify the wonder of this incarnation, playing upon both the translation and union of opposites:

> *To put on Clouds instead of light,*
> *And cloath the morning-starre with dust,*
> *Was a translation of such height*
> *As, but in thee, was ne'r exprest.*

> *Brave wormes and Earth! that thus could have*
> *A God Enclos'd within your Cell,*
> *Your maker pent up in a grave,*
> *Life lockt in death, heav'n in a shell!*

Only Vaughan could express this union by a translation like
'cloath the morning-starre with dust'.

Then another stanza amplifies the 'wofull story':

> *Ah, my deare Lord! what couldst thou spye*
> *In this impure, rebellious clay,*
> *That made thee thus resolve to dye*
> *For those that kill thee every day?*

Here the incarnation adds to the wonder of the martyrdom until
the ultimate cause answers the riddle.

> *O what strange wonders could thee move*
> *To slight thy precious bloud, and breath?*
> *Sure it was* Love, *my Lord; for* Love
> *Is only stronger far than death!*

Thus the motive is also the means to the end of the Passion, and
the means here surpasses its power in the Song of Solomon (viii, 6):
'for love is strong as death'.

To the consequence of this lyric theme, Vaughan's *Peace* gives
a more lilting tune. But peace, although 'Afar beyond the stars',
is defined by metaphors of war, its opposite. It is guarded by 'a
winged Sentrie' and 'Beauteous files', which are opposed to
'foolish ranges' or ranks; though a flower, it is also a fortress, and
only given by God. Again things become intelligible in terms of
their contradictions.

The Retreate laments the consequences of the soul's incarnation
in the world of time. His longing for the realm of eternity makes
him differ from other men:

> *Some men a forward motion love,*
> *But I by backward steps would move . . .*

Yet now he can go backward only by going forward:

> *And when this dust falls to the urn,*
> *In that state I came return.*

Only death can release the soul from time back to eternity, its
home. The poem deals with the soul's longing and sense of

alienation, with its frustration by the sinful flesh. Especially poig-
nant is the time

> *When on some gilded Cloud or flowre*
> *My gazing soul would dwell an houre,*
> *And in those weaker glories spy*
> *Some shadows of eternity;*

and before he lost this sense of eternity,

> *Or had the black art to dispence*
> *A sev'rall sinne to ev'ry sence,*
> *But felt through all this fleshly dresse*
> *Bright shootes of everlastingnesse.*

Eternity and time, light and shadow, backward and forward,
these are the contraries that define Vaughan's feeling in this poem.
Their conflict is resolved by the separation of body and soul in his
conclusion.

   In *Corruption* Vaughan expresses a similar sense of man's
heavenly origin against a darker background of his corruption.

> *He drew the Curse upon the world, and Crackt*
>   *The whole frame with his fall.*
> *This made him long for* home, *as loath to stay*
>   *With murmurers and foes;*
> *He sighed for* Eden, *and would often say*
>   Ah! what bright days were those!

Though he continues to find glimpses of his origin in nature, he
cannot feel at home there and longs for his first place of birth.

   Another fine poem on death, which laments a personal loss,
presents it in terms of a light gone out and the consequent darkness. But the loss is first approached in terms of days, the product of
light and the measure of time: 'Silence and stealth of dayes!' Their
stealth is multiplied into 'Twelve hundred houres', before the light
becomes a lamp 'To brave the night', and finally 'his Sun'. Then
time is again magnified into smaller parts:

> *So o'er fled minutes I retreat*
>   *Unto that hour,*
> *Which shew'd thee last, but did defeat*
>   *Thy light and pow'r.*

And he is conscious of nothing but the lamp gone out:

> *I search, and rack my soul to see*
> *Those beams again;*
> *But nothing but the snuff to me*
> *Appeareth plain.*

Now the lamp is translated into body and soul; first the 'snuff':

> *That, dark and dead sleeps in its known,*
> *And common urn;*
> *But those, fled to their Maker's throne,*
> *There shine and burn.*

And this flight deepens his sense of separation:

> *O could I track them! but souls must*
> *Track one the other;*
> *And now the spirit, not the dust,*
> *Must be thy brother.*

Yet he has a final recourse, which is the Gospel:

> *Yet I have one* Pearle, *by whose light*
> *All things I see;*
> *And in the heart of Earth and night*
> *Find Heaven, and thee.*

Thus he finds consolation in a spiritual source of light, which leads from earth and night to heaven and thee, and all in terms of the basic imagery of the poem.

It is a mistake to regard Vaughan's *Man* as a botched imitation of Herbert's *The Pulley*. Each poem is firmly based in its author's sense of spiritual conflict. Herbert has God withhold rest from man lest he succumb to the worldly gifts which are frequent temptations in Herbert's poetry. Desire for rest is the pulley that is ultimately to bring man to God; otherwise

> *He would adore my gifts in stead of me,*
> *And rest in Nature, not the God of Nature.*

For Vaughan man's desire is deeper than this, in *The Retreate* for example; and man cannot rest in nature, in *Corruption* for instance, because his home is elsewhere.

Moreover, each of the two poems is integrated in a manner

characteristic of its author. Vaughan begins by observing some
habits of nature that excite his envy; he finds 'stedfastness' and
'staidness' in nature as opposed to motion and restlessness in man.
His dialectic between man and nature produces a different answer
to man's restlessness. It arises from a comparison of their activities,
beginning with birds, bees, and flowers, and is related to time.
Nature shows its qualities with respect to time; for example,

> *Where birds like watchful Clocks the noiseless date*
> *And Intercourse of times divide . . .*

Nature is faithful 'To His divine appointments' and at peace with
itself.

Man's activities are then contrasted in two parallel stanzas.

> *Man hath still either toyes or Care;*
> *He hath no root, nor to one place is ty'd,*
> *But ever restless and Irregular*
> *About this Earth doth run and ride.*
> *He knows he hath a home, but scarce knows where;*
> *He sayes it is so far,*
> *That he hath quite forgot how to go there.*

Man lacks nature's attributes, but he knows he has a home, even
if he has lost his way. Indeed his restlessness suggests that his home
is not here, that he cannot rest in nature:

> *He knocks at all doors, strays and roams;*
> *Nay hath not so much wit as some stones have,*
> *Which in the darkest nights point to their homes*
> *By some hid sense their Maker gave.*

This comparison appears to leave the advantage with nature and
to rebuke man for his lack of wit.

But we must observe that the final lines remove the blame and
find purpose in man's restlessness:

> *Man is the shuttle, to whose winding quest*
> *And passage through these looms*
> *God order'd motion, but ordain'd no rest.*

Thus man is not governed by the law of nature, but obeys an
impulse of the soul. If anyone doubts the careful ordering of
Vaughan's contrast, he may reflect that man's resolving difference
is related to 'these looms' of time as nature is related to the

'Intercourse of times' in the first stanza. Nothing could be more fundamental, since the poem is concerned with a contrast between the powers of man and nature in the world of time.

The Night is pointed by its epigraph towards a religious context for its title. The epigraph, John iii, 2, relates to Nicodemus: 'The same came to Jesus by night, and said unto him, Rabbi, we know that thou art a teacher come from God: for no man can do these miracles that thou doest, except God be with him.' And the fifth stanza carries two Biblical references for 'Christ's progress, and his prayer time': Mark i, 35, 'And in the morning, rising up a great while before day, he went out, and departed into a solitary place, and there prayed.' Luke xxi, 37, 'And in the day time he was teaching in the temple; and at night he went out, and abode in the mount that is called the mount of Olives.'

These passages suggest the central theme of the poem: night versus day as ways to God. They also provide an answer to the question where Nicodemus found Jesus, a Silurian answer—nowhere

> *But his own living works, did my Lord hold*
> > *And lodge alone;*
> *Where trees and herbs did watch and peep*
> *And wonder, while the Jews did sleep.*

Of course Nicodemus had the vision of faith:

> *Most blest believer he!*
> *Who in that land of darkness and blinde eyes*
> *Thy long expected healing wings could see,*
> > *When thou didst rise;*
> *And, what can never more be done,*
> *Did at midnight speak with the Sun!*

And so he found the Son at night.

Then Vaughan salutes night with something of the thesaurus wit of Cowley's *Against Hope*. First as a relief from the diurnal round:

> *Dear night! this world's defeat;*
> *The stop to busie fools; care's check and curb;*
> *The day of Spirits; my soul's calm retreat*
> > *Which none disturb!*
> *Christ's progress, and his prayer time;*
> *The hours to which high Heaven doth chime.*

Then in terms of 'his own living works' and the Song of Solomon (v):

> *God's silent, searching flight:*
> *When my Lord's head is filled with dew, and all*
> *His locks are wet with the clear drops of night;*
> *His still, soft call;*
> *His knocking time; The soul's dumb watch,*
> *When Spirits their Fair Kindred catch.*

And he concludes that if all his 'loud, evil days' were 'Calm and
unhaunted as is thy dark Tent', then he would live in Heaven all
the year long, and never wander here.

But his life is not so blessed:

> *But living where the Sun*
> *Doth all things wake, and where all mix and tyre*
> *Themselves and others, I consent and run*
> *To ev'ry myre;*
> *And by this world's ill guiding light,*
> *Erre more than I can do by night.*

It is in the light that he goes astray, not in the 'dark Tent', whose
peace is rent only by 'some Angel's wing or voice'. It is there that
he, like Nicodemus, came to God:

> *There is in God, some say,*
> *A deep, but dazzling darkness; As men here*
> *Say it is late and dusky, because they*
> *See not all clear.*
> *O for that night! where I in him*
> *Might live invisible and dim!*

After his own paradoxical progress, this petition unites Vaughan's
Biblical passages in its emphasis on night as the devotional haunt
of the Lord.

In *The Water-Fall* Vaughan finds a parable of man's destiny;
it lends a voice to 'time's silent stealth'. First we have the identification or slow emergence of the parallel. The waters flow with
'deep murmurs', then 'chide and call' as if afraid of this steep place.
Here death begins to emerge:

> *The common pass,*
> *Where, clear as glass,*

> *All must descend*
> *Not to an end,*
> *But quickened by this deep and rocky grave,*
> *Rise to a longer course more bright and brave.*

As the grave becomes explicit, the course rises to a Christian destiny, ambiguously 'quickened'.

The second part draws inferences from the waterfall to man's fate based on parallels between them. As it had pleased his 'pensive eye', it had taught him Christian answers to man's fear of death. This analogy leads into a consideration of water as a religious symbol running from baptism to the Creation:

> *O useful Element and clear!*
> *My sacred wash and cleanser here;*
> *My first consigner unto those*
> *Fountains of life, where the Lamb goes!*
> *What sublime truths, and wholesome themes,*
> *Lodge in thy mystical, deep streams!*
> *Such as dull man can never finde,*
> *Unless that Spirit lead his minde,*
> *Which first upon thy face did move*
> *And hatch'd all with his quickening love.*

Even so, nature requires religious vision for its interpretation. Now Vaughan makes his parallel explicit:

> *As this loud brook's incessant fall*
> *In streaming rings restagnates all,*
> *Which reach by course the bank, and then*
> *Are no more seen, just so pass men.*

This passage leads him to reject the symbol for the meaning, which now exceeds the symbol:

> *O my invisible estate,*
> *My glorious liberty, still late!*
> *Thou art the Channel my soul seeks,*
> *Not this with Cataracts and Creeks.*

Thus his governing figure leads to its rejection because the natural ultimately fails to express the supernatural.

Vaughan can employ the neatness of form which is admired in Herbert, and he does so in one of his most characteristic poems,

Quickness. Here he contrasts false life and true life in two pairs of symmetrical stanzas, and then opposes their quickness in a final stanza. False life is a foil to the true, a 'foul deception . . . That would not have the true come on'. It has the appearance of quickness or life, but is blind, selfposing, full of contention. True life has less appearance of quickness and more of stability, is 'calm and full, yet doth not cloy'. It is a blissful state that quickens, 'and hath the skill / To please without Eternity'. Elements of the contrast in *The World* find their place in this poem.

But the conclusion seems to reflect the contrast between the natural state and the state of grace found in Ephesians ii, where God, 'for his great love wherewith he loved us, / Even when we were dead in sins, hath quickened us together with Christ'. These two states appear as a false and a true quickness:

> *Thou art a toylsom Mole, or less*
> *A moving mist.*
> *But life is, what none can express,*
> A quickness, which my God hath kist.

The physical veil has become a moving mist, and if none can express how man was quickened by divine love, Vaughan's last line can certainly suggest God's mercy. Moreover, this line would lose the force of its quickness if it did not rest on the contrast between appearance and reality that is elaborated in the poem. The quick and the dead have seldom been distinguished more paradoxically or more neatly.

It is not inappropriate to conclude with Vaughan's poem on his own pilgrim's progress, *Regeneration.* Its epigraph is from the Song of Solomon iv: 'Arise, O North, and come thou Southwind, and blow upon my garden, that the spices thereof may flow out.' This is a prayer for regeneration, and its imagery introduces the nature imagery of the poem, specifically wind and a garden. But Vaughan's title carries us to Nicodemus again, for Jesus taught him about regeneration in John iii, and in terms that supply the rest of Vaughan's nature imagery, especially in these verses:

'Jesus answered, Verily, verily, I say unto thee, Except a man be born of water and of the Spirit, he cannot enter into the kingdom of God . . .

'The wind bloweth where it listeth, and thou hearest the sound thereof, but canst not tell whence it cometh, and whither it goeth: so is every one that is born of the Spirit.'

A ward of the world, and still in bonds to sin, he stole abroad one day and found the appearance of spring:

> *It was high-spring, and all the way*
> *Primrosed, and hung with shade . . .*

'Primrosed' is perhaps ambiguous, but it is not spring within him:

> *Yet was it frost within;*
> *The surly wind*
> *Blasted my infant buds, and sinne*
> *Like clouds eclipsed my mind.*

Thus regeneration is to be presented as a progress towards spring or rebirth, and it begins by contrasting the external and internal, or appearance and reality.

'Storm'd thus', he straight perceived that his spring was only an appearance, and his walk in reality 'a monstrous, mountain'd thing'. In grief he struggles upwards, and at the top found a pair of scales which weighed his 'late paines' against 'smoake and pleasures', and proved the latter the heavier. Then he hears the command, 'Away', which he obeys, and is led 'full East' to holy land. Here he found a grove of stately height:

> *I entred, and once in,*
> *Amaz'd to see't,*
> *Found all was chang'd, and a new spring*
> *Did all my senses greet.*

Now the Biblical passages begin to impinge upon his experience. Instead of the primroses, 'The unthrift Sunne shot vitall gold':

> *The aire was all in spice,*
> *And every bush*
> *A garland wore; Thus fed my Eyes,*
> *But all the Eare lay hush.*

Here again the opposition of the seen and unseen, which was introduced at the beginning, appears in the opposition of eye and ear, organs of the seen and unseen. Although the spice now flows out, St John had said that one hears the wind of regeneration.

And now the poem emphasizes hearing:

> *Only a little Fountain lent*
> *Some use for Eares,*
> *And on the dumbe shades language spent,*
> *The Musick of her teares;*
> *I drew her neere, and found*
> *The Cisterne full*
> *Of divers stones, some bright and round,*
> *Others ill-shap'd and dull.*

So hearing leads him to St John's other requirement for regeneration, water, and to two kinds of stones.

The next stanza turns them into positive and negative responses to water:

> *The first (pray marke,) as quick as light*
> *Danc'd through the floud;*
> *But, th'last more heavy than the night*
> *Nail'd to the Centre stood;*
> *I wonder'd much, but tyr'd*
> *At last with thought,*
> *My restless Eye, that still desir'd,*
> *As strange an object brought.*

Vaughan makes the reader infer the lesson of the stones, but he repeats it for the eye:

> *It was a banke of flowers, where I descried*
> *(Though 'twas mid-day,)*
> *Some fast asleepe, others broad-eyed,*
> *And taking in the Ray . . .*

Here we have response and indifference to the 'vital gold' of the sun; but now his meditation is interrupted by another appeal to the ear:

> *Here musing long I heard*
> *A rushing wind,*
> *Which still increas'd, but whence it stirr'd,*
> *No where I could not find.*

Thus St John's wind of regeneration enters the poem, and Vaughan looks for any response in nature, thereby evoking the moral he has refused to draw.

> *I turn'd me round, and to each shade*
>   *Dispatch'd an Eye,*
> *To see if any leafe had made*
>   *Least motion or Reply;*
> *But while I listning sought*
>   *My mind to ease*
> *By knowing, where 'twas, or where not,*
>   *It whisper'd:* Where I please.

St John had said, 'The wind bloweth where it listeth', and so Vaughan utters the prayer of his epigraph:

> *Lord, then said I,* On me one breath,
> And let me dye before my death!

Thus, by God's grace, he too may be 'born of the Spirit'. And thus the wind and garden of the Song of Solomon unite with the water and wind of St John to develop this parable of regeneration. In its poetic integration the opposition of the seen and unseen, which served to state the conflict, also figures in the resolution.

It may be said in conclusion that Vaughan's poems are often built on fundamental antitheses explored by the wit that Samuel Butler called the 'expressing of Sense by Contradiction and Riddle'. Not only religious ideas and paradoxes but both the union and opposition of nature and the supernatural entered into the structure of his poems and left their stamp upon his language. In poems involving such patterns of thought it is hazardous indeed to neglect the whole for the part, or to detach them from their Scriptural epigraphs. Either course may throw the poem out of focus, and distort both the intention and the achievement of Vaughan. Some of these patterns have been illustrated in poems that, although among his better poems, have not escaped such unfortunate distortions by editors and critics.

11

THE PURPLE OF *URN BURIAL*

IT is paradoxical to treat the famous last chapter of *Hydriotaphia* as a great purple passage rather than a solution to a problem. Not without reason did Sir Thomas Browne conclude in this mourn‐ ing purple or funereal pomp. His Dedication gives us a plain warning: 'We were hinted by the occasion, not catched the oppor‐ tunity to write of old things, or intrude upon the Antiquary.' Yet the hint has too often been ignored. It was an occasion for melancholy: 'who knows the fate of his bones?' The problem of identifying the urns presented Browne with his theme; its solution required his intrusion upon antiquities; both theme and solution involved the rationale of burial customs. But it is his theme that governs his antiquities and modulates his prose. Although James M. Cline has rescued the unity of *Urn Burial*, he has not defined the rational structure that actually informs its eloquence.[1]

Like Donne in *Holy Sonnet X*, Browne deals with man's desire to conquer death; it is a desire that stirs his feeling and imagination to their depths. Bacon had crowned his plea for the advancement of learning with these words: 'Let us conclude with the dignity and excellency of knowledge and learning in that whereunto man's nature doth most aspire, which is, immortality or continuance: for to this tendeth generation, and raising of houses and families; to this buildings, foundations, and monu‐ ments; to this tendeth the desire of memory, fame, and celebration, and in effect the strength of all other human desires.'

But Browne in his contemplation of death in *Religio Medici* had concluded: 'Some, upon the courage of a fruitful issue, wherein, as in the truest Chronicle, they seem to outlive them‐ selves, can with greater patience away with death. This conceit and counterfeit subsisting in our progenies seems to me a meer

[1] See *University of California Publications in English*, Vol. 8, No. 1.

fallacy, unworthy the desires of a man that can but conceive a thought of the next World; who, in a nobler ambition, should desire to live in his substance in Heaven, rather than his name and shadow in the earth. And therefore at my death I mean to take a total adieu of the World, not caring for a Monument, History, or Epitaph; not so much as the bare memory of my name to be found any where but in the universal Register of God.'

This is the problem and the position that find their supreme expression in *Urn Burial*. The funeral sermon which began in *Religio Medici* had thus ended in fine purple. Donne's prose 'for whom the bell tolls' may strike more plangent notes, but the pageantry of death wears more splendid robes in Browne.

What was 'hinted by the occasion' or discovery of the urns was a meditation on man's attempts to subsist after death, to conquer time, to preserve his identity. The meditation is controlled by its occasion; hence it begins with the physical urn and its identifica- tion as a memorial. This investigation leads to the conclusion that mortality can be conquered only on the spiritual level, specifically the Christian.

The main topics may be summarized as follows: Chapter I considers the practices of burial followed by most nations, and reasons for them. Chapter II deals with the problem of identifying the urns with reference to national origin and time. In Chapter III the urns and their contents are considered in the light of ancient customs, and with respect to the advantages and disadvantages of urn burial. The latter consideration obliges Browne to enter the realm of belief—to regard the influence upon customs of a belief in a future being. But he is still pursuing the problem of identity. Chapter IV gives a 'rationall' of old funeral rites in relation to the idea of 'some future being'. Chapter V concludes that all at- tempts to subsist after death, to conquer oblivion, except by Christian immortality, are vain.

Browne moves from a consideration of the physical urn and body to the realm of shadows and soul in his quest for the pre- servation of identity. With respect to 'corporal dissolution' physi- cal memorials are explained by customs founded on reason. With respect to the 'soul upon disunion' funeral rites are explained by beliefs regardless of reason. Thus in considering man's attempts to conquer death and preserve his identity, Browne moves from the physical to the spiritual, from reason to belief, from pagan to

Christian—through the mediating belief in a future being. None of these realms can be kept absolutely distinct from the other, but the main emphasis passes from one to the other.

I

In his Dedication Browne shows his concern for the lessons of mortality that may be drawn from the discovery of these 'sad and sepulchral Pitchers'. Otherwise he is 'coldly drawn unto dis-courses of Antiquities'. This concern defines the right approach to his study. Let me try to make his argument obtrusive without rejecting his language, except as brevity requires. As in his *Religio Medici*, he begins Chapter I with the most general aspect of his subject; it is a discovery, but a discovery related to man: 'Nature hath furnished one part of the Earth, and man another. The treasures of time lie high, in Urnes, Coynes, and Monu-ments, scarce below the roots of some vegetables.'

In burial men have wished that 'the earth be light upon them; Even such as hope to rise again, would not be content with centrall interrment, or so desperately to place their reliques as to lie beyond discovery, and in no way to be seen again'. This human wish makes possible 'communication with our fore-fathers' and introduces the theme of *Urn Burial*. Although 'earth hath engrossed the name' of grave, some have conceived it most natural to end in fire, or water, or even air. For 'their corporall dissolution . . . the sobrest Nations have rested in two wayes, of simple inhumation and burning'. The Christians, however, ab-horred burning. Thus Browne begins the identification of his urns, which embody a basic human desire that becomes his theme.

In Chapter II Browne is not concerned with the practices of cremation or interment, but rather with urns and their contents. He conjectures that 'these were the urnes of Romanes', and con-siders the evidence of Roman occupation. The question of time is more difficult. 'Than the time of these Urnes deposited, or precise Antiquity of these Reliques, nothing of more uncertainty.' They contain no coins or 'appurtenances of affectionate superstition' that might date them. 'Some uncertainty there is from the period or term of burning, or the cessation of that practise.' The evidence syncopates his syntax: 'And perhaps not fully disused till Christianity fully established, which gave the finall extinction to these sepulchrall Bonefires.'

Then he considers the evidence of sex and age, concluding it 'not improbable that many thereof were persons of minor age, or women'. This conclusion is confirmed by the remains of cherished possessions found with the bones. Browne also considers the possibility that some of the urns might belong to 'our Brittish, Saxon, or Danish Forefathers'. But he concludes that 'the most assured account will fall upon the Romanes, or Brittains Roman/ized'. Although often expressed in the truncated syntax of an inventory, this investigation has not been concerned with antiqui/ties but with the evidence of human identity.

Chapter III continues to investigate the problems of identity. These seemed to be 'rurall Urnes'; they did not contain the objects that 'attended noble Ossuaries'. Yet the evidence shows their remains 'were not of the meanest carcasses'. In none did Browne find any mixture of bones or evidence of 'passionately endeavour/ing to continue their living Unions'. Identification is complicated by many factors. 'The certainty of death is attended with un/certainties, in time, manner, places. The variety of Monuments hath often obscured true graves; and cenotaphs confounded Sepulchres.' And they are subject to many hazards. They may be violated in search of riches: 'Bones, hairs, nails, and teeth of the dead, were the treasures of old Sorcerers.' Neither does Browne ignore the vicissitudes of decomposition.

And 'though we decline the Religious consideration', yet its consequences are not to be avoided in burial customs. This con/sideration leads him into the advantages and disadvantages of 'burning Burials'. Browne is not playing the gravedigger in *Hamlet* when he concludes: 'Teeth, bones, and hair, give the most lasting defiance to corruption.' For these set the limits of physical duration and identity. 'When Alexander opened the Tomb of Cyrus, the remaining bones discovered his proportion, whereof urnall fragments afford but a bad conjecture, and have this dis/advantage of grave enterrments, that they leave us ignorant of most personal discoveries.' For cremation destroys identity as 'carnall sepulture' does not. Thus 'physiognomy outlives our selves, and ends not in our graves'. But this leads to a further question: 'Severe contemplators observing these lasting reliques, may think them good monuments of persons past, little advantage to future beings. And considering that power which subdueth all things unto itself, that can resume the scattered Atomes, or identifie out of any thing, conceive it superfluous to expect a resurrection out of Reliques; But the soul subsisting, other matter, clothed with due accidents, may salve the individuality.' This is another solu⁄tion to the problem of preserving our identity, but it involves the conception of a future being.

Browne begins Chapter IV by observing that 'Christians have handsomely glossed the deformity of death, by careful considera⁄tion of the body, and civil rites which take off brutall termina⁄tions.' And this because 'they devolved not all upon the sufficiency of soul⁄existence'. For this reason 'Christian invention hath chiefly driven at Rites, which speak hopes of another life, and hints of a Resurrection. And if the ancient Gentiles held not the immortality of their better part, and some subsistence after death; in severall rites, customes, actions and expressions, they con⁄tradicted their own opinions.' Then he examines the influence of beliefs on funeral rites, and gives a variety of examples. Men are most irrational in religion, and hence a 'rationall of old Rites' requires no strict interpreter. Of course 'the particulars of future beings must needs be dark unto ancient Theories, which Christian Philosophy yet determines but in a Cloud of opinions'. Browne admires Epicurus's attitude towards life and death, but courage has more than one aspect: 'Were the happiness of the next world as closely apprehended as the felicities of this, it were a martyrdome to live; and unto such as consider none hereafter, it must be more than death to dye, which makes us amazed at those audacities, that durst be nothing, and return into their Chaos again. Cer⁄tainly such spirits as could contemn death, when they expected no better being after, would have scorned to live, had they known any.'

The 'virtuous heathen' are not to be scorned by Christians: 'all or most apprehensions rested in Opinions of some future being, which, ignorantly or coldly beleeved, begat those perverted conceptions, Ceremonies, Sayings, which Christians pity or laugh at. Happy are they, which live not in that disadvantage of time, when men could say little for futurity, but from reason.' All men have the same motivation: 'It is the heaviest stone that melancholy can throw at a man, to tell him he is at the end of his nature; or that there is no further state to come, unto which this seems progressionall, and otherwise made in vaine.' Browne ends this chapter on the threshold of the Christian answer to the desire that finds here 'no resting contentment'.

Chapter V opens and closes on a contrast of great and small, major and minor monuments, buildings and bones. Its theme is the vanity of human wishes with respect to continuance, for which there is only one answer. Time has spared 'these minor Monuments', which have outlasted the longest life of man, spacious buildings, and three conquests; but 'to be unknown was the means of their continuation and obscurity their protection'. Although 'puzling Questions are not beyond all conjecture . . . who were the proprietaries of these bones, or what bodies these ashes made up, were a question above Antiquarism'.

What was their mistake? 'Had they made as good provision for their names, as they have done for their Reliques, they had not so grosly erred in the art of perpetuation. But to subsist in bones, and be but Pyramidally extant, is a fallacy in duration. Vain ashes, which in the oblivion of names, persons, times, and sexes, have found unto themselves, a fruitless continuation, and only arise unto late posterity, as Emblemes of mortall vanities; Antidotes against pride, vain-glory, and madding vices.'

The pagans had one advantage over us: 'Pagan vain-glories which thought the world might last for ever, had encouragement for ambition; and, finding no Atropos unto the immortality of their Names, were never dampt with the necessity of oblivion.' But 'in this setting part of time' it is different: ' 'Tis too late to be ambitious. The great mutations of the world are acted, or time may be too short for our designes. To extend our memories by Monuments, whose death we daily pray for, and whose duration we cannot hope, without injury to our expectations, in the advent of the last day, were a contradiction to our beliefs.' The time of this world is running out. 'There is no antidote against the Opium of time, which temporally considereth all things'; and now gives them short measure.

To be remembered only as a name is a frigid ambition. 'To be namelesse in worthy deeds exceeds an infamous history.' 'But the iniquity of oblivion blindely scattereth her poppy, and deals with the memory of men without distinction to merit of perpetuity.' Our good names are only preserved in the 'everlasting Register'. Oblivion is not to be bribed: 'The greater part must be content to be as though they had not been, to be found in the Register of God, not in the record of man.' Only 'twenty-seven Names make up the first story before the flood'.

'Darknesse and light divide the course of time, and oblivion shares with memory, a great part even of our living beings.' Oblivion 'is a mercifull provision in nature, whereby we digest the mixture of our few and evil dayes'. But mankind has sought to escape oblivion in various ways. 'A great part of Antiquity con-tented their hopes of subsistency with a transmigration of their souls.' 'Others, rather then be lost in the uncomfortable night of nothing, were content to recede into the common being, and make one particle of the public soul of all things.' 'Aegyptian ingenuity was more unsatisfied, contriving their bodies in sweet consistencies, to attend the return of their souls.'

But 'in vain do individuals hope for Immortality, or any patent from oblivion, in preservations below the Moon'. Even those who have sought to perpetuate their names in the heavens have been deceived; for the heavens have proved to be 'like the Earth: Durable in their main bodies, alterable in their parts'. 'There is nothing strictly immortall, but immortality.' This paradox rebukes the vanity of human wishes: 'But the sufficiency of Christian Immortality frustrates all earthly glory, and the quality of either state after death makes a folly of posthumous memory.'

The next sentence does not betray Browne's scepticism but his knowledge of St Paul on the resurrection (1 Cor. xv). 'God who can only destroy our souls, and hath assured our resurrection, either of our bodies or names hath directly promised no duration.' St Paul said: 'It is sown a natural body; it is raised a spiritual body . . . For this corruptible must put on incorruption, and this mortal must put on immortality.' The natural body must give way to the spiritual, as Browne has already intimated about the resurrection of our relics. Now he adds a sentence worthy of man's vanity: 'But man is a Noble Animal, splendid in ashes, and pompous in the grave, solemnizing Nativities and Deaths with equal lustre, nor omitting Ceremonies of bravery in the infamy of his nature.'

From his infamy this noble animal rises to the most vain-glorious geometry: 'Pyramids, Arches, Obelisks, were but the irregularities of vain-glory, and wilde enormities of ancient mag-nanimity. But the most magnanimous resolution rests in the

Christian Religion, which trampleth upon pride, and sits on the neck of ambition, humbly pursuing that infallible perpetuity, unto which all others must diminish their diameters, and be poorly seen in Angles of contingency.' These words spell out the moral resolution of the problems of *Urn Burial*.

But the final triumph of the humble over the proud is celebrated in the last paragraph: 'To subsist in lasting Monuments, to live in their productions, to exist in their names and praedicament of Chymera's, was large satisfaction unto old expectations, and made one part of their Elyziums. But all this is nothing in the Metaphysicks of true belief. To live indeed is to be again our-selves, which being not only an hope but an evidence in noble beleevers; 'Tis all one to lye in St Innocents Churchyard, as in the Sands of Aegypt: Ready to be any thing, in the extasie of being ever, and as content with six foot as the Moles of Adrianus.' Thus it is a matter of indifference to lie either where our relics may be preserved or where we may be 'pompous in the grave', if we may 'be again ourselves' as described by St Paul.

II

Urn Burial does not live by style alone, but rather by its resonance in thought and feeling, however vaguely sensed. And its elo-quence develops as its thought and feeling deepen. At the end of Chapter III it turns to the issues of death in a future or resurrection: 'Severe contemplators observing these lasting reliques, may think them good monuments of persons past, little advantage to future beings.' Chapter IV divides the question: 'Nor were only many customes questionable in order to their Obsequies, but also sundry practises, fictions, and conceptions, discordant or obscure, of their state and future beings.' His feeling and eloquence mount as he considers man's attitude towards death, especially when it displays courage: 'Among all the set, Epicurus is most considerable, whom men make honest without an Elyzium, who contemned life with-out encouragement of immortality, and making nothing after death, yet made nothing of the King of terrours.'

Thus he confronted the basic emotion of human life: 'It is the heaviest stone that melancholy can throw at a man, to tell him he is at the end of his nature; or that there is no further state to come, unto which this seems progressionall, and otherwise made in vaine.' This is to make a vanity of life itself, and the triumph of man when he sees nothing after death is to make nothing of death. As rhetoric this stone reverberates four times in his last sentence: the end, no state to come, seems progressional, made in vain. Other creatures were 'framed below the circumference of these hopes'.

Of course the grand climax of Browne's style is Chapter V. His preface to *Pseudodoxia Epidemica* suggests one explanation of its character: 'Although I confess the quality of the subject will sometime carry us into expressions beyond mere English appre- hensions. And, indeed, if elegancy still proceedeth, and English pens maintain that stream we have of late observed to flow from many, we shall, within few years, be fain to learn Latin to under- stand English.' Thus the requirements of the subject could add a philosophical dimension to the language while Latin elegancy added a rhetorical dimension.

Another explanation of its style should be recalled. In *Religio Medici* he was content in matters of faith 'to understand a mystery without a rigid definition, in an easie and Platonick description'. Where he could not satisfy his reason, he loved to humour his fancy, and then preferred a metaphorical description to a meta- physical definition. He believed with Bacon that reason and faith made different demands upon style. Hence we should not be surprised that *Urn Burial* rises in emotional power as it nears the realm of its triumph—that is, the realm of belief. Moreover, one of the mysteries in which Browne loved to lose himself was the Resurrection.

In this last chapter he combined Latin elegancy and meta- phorical description. In the penultimate paragraph, for example, he uses five Latin abstractions and three metaphorical extensions to adumbrate the mystical experience: 'And if any have been so happy as truly to understand Christian annihilation, extasis, exolution, liquefaction, transformation, the kisse of the Spouse, gustation of God, and ingression into the divine shadow, they have already had an handsome anticipation of heaven.' In Chap- ter IV when Browne interprets the significance of 'old Rites' he falls into a stylistic formula, 'That they washed their bones. . . . That they . . . etc.', which nevertheless emphasizes the esoteric nature of their beliefs. In Chapter V as he prepares to treat the ultimate hypothesis of life after death, he begins with a series of hypotheses, 'If they . . . If they . . . If we . . . etc.', which leads to a resolution beyond reason or Antiquarism. Again the verbal parallelism magnifies the abstruseness of the problem.

But in this chapter the curt, elliptical movement of a Senecan style, appropriate to a compendium, finally disappears into the measured tread of a funeral march. As Browne expounds the Christian answer to death we may observe, in his search for expressiveness, his use of the striking metaphor and the striking abstraction, often together; or startling oppositions, either as antithesis or as seeming contradiction. In the rhetorical dimension his Latin abstractions also bring dignity to his style and make it splendid by numbers.

The opposition of life and death is presented in the opposition of concrete and abstract terms: 'If the nearnesse of our last necessity, brought a nearer conformity into it, there were a happinesse in hoary hairs, and no calamity in half senses.' In the paradox of feeling, nearness is not nearer. Whether the members of this period are numbered in syllables or accents, their relative equality measures the rhythm of the period. And to unite concrete and abstract terms offers no solution: 'But to subsist in bones, and be but Pyramidally extant, is a fallacy in duration.' Here there is more equality of stress than of syllables, but the tempo increases in the second member and decreases in the third. Bones become merely a *memento mori* lost 'in the oblivion of names'. All identity is lost in ashes. Thus the concrete may become too general to preserve the individual.

Yet Browne can reduce abstract oblivion to the concreteness of a choking gas: 'Pagan vain-glories . . . were never dampt with the necessity of oblivion.' And he can deflate these vainglories by an implied antithesis: 'But man is a Noble Animal, splendid in ashes, and pompous in the grave', rather than humble in Biblical 'sackcloth and ashes'. Here man's vainglory is also measured by balanced phrases. Browne describes not merely the frustration of death but the vanity of human wishes, and the vanity is magnified by his Latin diction. The Latin abstractions introduce into *Urn Burial* both a liturgical pomp and a majestic roll.

But true duration, being an abstraction, can be suggested only by a metaphorical reduction of the memorial pyramid: we 'being necessitated to eye the remaining particle of futurity, are naturally constituted unto thoughts of the next world, and cannot excusably decline the consideration of that duration, which maketh Pyra/ mids pillars of snow, and all that's past a moment'. Here the 'particle of futurity' both seizes and minimizes time, but time dwindles away in the last two members both in connotation and in rhythm.

The union and opposition of contraries can take a sententious form: 'To be namelesse in worthy deeds exceeds an infamous history.' Here 'nameless' is opposed to 'history' and 'worthy' to 'infamous', but the alternate terms are united to form a larger opposition which subordinates memory to virtue. And oblivion commonly separates them: 'But the iniquity of oblivion blindely scattereth her poppy, and deals with the memory of men without distinction to merit of perpetuity.' Here 'iniquity' is to 'blindely' as 'oblivion' is to 'poppy', and this union serves to separate 'memory' and 'merit'. But the rhythmic flow is impeded by the clash of alliterative syllables in 'oblivion blindely'. When he translates oblivion into 'the uncomfortable night of nothing' he concentrates spiritual and physical privation into a masterly epi/ thet. The contemporary wit of contradiction and riddle stands Browne in good stead as he explores the mystery of life and death.

For the last judgment this wit multiplies its paradoxes and even inverts his opening opposition between lying high and low in the earth: 'When many that feared to dye, shall groane that they can dye but once, the dismall state is the second and living death, when life puts despair on the damned; when men shall wish the cover/ ings of Mountaines, not of Monuments, and annihilations shall be courted.' Now waves of rhythm are supported by internal alliteration. Heresy finds no place here; nor does Browne have a 'party/colour'd Mind' in *Urn Burial*. But this opposition of moun/ tains and monuments recalls and inverts the opening sentiments of his essay.

The proud monuments of man to which the bones were op/ posed in the opening paragraphs of this chapter now are altered by moral perspective: 'Pyramids, Arches, Obelisks, were but the irregularities of vain/glory, and wilde enormities of ancient mag/ nanimity.' The new vision corrects the geometry of pride: 'But the most magnanimous resolution rests in the Christian Religion, which trampleth upon pride, and sits on the neck of ambition, humbly pursuing that infallible perpetuity, unto which all others must diminish their diameters, and be poorly seen in Angles of contingency.' In 'Angles of contingency' we hear a characteristic Browne cadence, which anticipates the final cadence of this chapter.

To Christian perpetuity all rivals must ultimately diminish their geometry. This is why the final paragraph summarizes the Christian answer to man's attempts to subsist after death by ending with the startling oppositions of humility: 'Ready to be any thing, in the extasie of being ever, and as content with six foot as the Moles of Adrianus.' Thus the poorest angle of contingency may produce the longest shadow. But the cadence of 'Moles of Adrianus' can be said, in Browne's words, to 'take off brutall terminations' like 'six foot'.

12

SENECAN STYLE IN THE
SEVENTEENTH CENTURY

As the reign of Elizabeth drew to a close, English prose style yielded to the pressure of a new movement. The Ciceronian movement had no sooner reached its climax in the formal periods of Hooker than the AntiCiceronian movement found a leader in Bacon, whose terse manner of expression became the hallmark of style among the later essay and character writers. In 1610 Bacon wrote to Tobie Matthew: 'They tell me my Latin is turn'd Silver, and become current.' By this time his English had, in fact, taken on a SilverLatin style and become current among the Senecan essayists. Even Polonius was a Senecan in theory when he observed that 'brevity is the soul of wit', and in practice when he recognized Hamlet's 'points' by remarking, 'How pregnant sometimes his replies are!' But since this is reading into Bacon and Shakespeare more than either intended, we may well ask to what extent the English seventeenth century was critically aware of the Senecan style.[1] To gather evidence of such awareness, either in the theory or in the criticism of rhetoric, will be the object of this essay.

Francis Thompson, who was sensitive to Renaissance style, recognized SilverLatin imitation in Browne: 'Browne was more idiomatic in structure than the Ciceronian Hooker. But the admirable knitting of his sentences was not due merely to a better study of English idiom. He was steeped in classic models more compact and pregnant than Cicero. Like his French contem

---

[1] M. W. Croll's excellent studies of 'Attic' or Senecan prose afford but a partial answer to this question; see *Studies in Philology*, vol. xviii; *Schelling Anniversary Papers*, 1923; *PMLA*, vol. xxxix; and *Studies in English Philology*, 1929. For the claim of science in the formation of seventeenthcentury prose see the articles by R. F. Jones, *The Seventeenth Century*, 1951.

poraries, he was influenced by the great Latin rhetoricians, Lucan, Ovid, and Seneca; whose rivalry it was to put an idea into the fewest possible words.'[1]

Elsewhere I have dealt with other aspects of the Jacobean cultiva-tion of Silver-Latin style: on the one hand, with the antithetic wit that was associated with the terse Senecan style;[2] on the other, with the development of a cult of obscurity which produced 'strong lines' after the example of Persius and Tacitus.[3] When brevity was the soul of wit, the points of wit often became so pregnant that 'significant darkness' or 'strong lines' were the result. In short, in Jacobean times the cult of brevity in Seneca was not unnaturally associated with the cult of obscurity in Tacitus. Enigmatic or cryp-tic expression, which both Chapman and Bacon allow, reached its extreme development in the poetry of this time under the form known as 'strong lines'.

At the close of the seventeenth century Shaftesbury felt that the Senecan style still prevailed, at least so far as the essayists were con-cerned. The prevailing style, in Shaftesbury's view, derived from the *Epistles* of Seneca: 'He falls into the random way of miscel-laneous writing, says everywhere great and noble things, in and out of the way, accidentally as words lead him (for with these he plays perpetually), with infinite wit, but with little or no coherence, without a shape or body to his work, without a real beginning, a middle, or an end.'[4]

The great and noble things, word-play, and wit concern Shaftes-bury less than Seneca's violation of unity and coherence. He

[1] *Works* (London, 1913), iii, 166–7. On the significance of Jacobean translation from Silver Latin see H. B. Lathrop, *Translations from the Classics into English from Caxton to Chapman, 1477–1620* (Madison, 1933), chap. IV, especially pp. 235, 244, 252, 304.

[2] See 'The Rhetorical Pattern of Neo-Classical Wit', *Seventeenth Century Contexts*.

[3] See 'Strong Lines', ibid.

Two versions of the same Horatian warning describe the nature and the name of these lines. First in Jonson's translation of Horace's *Art of Poetry*:

> *Myself for shortness labour, and I grow*
> *Obscure. This, striving to run smooth, and flow,*
> *Hath neither soul nor sinews.*

Second in Soame's translation of Boileau's *Art of Poetry*:

> *A verse was weak, you turn it much too strong,*
> *And grow obscure for fear you should be long.*

[4] *Characteristics*, ed. J. M. Robertson (London, 1900), ii, 170.

remarks that whole letters or pages may be divided or combined at pleasure; 'every period, every sentence almost, is independent, and may be taken asunder, transposed, postponed, anticipated, or set in any new order, as you fancy'. After this analysis of Seneca, Shaftesbury turns to his own time: 'This is the manner of writing so much admired and imitated in our age, that we have scarce the idea of any other model. We know little, indeed, of the difference between one model or character of writing and another. All runs to the same tune, and beats exactly one and the same measure. Nothing, one would think, could be more tedious than this uniform pace. The common amble or *canterbury* is not, I am persuaded, more tiresome to a good rider than this see-saw of essay writers is to an able reader.'[1]

Thus Shaftesbury disparages the style which not only clothed the work of the aphoristic essayists and character-writers, but corresponded to the Jacobean taste for mingled wit and *gravitas*. He is not struck by the aspect of this style which Professor Croll has analysed acutely: 'A prose-style that should adequately express this age must contrive, therefore, to mingle elements that in any other period would appear oddly contrasted. It must be at once ingenious and lofty, intense yet also profound, acute, realistic, revealing, but at the same time somewhat grave and mysterious.'[2]

Professor Croll, however, holds that Bacon naturalized such a style in English by imitating Tacitus rather than Seneca. But since Shaftesbury is not unaware that Seneca combined wit and gravity, we may leave the problem of discriminating between Senecan and Tacitean imitation to the testimony of the time.

Three tendencies of Anti-Ciceronian style have been associated by Professor Croll with three important names: the *curt* with Lipsius, the *loose* with Montaigne, and the *obscure* with Bacon. The curt and the loose tendencies, as Professor Croll observes, were both Senecan in pattern; but the curt and the obscure tendencies, which he is anxious to discriminate, were commonly confused in seventeenth-century Senecanism. And this is not unnatural, since the peculiar quality of Tacitus is brevity pushed to the verge of obscurity; moreover, his style offers more likeness than difference when compared with 'Seneca's own style—discon-

---

[1] Ibid., p. 171. This 'see-saw' suggests the antithetic wit of the Senecan essayists.
[2] 'Attic Prose: Lipsius, Montaigne, Bacon', *Schelling Anniversary Papers* (New York, 1923), p. 142.

nected, pointed, antithetic, metaphorical and piquant'.[1] Both differed from Cicero's polished and flowing amplitude chiefly in the abrupt terseness and jerky movement of their sentences. For English criticism, therefore, it will be erring on the right side to regard Senecan style in its most obvious character—as the cultiva- tion of sententious brevity and all the qualities that go with rhetorical *sententiae*. In general, the curt Senecan style is marked by a cultivation of brevity, gravity, and point in the essay manner; its rhythm is jerky and abrupt; in particular, the Tacitean variety is an extreme development of this style. For both Seneca and Tacitus brevity meant Sallust, and in the seventeenth century all three were distinguished for similar qualities. To the curt Senecan style our investigation will be restricted, since the English writers of this period were much less conscious of the loose Senecan style, though here and there that also may be noticed.

It is necessary to remark, however, that the curt style was gener- ally supplemented or relieved by the loose style. The two were commonly intermingled in the expression of Bacon or Browne. Both styles have been carefully analysed by Professor Croll in 'The Baroque Style in Prose', where he has summarized them as 'the concise, serried, abrupt *stile coupé*, and the informal, meditative, and "natural" loose style': 'It is necessary to repeat—once more— that in the best writers these two styles do not appear separately in passages of any length, and that in most of them they intermingle in relations far too complex for description. They represent two sides of the seventeenth-century mind: its sententiousness, its pene- trating wit, its Stoic intensity, on the one hand, and its dislike of formalism, its roving and self-exploring curiosity, in brief, its skeptical tendency, on the other. And these two habits of mind are generally not separated one from the other; nor are they even always exactly distinguishable.'[2]

[1] J. W. Duff, *A Literary History of Rome in the Silver Age* (London, 1927), p. 198; cf. pp. 228–9 and 593 ff. See Montaigne's account of the 'sharpe and witty fashion [d'une façon poinctue et subtile]' of Tacitus: 'He draweth somewhat neare to *Senecas* writing. I deeme *Tacitus*, more sinnowy, *Seneca* more sharpe' (*Essayes* (Everyman ed.), iii, 180). 'Il ne retire pas mal à l'escrire de Seneque: il me semble plus charnu; Seneque plus aigu.'
[2] *Studies in English Philology*, ed. Malone and Ruud (Minneapolis, 1929), pp. 452– 453. Croll describes four marks of the curt style: 'first, studied brevity of members; second, the hovering, imaginative order; third, asymmetry; and fourth, the omission of the ordinary syntactic ligatures' (ibid., p. 435); the loose style is differentiated by

The loose style was the more natural, and the curt style the more artful, for it did have to make its 'points' show. While the loose period may suggest the Ciceronian, it avoids or breaks the *con-cinnitas* or symmetry of structure of Cicero; while it may adumbrate a Latin mould, it follows a more organic order of thought. The curt style pre-empts attention before the Restoration, and the loose style predominates after, but both forms prepare the way for modern English prose. The separation or opposition of the curt style and the loose style distinguishes the Restoration from the first half of the century.

I

The rise of the Anti-Ciceronian cult which marks the seventeenth century has been traced by Professor Croll to Muretus,[1] and its dissemination to Lipsius, Montaigne, and Bacon. What these men discovered in Seneca and Tacitus, or disliked in Cicero, characterized the new taste in style—a taste that ran to the essay style rather than to the oratorical. In 1580 Muretus had defended Tacitus by going so far as to praise his obscurity and asperity of style. The passage which Professor Croll has quoted from this excellent appraisal of Tacitus found its way into late seventeenth-century English from the work of La Mothe Le Vayer: 'How-soever it be, it is no wonder if *Tacitus* (having imitated *Thucydides*, and both followed *Demosthenes*) retained something of that rough-ness and austerity, which is observed in the writings of those Two *Graecians*; and which all the Ancients accounted as a virtue, so far is it from deserving to be imputed as a fault, to him that should propose them to himself for imitation. And as some Wines are recommended to our palates by a little bitterness that is in them; and as many persons find that a dusky and obscure light in Churches is most sutable to their exercise of devotion: so others conceive the obscurity of an Author, mixed with a little roughness of Stile, is rather to be esteemed than otherwise; because it disposes the mind to attention, and elevates and transports it to notions, which it would not arrive at in a more easy composition.'[2] Muretus,

its relaxed syntactic ligatures, its 'linked' or 'trailing' period, and its 'natural' order (ibid., pp. 440–53).

[1] 'Muret and the History of "Attic" Prose', *PMLA*, xxxix (1924), 254–309.
[2] *Notitia Historicorum Selectorum*, translated by W.D. (William Davenant), Oxford, 1678, pp. 217–18. Cf. Croll, *PMLA*, xxxix, 300.

as Professor Croll remarks, 'stirs the ground about the roots of seventeenth-century style'; for the Jacobean cult of obscurity shares this doctrine with him.

Lipsius first employed the Anti-Ciceronian style in his *Quaestiones Epistolicae*, which appeared just before his edition of Tacitus. The character of his new style is best described by Lipsius himself in a letter to a friend: 'I am afraid of what you will think of this work [the *Quaestiones*]. For this is a different kind of writing from my earlier style, without showiness, without luxuriance, without the Tullian concinnities; condensed everywhere, and I know not whether of too studied a brevity. But this is what captivates me now. They celebrate Timanthes the painter because there was always something more to be understood in his works than was actually painted. I should like this in my style.'[1]

Professor Croll remarks that both the critical terms and the style of this passage come from Seneca, but it would be hard to show that the stylistic direction differs from that which Muretus discovered in Tacitus. Although Lipsius, as a Stoic, was eventually associated with the point and brevity of Seneca, he began by admiring the dark implications and studied ellipses of Tacitus. There is one kind of brevity which Seneca disparaged and which was more often associated with Tacitus, and that is obscurity, *obscura brevitas*. Seneca approved '*abruptae sententiae et suspiciosae*', or (in Lodge's words) 'abrupt Sentences and suspicious, in which more is to be understood than heard', so long as they were not carried to the point of obscurity. Although Seneca did not allow *copia* or superfluity, he did allow fluency, because it was unlaboured and because it revealed personality.[2] In fact, to him *fundere* meant to avoid affected and laboured composition, and to achieve the naturalness which he desired, but which was not without artifice.[3] It was this side of Seneca that encouraged the loose style at the same time that his cultivation of *sententiae* stimulated the curt style.

The difficulty of discriminating between Senecan and Tacitean imitation may be suggested by a contemporary criticism of the neostoic Lipsius. In Boccalini's *Ragguagli di Parnasso*, first translated

[1] Quoted by Croll, *Schelling Anniversary Papers*, p. 122.
[2] See *Epistles* 114, 59, 100. Cf. F. I. Merchant, 'Seneca the Philosopher and his Theory of Style', *American Journal of Philology*, xxvi (1905), 57 ff.
[3] See *Epistles* 75 and 115.

into English in 1626, Lipsius is brought before Apollo for his idolatry of Tacitus, and Muretus is one of those who jealously indict him as follows: 'Hee now loved to discourse with no other learned man: no conversation did more agrade him: he com/ mended no other *Historian*: and all with such partiality of inward affection, namely, for the elegancie of his speech, adorned more with choise conceits, than with words; for the succinctnesse of his close, nervous, and grave sententious Oratorie, cleare onely to those of best understanding, with the envy and hatred of other vertuous men of this dominion, dependents of *Cicero*, and of the mighty *Caesarean faction*, who approve it not. And did with such diligence labour to imitate him, that not onely with hatefull antonomasia, hee dared to call him his Auctor, but utterly scorn/ ing all other mens detections, he affected no other ambition, than to appeare unto the world a new *Tacitus*.'[1]

However, Lipsius 'is in the end by his *Maiestie* [Apollo], not only absolved, but highly commended and admired'. In this trial Lipsius, the great Neo/Stoic, is specifically a Tacitean, but gener/ ally an Anti/Ciceronian. If we were to distinguish Lipsius the Tacitean from Lipsius the Senecan, we should have to distinguish where the seventeenth century often confused; furthermore, as a Tacitean he could find merit in obscurity, as a Senecan he might condone word/play. Lipsius was the standard/bearer of Senecan style, but if his Anti/Ciceronian taste culminated in an edition of Seneca (1605) it had begun with an edition of Tacitus (1574).

In 1591 the first English translation of Tacitus, the work of Sir Henry Savile, was recommended to the reader by Anthony Bacon in these words: 'For Tacitus I may say without partiality, that hee hath writen the most matter with best conceyt in fewest wordes of anie Historiographer ancient or moderne. But he is harde. *Difficilia quae pulchra*: the second reading over will please thee more then the first, and the third then the second.'

In the second and enlarged edition of 1598 Richard Grenewey declared in his dedication that there is in Tacitus 'no woord not loaden with matter, and as himselfe speaketh of Galba, he useth

---

[1] *The New/found Politicke*, translated by Florio, W. Vaughan, and Another (London, 1626), p. 15 (Part I, *Rag.* 86). J. G. Robertson (*The Genesis of Romantic Theory*, p. 246) seems to think the 1656 translation by Henry, Earl of Monmouth, the first in English; but Monmouth claims only to have made the first complete English version.

Imperatoria brevitate: which although it breed difficultie, yet carrieth great gravitie'. Thus the words of Muretus came to partial fulfil-ment in recommendations to the readers of Tacitus in English, who received the sixth edition of this work in 1640.

When Thomas Lodge revised his translation of Seneca in 1620, he apologized to the reader for his own shortcomings: 'My businesse being great, and my distractions many; the Authour being seriously succinct, and full of *Laconisme*; no wonder if in somthings my omissions may seeme such, as some whose iudge-ment is mounted aboue the Epicycle of Mercurie, will find matter enough to carpe at, though not to condemne.'[1]

For Lodge Seneca was, above all, 'laconic'; but W.R., in his eulogy of Lodge, found other qualities to commend: 'You are his profitable Tutor, and haue instructed him to walke and talke in perfect English. If his matter held not still the Romane Majestie, I should mistake him one of Ours; he deliuers his mind so sig-nificantly and fitly. Surely, had hee chosen any other Tongue to write in, my affection thinkes, it had beene English; And in English, as you haue taught him in your Translation; you ex-presse him so liuely, being still the same Man in other garments . . . retaining still the natiue grauitie of his countenance. . . .'[2]

Although the praise goes to Lodge, it is for catching the quali-ties of Seneca, to whom Lodge becomes the '*Senec-Sybill* (or rather *Mercurie*) of his oraculous Discourses'. And thus Seneca emerges with qualities which are difficult to distinguish from those of Tacitus, for he too is succinct, majestic, grave, and oraculous; moreover, Lodge's English has taught Seneca a second native language, or so it seems to W.R. in Jacobean days. Whatever the origin, whether in the pregnant brevity of Seneca or in the obscure brevity of Tacitus, the virtue of difficulty suggested gravity of style to Anti-Ciceronian ears; weight rather than *copia* now trans-lated the Roman majesty.

While there is evidence for saying that gravity and obscurity were more commonly associated with Tacitus, and point and ingenuity with Seneca, these qualities are not very certain differen-tiae for writers who were celebrated for their succinctness. It is well to remember such differentiae, but it is more historical to accept the general identity of the two styles as Anti-Ciceronian or fundamen-tally Senecan in character. In Hakewill's *Apologie or Declaration*

---

[1] *Workes of Seneca* (London, 1620), sig. blr.   [2] Ibid., sigs. b2r–b2v.

of the Power and Providence of God, first published in 1627, we find important confirmation of such a view: 'Sr *Henry Savill* sharply censures [Tacitus] for his style, taking occasion from those words in the life of *Agricola, bonum virum facile crederes magnum libenter: at te* (saith he) *Corneli Tacite bonum historicum facile credimus, bonum oratorem crederemus libenter,* were it not for this & some other sayings of the like making: *Fuit illi viro,* saith Tacitus, (judging of *Seneca* as we may of him) *ingenium amaenum, & temporibus illius auribus accommodatum*: How that age was eared long or round I cannot define, but sure I am it yeelded a kinde of sophisticate eloquence and riming harmony of words; where-under was *small matter* in sense, when there seemed to be most in appearance, and divers instances he brings out of *Tacitus.* . . .'[1]

These very interesting remarks, involving the first English trans-lator of Tacitus, are essentially Bacon's indictment of the Senecan fashion, which we shall consider in due course. But this turning of the tables upon Tacitus, to which Hakewill subscribes, em-phasizes the resemblance (even in vices) between Seneca and Tacitus as they sounded to English ears.

II

Seneca, when he spoke of style, always preferred things to words—a preference which the seventeenth century remembered to his credit. And Bacon was the first to sound the seventeenth-century preference for things rather than words. That is the burden of his attack on Ciceronian style in 1605, when he condemns the Ciceronians for hunting 'more after the choiceness of the phrase, and the round and clean composition of the sentence, and the sweet falling of the clauses . . . than after the weight of matter'.[2] This Renaissance delight in style—'the whole inclination and bent of those times was rather towards copie than weight'—was fur-thered by hatred of the schoolmen, 'whose writings were alto-gether in a differing style and form'. Bacon admits the need to clothe philosophy in eloquence for civil occasions, but believes that 'to the severe inquisition of truth, and the deep progress into philosophy' such a dress offers some hindrance, for it gives a

[1] London, 1635, p. 285.
[2] *Philosophical Works,* ed. J. M. Robertson (London, 1905), p. 54.

premature satisfaction to the mind and quenches the desire of further search.[1]

The question of 'vain words' leads Bacon to 'vain matter', or the second distemper of learning, under which he attacks the schoolmen for crumbling knowledge into subtle distinctions and 'vermiculate questions'. Their unprofitable subtlety expressed itself in two ways: in fruitless matter and in a fruitless method of hand-ling knowledge, splitting the 'cummin seed'; 'whereas indeed the strength of all sciences is, as the strength of the old man's faggot, in the bond. For the harmony of a science, supporting each part the other, is and ought to be the true and brief confutation and suppression of all the smaller sort of objections; but on the other side, if you take out every axiom, as the sticks of the faggot, one by one, you may quarrel with them and bend them and break them at your pleasure: so that as was said of Seneca, *Verborum minutiis rerum frangit pondera* [that he broke up the weight and mass of the matter by verbal points and niceties]; so a man may truly say of the schoolmen, *Quaestionum minutiis scientiarum frangunt soliditatem* [they broke up the solidity and coherency of the sciences by the minuteness and nicety of their questions].'[2] And thus Quintilian's criticism of Seneca, slightly misquoted, is turned by Bacon into a criticism of the schoolmen. It might be concluded that a Senecan style would make a fitting dress for a scholastic habit of mind, and we shall have occasion to recall the suggestion. But for the present this must remain a criticism of the schoolmen rather than of Seneca.

In this connection we may wonder a little at what Bacon has to say of aphorisms, especially when we remember that he certainly knew Seneca as a master of *sententiae*, at which Quintilian had directed his criticism. Bacon's theory of the communication of knowledge is vital to his criticism of style, and revolves about the question of methods. The most real diversity of method concerns method as related to the use of knowledge and method as related to the progress of knowledge, or the delivery of knowledge as it may be best believed (the Magistral way), and as it may be best examined (the way of Probation).[3] Since knowledge is now

---

[1] Ibid., p. 55.

[2] Ibid., pp. 55–56. In the essay 'Of Seeming Wise' Bacon attributes this quotation to A. Gellius and applies it to those who 'are never without a difference, and com-monly by amusing men with a subtilty blanch the matter'.   [3] Ibid., p. 124.

delivered as it may be best believed, not as it may be best examined, 'there is a kind of contract of error between the deliverer and the receiver', because 'in this same anticipated and prevented know-ledge, no man knoweth how he came to the knowledge which he hath obtained'. This is the way of rhetoric and the oratorical style; the way of the essay style is quite different, for 'knowledge that is delivered as a thread to be spun on, ought to be delivered and intimated, if it were possible, *in the same method wherein it was in-vented*; and so is it possible of knowledge induced'. Here we have the philosophy which underlies the organic method of the 'loose' period found in the way of Probation; in the Magistral way, which merely announces the results of inquiry, one cannot see the thought grow.

This brings us to another diversity of great consequence—'the delivery of knowledge in Aphorisms, or in Methods'. Here Bacon begins by condemning the practice of spinning a few axioms or observations into a solemn and formal art; 'but the writing in Aphorisms hath many excellent virtues, whereto the writing in Method doth not approach. For first, it trieth the writer, whether he be superficial or solid: for Aphorisms, except they should be ridiculous, cannot be made but of the pith and heart of sciences; for discourse of illustration is cut off; recitals of examples are cut off; discourse of connection and order is cut off; descriptions of practice are cut off; so there remaineth nothing to fill the Aphorisms but some good quantity of observation: and therefore no man can suffice, nor in reason will attempt, to write aphorisms, but he that is sound and grounded. But in Methods,

> *Tantum series juncturaque pollet,*
> *Tantum de medio sumptis accedit honoris*

[the arrangement and connexion and joining of the parts has so much effect], as a man shall make a great shew of an art, which if it were disjointed would come to little. Secondly, Methods are more fit to win consent or belief, but less fit to point to action; for they carry a kind of demonstration in orb or circle, one part illuminating another, and therefore satisfy; but particulars, being dispersed, do best agree with dispersed directions. And lastly, Aphorisms, representing a knowledge broken, do invite men to enquire farther; whereas Methods, carrying the shew of a total, do secure men, as if they were at furthest.'[1]

[1] Ibid., p. 125.

If we recall the passage on the schoolmen, we must conclude that the vice of the schoolmen becomes a virtue in the realm of style; that aphorisms, which must be filled with 'some good quan⁄ tity of observation', belong to the method of inducing knowledge; and that a Senecan style represents a knowledge broken, and there⁄ fore avoids the 'contract of error between the deliverer and the receiver'. Here methods present knowledge as it may be best be⁄ lieved, and aphorisms as it may be best examined, with a view to further inquiry. They are different styles for different purposes, and so Bacon used them. But the method of probation is not the same as Methods of persuasion; rather, it belongs, with Aphorisms, to induction and the Senecan style.

Bacon wrote his severest philosophical work, the *Novum Organum,* in Aphorisms; but he clothed his popular *Advancement of Learning* in the rhetoric of persuasion or Methods. And yet it would be a mistake to say that 'discourse of illustration', 'discourse of connection and order', and 'descriptions of practice' are always cut off in the former and never in the latter. The habit of aphorism and the urge to persuade were too strong in Bacon to permit single⁄minded devotion to one manner of expression. The chief exception to this judgment is, of course, his early essays. They provide the best illustration of the aphorism in which his thought seems commonly to have been formulated. His change of style in the *Essays* reflects not so much a growing disapproval of Senecan style as a change from aphorisms to methods for a particular pur⁄ pose. In this instance the change seems to have derived from his meditation on the function of rhetoric in connection with the Stoic method in moral counsel. In the *Advancement of Learning* Bacon defends rhetoric by saying that virtue must be shown 'to the Imagination in lively representation, for to shew her to Reason only in subtilty of argument, was a thing ever derided in Chrysip⁄ pus and many of the Stoics; who thought to thrust virtue upon men by sharp disputations and conclusions, which have no sympathy with the will of man'.[1] But in the *De Augmentis Scien⁄ tiarum* he declares more specifically that virtue must be shown 'to the imagination in as lively representation as possible, by ornament of words. For the method of the Stoics, who thought to thrust virtue upon men by concise and sharp maxims and conclusions,

[1] Ibid., p. 128.

which have little sympathy with the imagination and will of man,
has been justly ridiculed by Cicero.'[1]

In 1623, then, Bacon condemns the method of the Stoics in
moral counsel expressly because aphorisms have little imaginative
appeal; then, having detected another vanity in the Senecan style,
he agrees with Cicero in ridiculing the Stoic method in moral
essays. That this objection was not so sharply defined for Bacon in
1605 or even in 1612 seems the plain inference from the change in
his essay style, since that change really does not appear until the
1625 edition. The difference between the parallel essays of 1597
and 1612 is chiefly one of slight revision or addition; it is not so
striking as the difference between the parallel essays of 1612 and
1625, for the latter can truly be said to be revised and even re-
written from the point of view of Methods.[2] Only in 1625 does
the aphoristic character of the *Essays* appear seriously modified, if
not forsaken. Aphorisms, Bacon seems to have concluded, are
appropriate to philosophy or science because they 'invite men to
enquire farther'; they are permissible to 'dispersed meditations' (his
early essays) because they give 'dispersed directions'; but Methods
are more appropriate to moral essays because 'methods are more
fit to win consent or belief'.

If the *Advancement of Learning* contained the seed of disapproval
of Senecan style, the *De Augmentis Scientiarum* brought the full-
grown plant. After his condemnation of the Ciceronian style,
Bacon now adds this criticism: 'Litle better is that kind of stile
(yet neither is that altogether exempt from vanity) which neer
about the same time succeeded this *Copy* and *superfluity of speech*.
The labour here is altogether, *That words may be aculeate, sentences
concise, and the whole contexture of the speech and discourse, rather rounding
into it selfe, than spread and dilated*: So that it comes to passe by this
Artifice, that every passage seemes more witty and waighty than
indeed it is. Such a stile as this we finde more excessively in
Seneca; more moderately in *Tacitus* and *Plinius Secundus*; and of
late it hath bin very pleasing unto the eares of our time. And this
kind of expression hath found such acceptance with meaner

[1] Ibid., p. 536.
[2] See E. Arber's *Harmony of the Essays* (London, 1871) for parallel versions. Bacon's
attitude towards rhetoric and Stoic method should be added to the explanation of
his change of style in R. S. Crane's article on the *Essays, Schelling Anniversary Papers*
(New York, 1923), pp. 98 ff.

capacities, as to be a dignity and ornament to Learning; never-thelesse, by the more exact judgements, it hath bin deservedly dispised, and may be set down *as a distemper of Learning*, seeing it is nothing else but a hunting after words, and fine placing of them.'[1]

One of 'the more exact judgements', as we have seen, was Sir Henry Savile; the 'meaner capacities' with whom this kind of ex-pression had found such favour were, as we know, actually the Senecan essayists and character-writers for whom Bacon had set the example. Perhaps Bacon only perceived the dangers of his own style when it fell into the hands of meaner talents; at any rate, he could not be charged with the 'vanity' of it, which is what he really condemns after all. Since he prized above all 'weight of matter', it is not surprising that he should condemn his own style when it merely disguised the lack of weight. But to be weighty in his day it was necessary to be Senecan, and Bacon moderated rather than deserted his own Senecanism.

III

The greatest vanity of Senecan style, however, appeared in the sermons of Bacon's friend, Bishop Lancelot Andrewes. As we have already observed, Bacon suggested (perhaps unintentionally) the propriety of Senecan style to the scholastic mind: 'as was said of Seneca, *Verborum minutiis rerum frangit pondera*; so a man may truly say of the schoolmen, *Quaestionum minutiis scientiarum frangunt soliditatem*'. Bacon fell upon the schoolmen's 'digladiation about subtilities', since all their thirst for truth proved only 'fierce with dark keeping'; 'in the inquiry of the divine truth their pride inclined to leave the oracle of God's word and to vanish in the mixture of their own inventions'.[2] The same charges were brought against preachers like Andrewes. Bacon also remarked that in contrast to the Ciceronian the scholastic 'writings were altogether in a differing style and form; taking liberty to coin and frame new terms of art to express their own sense and to avoid circuit of speech, without regard to the pureness, pleasantness, and (as I may call it) lawfulness of the phrase or word'.[3] In short, the

---

[1] *Advancement and Proficience of Learning*, translated by Gilbert Wats (Oxford, 1640), p. 29; cf. *Works*, ed. cit., p. 55 n.
[2] *Works*, ed. cit., p. 56.   [3] Ibid., p. 54.

schoolmen were guilty of Senecan faults when compared with the Ciceronians. Bacon's remarks on the schoolmen contain suggestions of two charges later brought against Andrewes's sermon style; both charges have a curious relevance to Quintilian's criticism that Seneca broke the weight of his matter by cultivating *sententiae*. One of these charges relates to Andrewes's practice of 'division', of 'crumbling' his text; and the other to his 'wit' or levity in serious matters.[1] These two aspects of *'rerum pondera minutissimis sententiis fregit'* are implied in Quintilian on Seneca;[2] they suggest the propriety of the Senecan style to the scholastic mind.

Both Andrewes and Donne were not only scholastic but also Senecan in their traits of style; they were both greatly influenced by the church fathers who had a Senecan bent, such as Tertullian.[3] The most striking trait of 'metaphysical' style, which has a close affinity to the Senecan, is the teasing out of ideas and figures so as to reveal their ambiguous, antithetic, or paradoxical aspects. This is present in Andrewes when he crumbles a text to pieces; it finds a place in the criticism which Dr Johnson directed against the 'metaphysical poets'; and it is not absent from the work of the characterwriters. Senecan brevity, abruptness, and point characterize the sentences of Andrewes, and affect those of Donne, though less obviously. The stylistic aims once expressed by Donne are clearly Senecan: '... with such succinctness and brevity, as may consist with clearness, and perspicuity, in such manner, and method, as may best enlighten your understandings, and least encumber your memories, I shall open unto you [the meaning of the text]'.[4]

In 1710 Steele remembers Donne in connection with such aims. Having remarked that Boccalini sentences a laconic writer, for using three words where two would have served, to read all the works of Guicciardini, Steele comments: 'This Guicciardini is so very prolix and circumstantial in his writings, that I remember our countryman, doctor Donne, speaking of that majestic and concise

[1] See W. F. Mitchell, *English Pulpit Oratory* (London, 1932), pp. 351–65, 'The Attack on the "Metaphysicals".'
[2] Quintilian, *Institutiones Oratoriae*, X, 1.
[3] On the Senecan cult in sermon style see W. F. Mitchell, op. cit., items indexed under 'Senecan' and 'Tertullian'.
[4] *Works*, ed. Alford (1839), vi, 146; quoted by Mitchell, op. cit., p. 191.

manner in which Moses has described the creation of the world, adds, "that if such an author as Guicciardini were to have written on such a subject, the world itself would not have been able to have contained the books that gave the history of its creation".'[1] The 'majestic and concise manner' is as brief a formulation of Jacobean ideals as one could find; only the wit is wanting.

But before the death of George Herbert the 'wit' and 'division' of Andrewes, which have their analogues in Seneca, had begun to provoke criticism. For his 'country parson' Herbert prescribes another style and method: 'The parson's method in handling of a text, consists of two parts: first, a plain and evident declaration of the meaning of the text; and secondly, some choice observations drawn out of the whole text, as it lies entire, and unbroken in the Scripture itself. This he thinks natural, and sweet, and grave. Whereas the other way of crumbling a text into small parts, as, the person speaking, or spoken to, the subject, and object, and the like, hath neither in it sweetness, nor gravity, nor variety, since the words apart are not Scripture, but a Dictionary, and may be considered alike in all the Scripture.'[2] Thus Herbert anticipates the method of Tillotson and condemns that of Andrewes, in which Donne was a lesser offender. Herbert begins his criticism of 'witty' preaching in these significant words: 'By these and other means the parson procures attention; but the character of his sermon is holiness; he is not witty, or learned, or eloquent, but holy. A character, that *Hermogenes* never dreamed of, and therefore he could give no precept thereof.'[3] But while Herbert deplores the wit he reveals the profit to be derived from Senecan brevity. Of course Senecan wit was not 'metaphysical' wit, but Seneca provided the chief classical model of a witty prose style.

By the time of Robert South there was something like a general disapproval of the witty preaching represented by Andrewes. At the same time that South cultivates the Senecan qualities which pass into Restoration style, he succumbs to some of the wit that he condemns in Andrewes or disparages by association with Seneca. In *The Scribe Instructed*, preached in 1660, South administers severe reproof to two kinds of preaching: that which

---

[1] *Tatler*, No. 264, 16 December 1710. Cf. Donne, ed. Alford, iv, 491.
[2] *Works* (London, 1836), i, 17–18. The *Priest to the Temple* was first printed in 1652. Herbert, it may be recalled, had acted as Latin scribe for Bacon.
[3] Ibid., pp. 15–16. The witty preacher used his 'pyrotechnics' to procure attention.

sponsors 'a puerile and indecent sort of levity', and that which follows a 'mean, heavy, careless, and insipid way of handling things sacred', or the manner of the school of Andrewes and that of the Puritans. Of the former he declares: 'What Quintilian most discreetly says of Seneca's handling philosophy, that he did *rerum pondera minutissimis sententiis frangere*, break, and, as it were, emasculate the weight of his subject by little affected sentences, the same may with much more reason be applied to the practice of those, who detract from the excellency of things sacred by a comical lightness of expression: as when their prayers shall be set out in such dress, as if they did not supplicate, but compliment Almighty God; and their sermons so garnished with quibbles and trifles, as if they played with truth and immortality; and neither believed these things themselves, nor were willing that others should.'[1]

Quintilian speaks to South even more pertinently about the wit of Andrewes than about that of Seneca, and South finds Quintilian relevant to the practice of 'division': 'Such are wholly mistaken in the nature of wit: for true wit is a severe and manly thing. Wit in divinity is nothing else, but sacred truths suitably expressed. It is not shreds of Latin or Greek, nor a *Deus dixit*, and a *Deus benedixit*, nor those little quirks, or divisions into the ὅτι, the διότι, and the καθότι, or the *egress, regress,* and *progress,* and other such stuff, (much like the style of a lease,) that can properly be called wit. For that is not wit which consists not with wisdom.'[2] South is here purging the Senecan or 'differing' sermon style of its 'levity'—in both of the senses in which Quintilian suggested that it was an enemy to *gravitas*. The standards by which South reproves this wit are obviously Restoration.

But it would be a mistake to conclude that South was not Senecan in style, or that his ideals of style were not definitely Senecan, in the better sense of brevity and plainness rather than 'point'. No one can overlook his clearly Senecan requirements for style in *A Discourse against Long and Extempore Prayers.*[3] His thoroughly Baconian view and an epitome of Jacobean stylistic ambitions find expression in one short paragraph: 'In fine, brevity and succinctness of speech is that, which, in philosophy or speculation, we call *maxim*, and first principle; in the counsels and resolves of practical wisdom, and the deep mysteries of religion,

[1] *Sermons* (Oxford, 1842), ii, 359.   [2] Ibid.   [3] Ibid., i, 334–56.

oracle; and lastly, in matters of wit, and the finenesses of imagination, *epigram*. All of them, severally and in their kinds, the greatest
and the noblest things that the mind of man can shew the force
and dexterity of its faculties in.'[1] Here we are reminded of the
advantage of 'aphorisms' over 'methods', and we should not forget
that 'oracle' and 'epigram' led into 'strong lines'. It is significant
that in condemning the 'vanity' of the school of Andrewes, South
confuses the 'metaphysical' and 'Senecan' aspects of their levity;
it is not less significant that he himself remains stoutly Senecan in
the plainer fashion of Bishop Hall.

Before we return to the secular prose, we should recall that
clearness or perspicuity is not a trustworthy guide to the ideals or
affinities of styles, since perspicuity is the constant of language as a
vehicle of communication. It is rather the variants, or the qualities
associated with perspicuity, that give styles their peculiar character. Thus when John Hughes tells us, in his essay *Of Style*, that
the qualifications of a good style are propriety, perspicuity, elegance, and cadence, it is the propriety, elegance, and cadence that
are significant. When Ben Jonson likewise names perspicuity,
but in connection with other qualities, it is the other qualities that
differentiate the ideals of Jonson from those of Hughes; the difference will tell us much of the evolution of style between Jonson
and Hughes. Of course an emphasis upon brevity endangers
perspicuity, and obscurity flies in the face of this constant of
language; otherwise, the presence or absence of that constant is
not in itself very significant. With this reminder, we may return
to the seventeenth-century awareness of Senecan style in secular
prose.

IV

Both Seneca and Tacitus were great favourites of the first half of
the seventeenth century. Seneca appealed as a moralist who could
put even the Christian to shame, and Tacitus rivalled Machiavelli
for shrewd political wisdom. As Jonson's 'New Cry' puts it,
Tacitus appealed to 'ripe statesmen, ripe!':

> *They carry in their pockets Tacitus,*
> *And the Gazetti, or Gallo-Belgicus.*

[1] Ibid., p. 338. South, like Donne, praises the style of Genesis for its brevity; unlike
Donne, he refers to Longinus in this connection.

One of the first essayists, Robert Johnson, finds Tacitus the perfect historian and remarks his 'iudiciall, but strangelie briefe sen/tences'.[1] Seneca and Tacitus, as we have already observed, were the Jacobean models for such sentences.

But Seneca was also a model of another sort—the kind that Burton found in him. When Burton explains his own style in 'Democritus to the Reader', he comments on the difference of tastes in style: 'He respects matter, thou art wholly for words, he loves a loose and free style, thou art all for neat composition, strong lines, hyperboles, allegories . . .'[2] To Burton the alternatives are the 'loose' style, which respects matter, and the 'neat' style, which employs strong lines; for both of which Seneca provided a model. Respecting matter rather than words, Burton calls upon Seneca to support his 'extemporean style': 'Besides, it was the observation of the wise *Seneca, when you see a fellow careful about his words, and neat in his speech, know this for a certainty, that man's mind is busied about toys, there's no solidity in him. Non est ornamentum virile con/cinnitas.*'[3] The seventeenth century did not forget this other side of Seneca, but his 'curt' style attracted more attention. Somewhat later a more elaborate Latin mould engaged the attention of Browne and Milton; it cannot be called loose in quite the same sense that Burton is loose, for it endeavoured to suggest *concinnitas*.

In 1615 when Nicholas Breton, a belated Elizabethan, wrote *Characters upon Essaies*, he dedicated his work to Bacon, but it was a feeble imitation. Nevertheless, it received significant praise in the eulogistic verse of I.B. '*In Laudem Operis*':

> *I herein finde few words, great worth involve:*
> *A Lipsian stile, terse Phrase. . . .*

But the praise was not significant enough for a modern editor,[4] who explains 'Lipsian' by the note 'lip salve, flattering speech'. A 'Lipsian stile, terse Phrase', refers of course to the Senecan style of Justus Lipsius. Less flattering is another reference to Lipsian style which appears in John Earle's character of 'A selfe/conceited Man' as set forth in 1628: 'His tenent is always singular, and

[1] *Essaies, or Rather Imperfect Offers* (London, 1601), 'Of Histories'.
[2] *Anatomy of Melancholy* (Bohn ed.), i, 25.
[3] Ibid., pp. 30–31.
[4] Ursula Kentish/Wright (ed.), *A Mad World My Masters and Other Prose Works* (London, 1929), i, 151.

aloofe from the vulgar as hee can, from which you must not hope to wrest him. He ha's an excellent humor, for an Heretique, and in these dayes made the first Arminian. He prefers *Ramus* before *Aristotle*, & *Paracelsus* before *Galen*, and whosoever with most Paradox is commended & *Lipsius* his hopping stile, before either *Tully* or *Quintilian*.'[1] In later editions the Lipsian passage is deleted. Earle must have realized either that this style had become too common to be a paradox or that his own style made the paradox invidious. At any rate, Earle shows us that the abrupt or 'hopping' style of Lipsius was the smart fashion as opposed to the correct Ciceronian. These two references to Lipsius give us the cardinal features of the Senecan style as it seemed to the seventeenth century: it was terse in phrase and abrupt in movement.

   Owen Feltham, who bears the clear imprint of Baconian imitation, speaks of style in his essay 'Of Preaching', which was added to his *Resolves* in 1628. His preferences in style are plainly Senecan: 'A man can never speak too well, where he speaks not too obscure. Long and distended clauses, are both tedious to the ear, and difficult for their retaining. A sentence well couched, takes both the sense and the understanding. I love not those cart-rope speeches, that are longer than the memory of man can fathom.... The weighty lines men find upon the stage, I am persuaded, have been the lures, to draw away the pulpit-followers.'[2] Sententious but not obscure, such is the good style: apparently the pulpit had not been Senecan enough. Feltham feels that besides the advantage of action, the stage has the benefit of a 'more compassed language: the *dulcia sermonis*, moulded into curious phrase'. Echoing the opinion that action is 'the chiefest part of an Orator', Feltham adds: 'And this is *Seneca's* opinion: Fit words are better than fine ones. I like not those that are injudiciously made, but such as be expressively significant; that lead the mind to something, besides the naked term.'[3] But judgment is necessary

[1] *Micro-cosmographie* (London, 1628), 'Character 12'. Note that a love of paradox goes with a Senecan style.
[2] *Resolves* (Temple Classics ed.), p. 62. 'In the development of English style', says Joseph Jacobs, 'the decisive and critical moment is the introduction of the easy short sentence' (Howell's *Familiar Letters* (London, 1892), I, lxi). But the curt style brought premeditated shortness rather than extemporary ease; cf. Howell's emphasis on brevity in his first letter.
[3] Ibid., p. 63.

for depth: as 'Saint *Augustine* says, *Tully* was admired more for his tongue, than his mind.' And yet studied language is not altogether vain, for 'he that reads the Fathers, shall find them, as if written with a crisped pen'. Fit words do not preclude study, but rather enjoin it. 'He prodigals a mine of excellency,' says Feltham, 'that lavishes a terse oration to an aproned auditory'; but if the orator must have judgment, still a terse oration was a mine of excellency to Feltham.

If we have any doubt of Feltham's Senecanism, Thomas Randolph sets it at rest. His *Conceited Peddler* (1630), which W. C. Hazlitt calls 'a shrewd satire on the follies and vices of the age', makes much of 'points' and of 'a sovereign box of cerebrum' produced by alchemy, 'the fire being blown with the long-winded blast of a Ciceronian sentence, and the whole confection boiled from a pottle to a pint in the pipkin of Seneca'.[1] Of course 'points' were the favourite form of Senecan wit, and the brevity of Seneca appeared by contrast with Ciceronian length. Randolph shows that for his age the Senecan and the Ciceronian were the two poles between which style turned. His verses 'To Master Feltham on his book of Resolves' place Feltham accordingly: 'Nor doth the cinnamon-bark deserve less praise':

> *I mean, the style being pure, and strong and round;*
> *Not long, but pithy; being short-breath'd, but sound,*
> *Such as the grave, acute, wise Seneca sings—*
> *That best of tutors to the worst of kings.*
> *Not long and empty; lofty, but not proud;*
> *Subtle, but sweet; high, but without a cloud.*
> *Well-settled, full of nerves—in brief 'tis such,*
> *That in a little bath comprised much.*[2]

Little could be added to this character of Senecan style, for such it appeared to that age; pithy, short-breathed, grave, acute, and nervous—such was Seneca and such Feltham. 'Round', here and elsewhere, seems to acquire an Anti-Ciceronian significance if we recall Wats's translation of Bacon on Senecan style: 'The labour here is altogether, That words may be aculeate, sentences concise,

[1] *Works*, ed. W. C. Hazlitt (London, 1875), i, 40 and 44.
[2] Ibid., ii, 575. This passage clearly suggests the pattern of Denham's apostrophe to the Thames; cf. 'The Rhetorical Pattern of Neo-Classical Wit', *Seventeenth Century Contexts*.

and the whole contexture of the speech and discourse, rather rounding into it selfe, than spread and dilated.' The Senecan style was concise and 'round' rather than 'spread and dilated' like the Ciceronian; in Bacon's Latin, '*oratio denique potius versa quam fusa*'. Jonson, modifying Vives, gives similar associations to 'round': 'The next thing to the stature, is the figure and feature in Language: that is, whether it be round, and streight, which consists of short and succinct *Periods*, numerous, and polished, or square and firme, which is to have equall and strong parts, everywhere answerable, and weighed.'[1] Here 'round' goes with short and succinct periods, while 'square' goes with *concinnitas* or symmetry of structure.

Jonson pauses in his *Discoveries* (1641) to condemn all the essayists,[2] but a few pages later he eulogizes Bacon: 'Yet there hapn'd, in my time, one noble *Speaker*, who was full of gravity in his speaking. His language (where hee could spare, or pass by a jest) was nobly *censorious*. No man ever spake more neatly, more pressly, more weightily, or suffer'd lesse emptinesse, lesse idlenesse, in what hee utter'd. No member of his speech, but consisted of his owne graces. His hearers could not cough, or looke aside from him, without losse.'[3] Of course, Jonson is speaking of Bacon as an orator, but it was for speaking thus 'prestly' that Cicero condemned the Stoics.[4] For Jonson, however, Bacon may 'stand as the mark and acme of our language', and of the style which Jonson favoured.

Much of his most personal stylistic doctrine Jonson draws from Seneca's famous *Epistles* (114, 115) and from similar matter in Vives's *De Ratione Dicendi*. Out of Vives comes his summary of the varieties of succinct style: 'A strict and succinct style is that, where you can take away nothing without losse, and that losse to be manifest. The briefe style is that which expresseth much in little. The concise style, which expresseth not enough, but leaves somewhat to bee understood. The abrupt style, which hath many breaches, and doth not seeme to end, but fall.'[5]

[1] *Discoveries*, ed. M. Castelain (Paris, 1906), pp. 105 and 106 n.
[2] Ibid., p. 39.
[3] Ibid., p. 47. Bacon, like Seneca, was nobly censorious 'where he could spare, or pass by a jest'.
[4] Cf. *Brutus*, xxxi.
[5] Ibid., pp. 100–1. Quintilian (X, i, 106) says that 'from Demosthenes nothing can be taken away, to Cicero nothing can be added'.

Against this passage Jonson sets the names *Tacitus, The Laconic, Suetonius, Seneca and Fabianus*; Vives refers to Seneca for the remark that Fabianus inclines to the abrupt style but Cicero ends every‑ thing. Jonson does not borrow intact one of Vives's most Senecan comments: '*Venustissimae sunt periodi, quae fiunt vel ex antithetis, vel acutè concluso argumento.*' While Jonson echoes Bacon's words on Ciceronian style, he removes their sting.[1] However, when Jonson writes on epistolary style, his remarks are thoroughly Senecan. These remarks present his most complete statement on style, and although apparently drawn from John Hoskins's *Directions for Speech and Style*,[2] are parallel to the requirements laid down in the *Epistolica Institutio* of Justus Lipsius.

In the Lipsian scheme five qualities were necessary: *brevitas, perspicuitas, simplicitas, venustas,* and *decentia*. These are subsumed under four heads by Hoskins, whose statement of the Lipsian doctrine is retailed by Jonson.[3] 'The first is brevity': '*Brevity* is attained in matter, by avoiding idle Complements, Prefaces, Protestations, Parentheses, superfluous circuit of figures, and digressions: In the composition, by omitting Conjunctions (*Not onely; But also; Both the one, and the other, whereby it commeth to passe*) and such like idle Particles, that have no great business in a serious Letter, but breaking of sentences; as often times a short journey is made long, by unnecessary baits.'[4] Remembering that Jonson on epistolary style was merely the public voice of Hoskins, we may say that Jonson particularizes the means by which the disjunctive or disconnected Senecan style was achieved.[5] But he remembers that Quintilian says 'there is a briefnesse of the parts sometimes, that makes the whole long'; and comments thus: 'This is the fault of some Latine Writers, within these last hundred years, of my reading, and perhaps *Seneca* may be appeacht of it; I accuse him not.'

[1] Ibid., pp. 108–9.
[2] Edited from manuscript by Hoyt H. Hudson (Princeton, 1935). Although the *Directions* (1599?) was not printed under Hoskins's name, it was given to the public partially by Jonson and almost completely by Blount. The section 'For Penning of Letters', which Hoskins adapted from Lipsius, is found almost verbatim in Jonson, and with some modification in Blount, whose version will be discussed later.
[3] Op. cit., pp. 112–16.   [4] Ibid., p. 113.
[5] Suetonius records Caligula's contempt for Seneca's style as 'sand minus mortar' (*Cal.*, liii).

'The next property of *Epistolarie* style is *Perspicuity*', and with this Jonson combines 'Plainenesse', which is *simplicitas* in Lipsius. Following Lipsius, who quotes Seneca's wish that his epistles might be '*illaboratus et facilis*', Jonson counsels informality or 'a diligent kind of negligence'. The third quality is vigour or '*Life and Quickness*'; Lipsius says, '*Venustatem appello; cum sermo totus alacer, vivus, erectus est.*' Here Lipsius names and Jonson suggests the '*argutae sententiae*' of Senecan style. The last quality, the *decentia* of Lipsius, becomes *discretio*, 'respect to discerne', or propriety in Jonson. In all these matters, however, Jonson was merely repeating Hoskins, who noted with some disapproval the new tendency towards a 'sententious' or Senecan style.

But this hierarchy of stylistic qualities, with brevity heading the list, is Senecan; and perspicuity, being a constant in communica-tion, is less significant than vigour, which receives a Senecan definition. Although Jonson is given to quoting Quintilian, his own practice shows that Senecan doctrine was more persuasive in moulding his style.[1]

The 'English Seneca', Bishop Hall, was criticized by the eigh-teenth century because 'he abounds rather too much with anti-theses and witty turns';[2] but his Senecanism had already been criticized by Milton. In the Smectymnuan controversy Hall referred to his own style in his *Answer to Smectymnuus's Vindication*: 'In the sequel, my words, which were never yet taxed for an offensive superfluity, shall be very few; and such as, to your greater wonder, I shall be beholden for, to my kind adversaries.' While defending the authors of Smectymnuus in his *Apology*, Milton declares that Hall's design was 'with quips and snapping adages to vapour them out', and that he could not endure that they 'should thus lie at the mercy of a coy flirting style; to be girded with frumps and curtal gibes, by one who makes sentences by the statute, as if all above three inches long were confiscate'.[3] Although his opponent was anonymous (Hall's son?), Milton was here answering Bishop Hall directly, and criticizing his style for its Senecan traits. Milton

[1] See Dryden's character of Jonson in the *Essay of Dramatic Poesy*: 'If there was any fault in his language, 'twas that he weaved it too closely and laboriously, in his serious plays: perhaps too, he did a little too much Romanize our tongue, leaving the words which he translated almost as much Latin as he found them: wherein, though he learnedly followed the idiom of their language, he did not enough comply with the idiom of ours.'

[2] Cf. W. F. Mitchell, op. cit., p. 367.   [3] *Prose Works* (Bohn ed.), iii, 99.

returns to the attack in a stronger vein when he declares that the Remonstrant 'sobs me out half⁄a⁄dozen phthisical mottoes, wherever he had them, hopping short in the measure of convulsion⁄ fits; in which labour the agony of his wit having escaped narrowly, instead of well⁄sized periods, he greets us with a quantity of thumb⁄ring posies'.[1] Milton, who believed in well⁄sized periods, thus condemns 'Lipsius his hopping style' and 'this tormentor of semicolons'.

Milton's own taste comes out more clearly in a later statement about the clerks of the university who are to be ministers: 'How few among them that know to write or speak in a pure style; much less to distinguish the ideas and various kinds of style in Latin barbarous, and oft not without solecisms, declaiming in rugged and miscellaneous gear blown together by the four winds, and in their choice preferring the gay rankness of Apuleius, Arnobius, or any modern fustianist, before the native Latinisms of Cicero.'[2] Here is clear disapproval of the 'modern fustianist', who was commonly an Anti⁄Ciceronian. In 1622 Archbishop Abbot, in a letter to All Souls College, had found fault with the general deterioration of Latin style at Oxford: 'The style of your letter is somewhat abrupt and harsh, and doth rather express an affected brevity than the old Ciceronian oratory. And I am sorry to hear that this new way of writing is not only become the fault of the College, but of the University itself.'[3] Likewise, to Milton the humanist a pure style meant Cicero, and neither 'the knotty Africanisms, the pampered metaphors, the intricate and involved sentences of the fathers',[4] nor the Senecan style condemned by Abbot. As a humanist Milton scorned not only those who con⁄ fused 'the ideas and various kinds of style in Latin barbarous', but also those who introduced Senecan style into English prose.

The Latin mould of Milton's style is so obvious that we may pause to consider the contemporary awareness of such a mould in

[1] Ibid., p. 135. This passage does not refer directly to Hall, but it repeats the charges already made against his style.

[2] Ibid., p. 155.

[3] Quoted from the *Archives of All Souls* by Montagu Burrows in his edition of *The Register of the Visitors of the University of Oxford, 1647 to 1658* (Camden Society, 1881), p. xcvii.

[4] *Prose Works*, ii, 388. The effect of academic Latin composition upon English prose is often neglected in modern accounts of seventeenth⁄century style. Both Lipsius and Muretus were read in the schools.

English. In 'A Discourse of Languages' Richard Flecknoe attributes the variations of English style 'to the severall Inclinations and
Dispositions of *Princes* and of *Times*': 'That of our *Ancestors*
having been plain and simple: That of Queen *Elizabeths* dayes,
flaunting and *pufted* like her *Apparell*: That of King *Jame's, Regis
ad exemplum*, inclining much to the *Learned* and *Erudite*, as (if you
observe it) in the late Kings dayes, the *Queen* having a mayne
ascendancy and *predominance* in the Court, the *French style* with the
Courtyers was chiefly in *vogue* and Fashion.'[1]

Flecknoe goes on to say that the inclination of the times has
corrupted their metaphors with military terms; 'much of the
Chican having likewise entred for its part, even to the *Scripture*
style amongst the common *Rabble*, who are our *Rabbies* now, and
Gypsies cant it in the *Hebrew* phrase'. The consequence of all this
appears in another passage: 'For the differencing of *Stiles* (to go
on with this matter, since we have begun) wee may divide them
into the *Vulgar*, or that of the *Time*, and the *Learned* and *Erudite*:
which he, who writes for *Fame* and *lasting*, should principally
affect: It bearing Translation best, being cast in the *Latine mould*,
which never varies: whilst that of the Time changes perpetually,
according to the various humors of the *Time*.'[2]

Those who would write for posterity must now write, not in
Latin, but in the learned and erudite style which is cast in the
Latin mould. Since the Jacobean style was of this persuasion, we
might expect that a Jacobean writer would offer a suitable model;
and in the refinement of English no name stood higher than that
of Bacon at this time. In 1644 the writer of *Vindex Anglicus* tells us
that 'the renowned Lord Bacon taught us to speak the terms of art
in our own language';[3] in 1650 Dr Walter Charleton links
Browne with Bacon in the '*Carmination* or refinement of English';[4]
and in 1653 S.S. (probably Samuel Sheppard) praises Bacon for
being 'so succinct, elaborate, and sententious' that the best foreign
wits think it the highest honour to translate him into their native
languages.[5] If Bacon set a popular example in his *Essays*, he set
a more learned example in his *Advancement of Learning*; for his

---

[1] *Miscellania* (London, 1653), p. 77.
[2] Ibid., p. 78.
[3] *Harleian Miscellany* (London, 1810), v, 431.
[4] Epistle Dedicatory to Helmont's *Ternary of Paradoxes* (London, 1650), sig. clr.
[5] *Paradoxes or Encomions* (London, 1653), p. 10.

terms of art carried from Jonson to Browne, and his period sup-
plied an Anti-Ciceronian but Latin mould for more elaborate
writing.

Sir Thomas Browne seems to have been of Flecknoe's mind
when he explained why he wrote the *Pseudodoxia Epidemica* in
English rather than Latin, and how the 'paradoxology' of his
subject sometimes carried him into 'expressions beyond mere
English apprehensions. And, indeed, if elegancy still proceedeth,
and English pens maintain that stream we have of late observed to
flow from many, we shall, within few years, be fain to learn Latin
to understand English, and a work will prove of equal facility in
either. Nor have we addressed our pen or style unto the people,
(whom books do not redress, and [who] are this way incapable of
reduction,) but unto the knowing and leading part of learning.'[1]
Thus, in Milton's time, Browne suggests that there was an unusual
effort to cast English into a Latin mould, or to bring Latin terms
into English, at least when a writer was not addressing the vulgar.
But where Browne went to extremes in the terms of art, Milton
went to extremes in the Latin mould, setting his Latin construc-
tions against the idiom of the 'loose' period in English. This more
elaborate Latin mould, which suggested *concinnitas*, was the result
of an effort to stem the idiomatic current of the time.

In 1654 Richard Whitlock, in his preface to *Zootomia*, declared
that Plutarch's discourses most invite imitation for the form, and
are not behind any for matter, '*if mixt sometimes with those* Mucrones
Sermonum, Enlivening Touches *of* Seneca *full of* smart Fancy,
solid sense *and* accurate reason'. The wit of Seneca was for Whitlock still a desirable addition to the essay; but 'Exactness *of writing
on any* Subject *in* Poetick heights *of* Fancy, *or* Rhetoricall Descants
of Application', he left to others: '*For my own part I may say, as*
Lipsius *in his* Epistle; Rationem meam scribendi scire vis? fundo,
non scribo, nec id nisi in Calore & interno quodam Impetu, haud
aliter quam Poetae. *Would you know (saith he) my manner of writing?
it is a kind of voluntary* Tiding of, *not* Pumping for; Notions
flowing, *not* forced; *like* Poets unconstrained Heats *and* Raptures:
such is mine, rather a running Discourse *than a* Grave-paced
Exactnes. . . .'[2]

Fundere, if we remember, was the aim of Seneca's 'loose' style;
and Lipsius here echoes Seneca no less than when he subscribed

[1] *Works*, ed. S. Wilkin (Bohn ed.), i, 3.   [2] *Zootomia* (London, 1654), sig. a5r.

to the curt style in his *Quaestiones*. But Whitlock's subscription to this aim suggests that the loose rather than the curt style was proving congenial to the essay as the product of 'a mind thinking'. Informality is the effect of this style and the aim of the personal essay.

If Whitlock suggests that the loose style is to triumph in the Restoration, Thomas Blount's *Academie of Eloquence* shows that the curt style still has some life before it. This rhetoric, which adopts almost in full the *Directions* of Hoskins and borrows considerably from Bacon, ran through five editions between 1654 and 1684; in fact, no other rhetoric of that time seems to have been quite so popular. If we examine a passage in the *Academie* on *sententiae* (borrowed with some modernization from Hoskins), we shall discover notwithstanding that the ideal form of the curt style is seriously threatened: 'Sententia, if it be well used, is a Figure; if ill and too much, a Style, of which none that write humorously and factiously, can be clear in these days, when there are so many Schismes of Eloquence. We study now-a-days according to the predominancy of Criticall fancies. Whilst *Moral Philosophy* was in request, it was rudeness, not to be sententious; whilst *Mathematics* were of late in vogue, all similitudes came from *Lines, Circles* and *Angles*; But now that *Mars* is predominant, we must *recruit* our wits, and give our words a new *Quarter*.'[1] The *sententia*, which is still acceptable as a figure, is no longer quite approved when used so much as to make a style, although it is still popular in certain kinds of writing. Its association with moral philosophy, and so with the moral essay, is specified. But this wariness towards the pure form of the curt style does not prevent Blount, any more than it prevented Hoskins, from retailing Senecan instructions for an epistolary style.

Blount, who repeats the instructions of Hoskins and Jonson, begins with their opening remark on the fashion of this style: 'Now for Fashion, it consists in four qualities of your Style. The first is *Brevity*.'[2] As a sample of Blount's borrowing, let me quote the passage which I have already cited from Jonson: 'Brevity is attain'd upon the matter, by avoiding idle complements, prefaces,

---

[1] *Academie of Eloquence* (London, 1654), p. 34. Cf. Hoskins, op. cit., pp. 38–40. Although Hoskins retailed Senecan doctrine, he was critical of it; and Blount adapted this criticism to his own time. Jonson borrowed some of this dispraise, which is more discordant in him.

[2] Ibid., p. 142; cf. *Discoveries*, ed. cit., p. 112.

protestations, long Parentheses, supplications, wanton circuits of Figures, and digressions, by composition, omitting conjunctions, *Not onely but also, the one and the other, whereby it comes to passe, etc.* and such like particles, that have no great business in a serious Letter; By breaking off sentences; as oftentimes a short journey is made long by many baits.'[1] 'Omitting conjunctions' and 'breaking off sentences', though garbled by Blount, could describe the disconnected 'curt period' that Professor Croll has analysed.

Blount, however, looks ahead when he adds a remark that is much more explicit than any similar idea in Jonson, not to mention Hoskins: 'Under this Notion somewhat may be said of Periods, which ought not to bee too long, nor yet too short, *QUO MAGIS VIRTUS, EO MAGIS MEDIETAS.* All vertue consists in a certain Geometrical mediocrity, equally distant from excess and default.' Again reflecting his time, Blount quotes Longinus in support of another requirement which suggests that the reign of abruptness is over: 'There ought likewise to be a speciall regard had to the cadence of the words, that the whole contexture of the *Period* may yeeld a certain kind of harmony to the ear.'[2]

But the next requirement carries Blount back to the text of Hoskins and Jonson: 'The next property of Epistolary Style, is, *Perspicuity*, which is not seldom endangered by the former quality.'[3] 'Under this vertue', echoes Blount, 'may come *Plainness*, which is, not to be too curious in the order', but to use 'a diligent kind of negligence'.[4] Blount likewise frowns upon 'perfumed moding terms', but goes beyond Hoskins and Jonson by referring explicitly to Seneca: 'Besides, a vain curiosity of words hath so scandalized some Philosophers, that *Seneca* (in one of his epistles) says, Had it been possible to make himself understood by signes, he would rather serve himself of them, then of discourse, to the end he might the better avoid all manner of affectation.'[5] Blount's third and fourth qualities are identical with those of Hoskins and Jonson, the third being 'Life' or 'Vigor', and the fourth 'Respect' or Propriety.[6] Thus Blount fulfils the promise of his Epistle

---

[1] Ibid., p. 143; cf. *Discoveries*, p. 113.   [2] Ibid., pp. 143–4.
[3] Ibid., p. 144; cf. *Discoveries*, p. 114.   [4] Ibid., p. 145; cf. *Discoveries*, p. 115.
[5] Ibid., pp. 145–6; cf. *Discoveries*, p. 116. John Wilkins's *Essay towards a Real Character and a Philosophical Language* (1668) was an effort in this direction.
[6] Ibid., p. 146; cf. *Discoveries*, p. 116.

Dedicatory 'with some particular *Instructions* and Rules premised, for the better attaining to a Pen-perfection'. As this Senecan scheme of style passed from Hoskins and Jonson to Blount it received important though slight alterations; and the *Academie of Eloquence*, perhaps because of this modification, renewed the life of Senecan ideals in the early days of the Royal Society—a fact which cannot be without significance.

V

In conclusion, we may attempt to place the curt Senecan style by comparing the stylistic aims expressed by Jonson, Blount, Glanvill, and Hughes. In these aims we shall find a simple graph or outline of the evolution of prose style during the century.

Jonson and Blount both advocate brevity, perspicuity (and plainness), vigour, and propriety; but Blount adds the require-ments of cadence and medium length in the period. By placing brevity first, both testify to the reign of the terse Senecan style; but by advancing cadence and 'mediocrity' in the period, Blount looks beyond that style. In the quality of plainness, which Jonson and Blount place under the head of perspicuity, we find the aim of style which becomes dominant after the reign of brevity.

Joseph Glanvill has as good a right as any to speak for the plain style, and his general theme is that 'plainness is for ever the best eloquence'. After such works as Sprat's *History of the Royal Society* (1667), Eachard's *Grounds and Occasions of the Contempt of the Clergy* (1670), and Arderne's *Directions concerning the Matter and Stile of Sermons* (1671), Glanvill gave vigorous expression to the doctrine of plainness in *An Essay concerning Preaching* and *A Seasonable Defence of Preaching; And the Plain Way of it*, both published in 1678. Plainness is the watchword at this time, and Glanvill would have sermon style plain, natural, adequate, familiar but not mean; 'obvious' rather than 'Cryptick'. Glanvill knew what the terse Senecan style was, for he had practised it; hence the significance of his remarks on wit. While 'some Sermons lose their efficacy and force by being too full, and close', he would not go so far as 'what M. *Cowley* saith of Wit in Poetry',

Rather than all be Wit, let none be there.

Associating wit with 'closeness', he concludes that the right course is to seek a mean between prolixity and brevity.[1] For Glanvill, who would not be dull, the 'proper, grave, and manly wit' is still 'sharp, and quick thoughts' set out in lively colours;[2] his wit still comes under the head of 'vigor' or 'life'.

But Glanvill emphasizes Blount's new requirement of a mean between prolixity and brevity, and he elevates the rather subordinate plainness of Jonson and Blount to first place in the hierarchy of style. With Glanvill the reign of brevity has definitely given way to the reign of plainness; and plainness, 'the best Character of Speech', is not 'Bluntness', but rather a simplicity in which there are no 'words without sence'. Of the other qualities specified by Jonson and Blount, vigour outweighs propriety with Glanvill. If he believes that the wit which consists in 'playing with words' is 'vile and contemptible fooling', he points out that 'there is a vice in Preaching quite opposite to this, and that is a certain road-dulness, and want of wit', which only philosophy will cure.[3]

In 1698 John Hughes is much more concerned that a man's learning be 'polite'; the philosopher is now to be saved from the 'Rust of the Academy' by 'Polite Learning', which gives the mind a 'free Air and genteel Motion'. 'In a Word,' says Hughes, 'it adds the Gentleman to the Scholar';[4] and Henry Felton soon found Dryden too much the scholar.[5] The qualifications of a good style are now these four: propriety, perspicuity, elegance, and cadence. 'Propriety of Words, the first Qualification of a good Style', is to be learned from the 'most correct Writers' and 'People of Fashion'.[6] As usual, perspicuity is necessary rather than significant: 'Little need be said of the second Qualification, *viz. Perspicuity*. If your Thoughts be not clear, 'tis impossible your Words shou'd, and consequently you can't be understood.'[7] For

---

[1] *An Essay concerning Preaching* (London, 1678), p. 63. This is not, to be sure, his first word on the plain style, but it is one of the best statements of that style.

[2] Ibid., p. 72. Cowley had also said that wit is not 'the dry chips of short lung'd *Seneca*'.

[3] Ibid., pp. 72–73.

[4] 'Of Style', *Critical Essays of the Eighteenth Century*, ed. W. H. Durham (New Haven, 1915), p. 79.

[5] *A Dissertation on Reading the Classics and Forming a Just Style* (London, 1715), pp. 64–65. See pp. 92–93 for a condemnation of the close, contracted style of sententious writers.

[6] Hughes, op. cit., p. 80.

[7] Ibid., p. 81.

Hughes 'Elegance of Thought is what we commonly call Wit', or 'Curiosa Felicitas';[1] for Jonson it came under the head of 'Life' or 'Vigor'. Cadence is 'a sort of musical Delight' in the periods, but this had been anticipated by Blount. In Hughes the plainness of Glanvill gives way to propriety as the quality of prime importance. Elegance comes from the gentleman and may be called 'ease'; it is the genteel and proper 'Motion' of a polite mind.

The style which discovers a mean between brevity and prolixity was suggested in Blount, established in Glanvill, and maintained in Hughes; it developed out of the loose 'unexpected' period of Seneca rather than out of the formal 'expected' period of Cicero. To Henry Felton at the beginning of the eighteenth century a just style was threatened by obscurity from two directions: either by labouring to be concise, or by running into a 'Prodigality of Words'. Of course, Jonson had been aware of this, but he had, nevertheless, emphasized brevity. Studying to be concise produced 'close contracted Periods', which were now outlawed; on the other hand, there could be no return to the copiousness that Bacon had condemned in the Ciceronians. Moreover, since the terse Senecan style often produced a tissue of epigrams, Shaftesbury could object that 'every period, every sentence almost, is independent, and may be taken asunder, transposed, postponed, anticipated, or set in any new order, as you fancy'. But the neo-classical impulse to order modified this 'random way of miscellaneous writing' just as the neo-classical regard for 'ease' rebuked what Hobbes had called 'the ambitious obscurity of expressing more then is perfectly conceived, or perfect conception in fewer words then it requires'.

[1] Ibid., p. 82.

Index

Index

DATE DUE
